Welcome,
Foolish Mortals...

Welcome, Foolish Mortals...

The Life and Voices of Paul Frees

by Ben Ohmart
Foreword by June Foray
Afterword by Keith Scott

BearManor Media
2014

Published in the USA by

BearManor Media
P. O. Box 1129
Duncan, OK 73534-1129

bearmanormedia.com

Cover design by John Teehan

Typesetting and layout by John Teehan

ISBN—1-59393-434-3
978-1-59393-434-7

For my father,
for all your loving support.

Table of Contents

Foreword by June Foray ix

Introduction...1

LITTLE BUDDY GREEN 5
The 1920s–1930s

THE PLAYER 15
The 1940s

THE MILLIONAIRE 65
The 1950s

I'M SPARTACUS!..123
The 1960s

THE BURGERMEISTER MEISTERBURGER 207
The 1970s

THE ETERNAL DOUGHBOY 255
The 1980s

Afterword by Keith Scott...283

Photos...287

References 293

Credits 295

Appendix: The Beatniks 45s and Press Kit.............................333

Index..341

Foreword

SURPRISINGLY, I hadn't met Paul Frees until we came together for the *Rocky and Bullwinkle* sessions. Even though I had done a plethora of radio - *Lux Radio Theatre, The Danny Thomas Show, The Jimmy Durante Show*, etc. - and though Paul had done thousands of shows himself, somehow we never met up until Jay Ward put together his all-star team: Bill Conrad, Daws Butler, Hans Conried, Bill Scott, Paul and I—and now I'm the only one left.

Looking back at that series, I really do believe those were the Golden Years. It's often said that that show might have contained the Dream Team of cartoon voice talent. It's true that I've never before or since found myself in company to rival or surpass what we had together. Especially Boris—I mean Paul and I. It was always a true joy working with him. Always a laugh. He was constantly *on*, and had the quickest wit around. Joking. All the time. But in a friendly sort of way. He would put you down but only in a humorous manner because he didn't intend to be malicious or frightening. When you got to know him, when you could pierce that arrogance that he showed on the outside, he was a very gentle and a very giving man.

I loved Paul, and he was short. He, Daws and I were comparable as far as height was concerned. But I hope we were equal as far as talent, too. We had fun at and with the Bullwinkle sessions! The longer we stayed there, the better. The recording was only incidental. We enjoyed every moment, since we all grew up together. After we did *Rocky and His Friends*, we did *George of the Jungle*, and *Tom Slick* and *Super Chicken*. And we did all those Cap'n Crunch commercials (I was Brunhilde). We were just a wonderful, close-knit company, and family. And we knew all of Paul's wives, except the first one, since she died so early.

For *Rocky*, we always read the script first around the table, and then we did only one take. That's what professional people do. We were from radio. We would read a script through for time, then we just did it. The only time we had to do it again was if we were over a minute or so. We were locked in as far as time was concerned, because we did two *Bullwinkles* and then a *Fractured Fairy Tale* or *Aesop's Fables* per palaver.

Paul might joke around for half an hour then do the whole scene in two minutes. He and Bill Conrad would just go crazy during the recordings, ribbing each other, joking and reducing each other—especially Bill—to hysterical fits of giggles. It was wild!

Paul had an old Rolls Royce that he used to drive up in. He would get out and would be dressed to the 9's, being very superior in his speech and the way he looked at people, but underneath he was a very sensitive human being.

I didn't realize that Paul painted and made furniture and everything else until Ben told me when we talked about the book. But it doesn't surprise me too much. I've always thought that when you're brilliant in one aspect in your life, it shines in other ways, too.

All I can say is that Paul had a wonderful sense of humor, and was a magnificent talent, as far as his impersonations and his acting ability. No one could match him at Orson Welles—not even Orson himself much of the time. And of course his singularly perfect Peter Lorre impression for the Spike Jones recordings made even Peter himself bow down in homage.

I do miss Paul. Not only his breadth of characterizations and intense vocal variations, but as a warm and MUCH larger than life personality that will never pass this way again. Some called him The Voice of God. And I'm pretty sure God is laughing at his wicked impression of Him right at this very moment.

June Foray
November 2003

Introduction

WRITING A BOOK ON PAUL FREES is a bit like trying to author an encyclopedia from scratch using only six books and bad lighting. It is a nearly impossible task, for as soon as you conquer his first 5,000 credits, another three grand are bubbling below the surface awaiting excavation. This puny book is the closest I could come in a mere three years of research to the 'essence' of the Master of Voices.

Paul must have never slept until the latter part of his career. He did enough work to keep an entire platoon of voice actors happy, rich and artistically satisfied. Whatever drove him on to achieve such a mind-boggling array of film, TV, commercial, radio and etc. credits would probably be a sociology book in itself. He was indeed the master of everything he attempted. But he was also a Mystery Man who delighted in remaining as such.

Uncovering the enigma of his private life, including the elusive "government work," commiserated well with tracking down his thousands of voice credits. Fred Frees himself admitted that he'd considered doing a book on his father, but by the time he got around to it, most of the witnesses, friends and co-workers had passed on. I could only locate one of Paul's ex-wives, and though many acquaintances and colleagues were found and interviewed, few die-hard *friends* (the ones who knew the *real* Paul Frees) could be found for in-depth personal information. Not even the last names of some of his wives could be uncovered. And almost nothing of Paul's years working for the FBI could be unmasked with any degree of certainty. Perhaps reading this book will bring some of these undiscovered souls out.

Since Frees went all over the map, rather than group his work by category (cartoons, on-camera, narration), I decided to assemble this tome in chronological order. I tried to give a better account than "and then he did...and then he did..." but if the contents herein read more like a list, please forgive, since the man, like God, was everywhere. (Indeed, one of

1

his nicknames was The Voice of God—which I dropped as a possibility for the book's title, fearing religious reprisals.) So, for the sake of staying sane throughout the construction of this biography, I elected to give each decade its own chapter.

Paul Frees was a complex character; not merely as the artistic soul who could paint beautifully, build furniture, compose catchy songs and had faultless timing, but as a fashion-conscious man about town, local curiosity with cape and vocal disguises, fastidious collector of antiques, guns and watches, and lover of fine wine and finer cuisine. He was also the wittiest of raconteurs whose famed recording sessions would overflow with countless stories and jokes, causing either chronic side-splitting or professional consternation. Perhaps it was his short stature that made him feel he had to keep 'em laughing to be loved. Some said it was ego, his need to dominate whatever situation he inhabited, though, professionally, he was no control freak. He did love the attention, of course, and sought out his own hue of limelight once he realized working on camera would not make him a star, and that putting a voice in *almost* every recording ever made would make him, literally, *The Millionaire.*

For every project there is a point of origin from which all success stems. For me this was *Hardware Wars* writer/director Ernie Fosselius. Ernie gave me contact information for the ever-helpful session recorder Luther Green, who gave me contact information for kindly commercial producer, Bob Lindner, who gave me contact information for Paul's last love, Joyce Post, who gave me contact information for Paul's daughter, Sabrina Perrin-Frees, and so on. It was a research journey made of happy coincidences. Each person was incredibly helpful and receptive to so monumental a task as a chronicle of the great Paul Frees. There would be no book without all of you.

Independent of that strain was Keith Scott, author of *The Moose That Roared* (and who really should've written *this* book as well), who donated a wealth of material. Another year would have been added to this project if he hadn't supplied me with interviews, articles, photos, credits, and all the rare audio goodies at his command. This selfless Aussie has made this a much better biography. Not only has he let me steal from his book, but I can make no greater compliment to his achievements than say: don't buy this book for Rocky and Bullwinkle. The entire story is in the *Moose.*

Joy Terry Frees and Fred Frees have given hours and hours of their collective time in answering every question I could (and couldn't) imagine. Their generosity was unwavering, and patient. If there were more people like these to interview, there would be more and better biographies on the market.

I'd also like to thank Mitch Axelrod, X. Atencio, Buddy & Charlotte Baker, Wade Ballard, Harry Bartell, Terry Bellows, Eddie Brandt, Ryan Brennan, Big Jim Buchanan, Robert Burrill, Corey Burton, Kevin Butler, Skip Craig, Jim D., Gerald D'onofrio, Peter Davis (one of the champions of this book; your generosity has increased these contents a hundred fold), Roger Dorfman, John Dunning, Walker Edmiston, Greg Ehrbar, Dan Fiebiger, Janice Fishbein, Pete Fitzgerald, Carol Lynn Fletcher (for the wonderful insight into Paul's later life), June Foray (you know why!), Joseph Fotinos, Vikki Franks, Stan Freberg (thanks for writing your book), Dave Frees (for priceless stories and photos of your brother and the Frees family), Helen Frees, Sharon Frees, Jeff Frentzen, Charles Fretzin (for your fantastic interviews and a superb photo session; see www.fretzinphoto.com), Didier Ghez, Rick Goldschmidt (for all things Rankin/Bass), Martin Grams, Jr. (the master of radio credits!), Bob Gutowski, John Hall, Lee Harris, Chris Hayward, Carl Hixon, Tim Hollis, Walden Hughes, Justin Humphreys, imdb.com, Warren Jones, Brian Kistler, Walt Kraemer, Greg Krieger, Tim Lawson, Andrew Leal, Steve Lee, Arnold Leibovit, Jerry Lewine (gushing thanks for many hours of footwork), June Lewis and family, Bob Lloyd, Tim Lucas, Bob Martin (for *lots* of photo help!), Marty McKee, Mobius' Home Video Forum, Ed Newmann, Nohitters Records, Floyd Norman, Gary Owens (you're the wittiest man alive), Don Pitts (for some great stories), Chris Poggiali, Joyce Post (I must *thank you* again for *everything*, including a third of the photos here and the priceless scripts), Frederick Rappaport, Thurl Ravenscroft, Rick Reid, Bill Schallert, Jeff Schwedhelm, Lurene Schwedhelm, Al Scoma, Special Collections at the Thousand Oaks (California) Library, Chris Stone, Michael Streeter, Charles Stumpf (nature's gentleman), Richard Synchef, Al Teixeira, John Thompson, Randy Thornton, Gail Thorpe, Charles Ulrich, Voice Chasers, Don Webber (you shared a *lot* of goodies), Laura Wagner (for knowing everything, and for *two tons* of help), Tom Wagner, Stephen C. Wathen, Tom Weaver (Mr. Interview), Steve Wesson, Dave White, Morgan White, Jr., William Wickerson, Michael Wiese, Beth Williams, John Willyard, Jordan R. Young (for the golden Spike Jones info and scripts), and Chuck Zigman.

And many apologetic thanks to the hundreds of people who have helped during these Frees years; you weren't left out intentionally.

I never met Paul Frees. And since many credits at the end of TV cartoons were run so *fast* (and still are; or shrunk so small to edge in another commercial, they are unreadable), I never even knew his name until years after I'd been influenced by him - first by *The Haunted Mansion* ride, in which I would cry and scream my guts out when the lights went off in the elevator; then by the world's most perfect cartoon, *Santa Claus Is Comin' To Town*; then by the cleverness and matchless voice cast of *Rocky and His Friends*. Therefore, when possible, I have let those who *did* know him tell the story as much as possible. Their views may conflict with each other at times, but they all knew Paul in their way.

This book will remain incomplete; it could never be as hefty and grand as Paul's autobiography would have been, had he delighted us all by inventing one. And inventing must be the word. With brush, Russian accent, nails, microphone and a *lot* of color. My great regret is that the man never got around to it.

Had I waited until every piece of the puzzle fit into this book, I would be too old to type it up. Probably every reader who finds himself dazzled by this text and this huge stack of credits will instantly find one or two items not listed. Okay. I'm ready for that. Please get in touch. I'm already resigned to a second edition of this book if significantly more information is found, and if some of the missing people of his life – friends and wives—come forward, I welcome you. If this is indeed meant to be the definitive biography of such a high-grade, over-worked talent, I need all the leads I can get.

Until then, enjoy the book. Enjoy the life and voices of the one, the only, the mysterious, your Ghost Host, Paul Frees.

Ben Ohmart
November 2003

Little Buddy Green
The 1920s – 1930s

WHEN ONCE ASKED how he came to discover his first voice, Paul Frees responded that it was the fault of the doctor who spanked his new baby behind. "How does that feel?" the doc asked, to which the young prodigy replied something unintelligible in a Swedish dialect. Or perhaps he giggled like the Pillsbury Doughboy; his memory was a little hazy on that point.

In the early 1900s Russian immigrants Sarah Cohen and Abe (Abraham) Frees married and settled in Chicago, Illinois. On June 27, 1912 their first child, Emmanuel ("Manny"), was born, followed by Rose, and David. The baby of the family, Soloman Hersh Frees, voiced to life on June 22, 1920. Soloman was quickly shortened to Solly, then Paul. Eventually he would give himself the middle name Harcourt, as he thought it sounded more impressive.

Dave Frees recalls: "My parents never talked about their parents. My father was a jobber in dry goods. He'd buy up defunct stock - he had a store where he'd put all this merchandise on sale. He made a fair living. We weren't wealthy but we never went hungry. Even in the deepest days of the Depression, we did all right.

"My mother loved good things. She was dramatic. She wasn't *in* drama, but when anything would happen she would be very dramatic about it. Today she'd probably be in Hollywood getting acting jobs; there's where he probably got the acting bug from. The voice, I don't know where that came from. Neither one of my parents

Sarah Cohen.

5

Sarah and Abraham Frees.

sang, and I can't sing worth a damn. My sister sang and played piano. Paul used to accompany her, he'd sing and she'd play the piano. My older brother had a little combo, he played piano. They played for neighborhood people. The house was always filled with people. My mother loved people, loved to entertain.

"When Paul was about four or five he had this deep voice already. The relatives would come over every week or we'd go over to them, and invariably they would ask him to sing, because this little kid had this great voice and he would blast out."

"Paul and Dave were very close," explains Dave's wife, Helen Frees. "Dave was four years older than Paul. When they were small they would sleep in the same bed. Dave would tell Paul stories at bedtime such as the two of them traveling to the moon in a rocket. When he was 2 or 3 the family would put Paul up on a table and he would sing for them. He loved the limelight—and being the center of attention. That came to Paul at a very early age."

There are differing opinions as to where Paul Frees inherited his impressive talents. According to Rose's daughter, Janice Fishbein, it ran in the family. "My mother had his storytelling ability. She was like Paul with accents. She spoke several languages and always gave her stories with the correct accent. They were all very artistic. Manny and David were painters, and my mother was from Russia and did sculpting. My grandfather Abe was from Russia and had a store where he sculpted heads of some kind.

"My grandmother had a very sad life. She was fifteen when she went to London to live with her older sister who was a horrible, horrible person. She was very mean to Sarah, so at sixteen she decided to come to the United States. How she got the money, I don't know. In the bottom of that ship she got very, very seasick and she met a boy who took care of her the whole trip. They fell in love. When they got to Ellis Island, they got separated and never saw each other again.

Paul playing hooky in Chicago.

"It was really an arranged marriage with my grandfather, arranged in Chicago. I don't think they were ever in love. My grandmother was very funny and had a great sense of humor."

In the early 1940s, they moved from Chicago to 20 Dudley Avenue in Venice, California, but Paul had left home nearly a decade before that.

Growing up in Chicago, Paul wasn't sure if he wanted to be an artist or a gangster. "There's something glamorous about the life of a gangster when you're an 11-year-old," he later said, taking great pride in his city, when it wasn't deplorable to be a racketeer. "They were in vogue."

He attended Von Steuben Junior High in Albany Park, but frequently skipped classes for the sake of attending theatre matinees. He began duplicating the voices and dialects of those on the stage, just for fun, but found he had a real talent for impersonations. When school authorities would

Spring in Chicago.

call the house to inquire why Paul wasn't in school that day, he would invent a house full of relatives who couldn't speak English. He didn't care much for school, calling it dull. "Besides, they wouldn't let me talk, and talking is what I like to do most."

"He had lots of friends at school," says Dave Frees. "He was always on. But he didn't care much for school. And my parents were always telling him to get out there and get a job. He always just wanted to go on the road."

Paul himself admitted, "My parents didn't want me to go into showbiz. They tried to get me to sell shirts with my big brother. I've always felt I must be a scatterbrain. I do everything, but never in the same way. It's taken me years to realize there's nothing wrong in being versatile. Why should I spend my life looking for an identity? For a diamond to sparkle it must have many facets."

Paul's son, Fred Frees: "I don't think dad did well or cared much for school. His talent was natural and enhanced through experience, but he never took classes as far as I know. He was not actually knowledgeable about certain things, like science, but he was the best in recognizing talent. I don't even think he finished high school."

In 1991, Paul's older sister Rose was interviewed by Keith Scott. She remembered one long-ago childhood incident that seemed to point to his future career. "One time my mother and I took Paul on a train trip. He was only about ten or eleven at the time. And he was amusing several of the passengers—total strangers—by drawing pictures, and singing, and doing imitations. In those days his earliest imitations were the first ones he ever did on stage—he imitated musical instruments with his mouth, like the four Mills Brothers did—trumpet, trombone, clarinet, the bass guitar. As we got off the train a very distinguished, wealthy-looking, elderly man came up to us and said, 'That little boy is the most talented child I've ever seen. He should be performing on stage.' The way this man talked, we were sure we had just met a famous, legitimate Broadway producer."

Paul left home and school at age thirteen because, some family members said, he wasn't happy at home. He was beginning to love the show business life,

An early audition in Chicago.

which was far removed from his parents' natural habitat.

Fred Frees: "Nobody else had what dad had. No one else in the family had a booming voice. He was one of a kind. They were very simple people—my dad's parents came here from Russia, and they were even simpler people than dad's siblings."

According to Dave Frees, "When Paul was about thirteen, fourteen, he asked me if I could get him an audition at WGN (which stood for World's Greatest Newspaper), the *Tribune*'s radio station in Chicago. I got him an audition there. He was supposed to sing two songs, one of which was 'Starry Night.' We rehearsed together, since my older brother played piano. We rehearsed it, and rehearsed it, and *rehearsed* it, and warned him to memorize it, but he says, 'Oh, I've got it down pat.' Anyway, when we got to the radio station, he sang part of it and forgot the rest of it. But they did say he had a beautiful voice. But at that time it was untrained."

As a teenager in Chicago, Paul got a part-time job cleaning an artist's studio in the Loop. "I wasn't studying art in the sense of studying art. I was working in an artist's studio, cleaning up, and I was trying to learn

as much as I could, unofficially, while cleaning his palette. I would watch his technique and all of the various things that he did.

"But at the same time, in the same building, a 35-story building in Chicago, I would go down and watch the amateur hours. There were two shows in Chicago: *The Marsby Sax Amateur Hour*, and *Reuben's*. And in those days the amateur hours were all the rage. I was originally going to be a painter. By a fluke I got into auditioning for this amateur hour, which was on the 8th floor of where I was learning to be a painter on the 23rd floor. The next thing I knew, they

Buddy Green.

had me in front of the microphone and I did *fantastic* things. I was doing Al Jolson, Wee Bonnie Baker, a scene from *Heidi* with Jean Hersholt (that might have come later in my career), Wallace Beery and Charles Boyer.

"I do not remember my having the ability to impersonate, but I did quite a few. I was on one amateur show and won first prize: $75 and a wristwatch. The following week I was on another show, and soon I thought, boy, this is a pretty good touch, getting money and everything else. And that's how I started in show business."

Touring as Buddy Green.

He talked his parents and high school teachers into letting him go on the road with a variety troupe for a year.

"He went in for all the amateur shows in Chicago," recalls Dave Frees, "and every time he went, he'd win something, a watch or whatever. He did impersonations, not singing. From there, he went on the road with a show called *Fun's-A-Poppin'*. They'd always get stuck someplace on the road, and close the show. And he always came back broke. The first thing he'd ever do when he got paid was to buy jewelry. The reason for that was that if the show went broke, as it did, he'd hock the jewelry and have enough money to come home."

To keep from starving and to fight off the constant competition of the many acts that kept popping up on tour, Paul became a singer, dancer, nightclub emcee and nightclub impersonator. He toured briefly with the Hull House troupe, and played many solo engagements for a whopping $8 a week. He even had a stint at tap dancing, and stooged for other comics. Frees was doing well enough, but not setting Chicago nightclubs on fire. Orchestra leader Benny Meroff thought the talented teen might have better luck with a "less square name," claiming, "you'll never get anywhere with a name like Paul Frees." Benny thought "Buddy Green" sounded hip and showbiz enough to stick in theater managers' minds, so the "Prince of Impersonators" was born, with new material, written by Frees himself, and new impressions added.

AS USUAL . . .
CLUB FORTUNE
Brings You Outstanding Talent in the Field of Entertainment

VERSATILE MASTER OF CEREMONIES

BUDDY GREEN

Direct from CHEZ PAREE Chicago

But being a comic in those days was tough. Eddie Brandt, who would work with Paul later on Spike Jones recordings, remembered: "Buddy Green. He was a comic in the B clubs, in between the strippers in Chicago. The toughest job in the world. A comic - no one wants to see the *comic*. They want to see the girls. They want you to bring on the girls, the naked girls!"

Times were tough. Frees later told a reporter that upon one disastrous return to Chicago, he was broke, sleeping in the park, washing in bus stations, and existed on pickles, sauerkraut and hot water (given free at a hamburger joint) for five days. Then he met Bert Wheeler, one-half of the popular comedy team Wheeler and Woolsey. Paul put on the happiness act for him, but after Bert had bought him a single gin fizz, Paul broke into tears and cried out his entire story. Wheeler gave him $10 and enough words of encouragement to carry on. Twenty-four hours later, he got a job at The Oriental Theatre.

Frees/Green had the mind of a copywriter, often thinking up clever gimmicks to secure just one more booking. Though he didn't work for Disney until many years later, 14-year-old Buddy Green would bill himself as "The Boy Who Does Some of the Voices for Walt Disney," then "Most of the Voices," and then "All of the Voices" to improve the crowds. Disney didn't know it then, but they both laughed about it in the early '60s.

The gratification of the applause and the positive response to his writing and vocal skills outweighed any financial doubts he had about his new obsession: entertaining. In front of riotous or passive audiences nightly gave him the opportunity to hone his skills of timing, comedy and song, and flex his three-octave range.

Then, the war came.

The Player
The 1940s

ENLISTING IN WORLD WAR II did little to curb Paul Frees' voracious creative output. *The Camp Rucker*, the Army's Alabama newspaper, reported on one of Frees' early songwriting efforts: "Sgt. Schmidt and Cpl. Frees presented the [regimental] marching song to the [137ᵗʰ Infantry] Regiment. It was their own composition and the Colonel [Col. Grant Layng, commanding officer] accepted it and extended the Regiment's thanks to the donors. Cpl. Frees led in singing the martial song, and the officers and men sang it heartily."

It started with the Civil War
Eighty years ago or more,
Our regiment became united.
Altho' it may have changed it's name
It's spirit still remains the same
(part missing)

In the Philippines and Meuse... (missing)
Mexico we fought and won.
We thought our job was thru,
Now it's started once again.

When work must be done (missing)
We're there to do it.
We're the Hundred Thirty Seventh Infantry.

To say that we're tough
It isn't enough

15

We're here to show it
We're the Hundred and Thirty Seventh Infantry.

At sight of our guns the enemy runs
They know we're coming
We will be ready for all emergencies
And we're proud to say that we're on our way.
We're the Hundred and Thirty Seventh Infantry.

Our regiments (missing)
We're the Hundred Thirty Seventh Infantry.
Like fighters of old
We're tough and we're bold
Join in the chorus
We're the Hundred Thirty Seventh Infantry.

When there is a fray
You'll find we will stay
'till it is over
Our final word will always be victory
And where e're we go
Oh the world will know
We're the Hundred and
    Thirty Seventh Infantry.

Dave Frees: "I think very highly of my brother. He was a real patriot. He was in the infantry. He told me a bunch of stories about what happened, but they weren't fond ones. Horror stories. And some funny ones. He was out on patrol with another soldier. All of a sudden there was some shooting. He dropped to the ground, as did his buddy, who wore glasses. And all of a sudden he's rummaging around and the guy says, 'I'm look-

137TH INF. MARCH

VALOR FOR SERVICE

WORDS BY
PT. BUDDY FREES

MUSIC BY
SGT. R. W. SCHMIDT

ing for my glasses.' They did find them and they had just started back on patrol when the shooting started again. So he dropped to the ground and his friend says, 'Are you hit?' And Paul says, 'No, I found your glasses.'"

Studio engineer Bob Lindner, who would work with Frees many years later, recalled Paul speaking of his war duty: "He said it was the most terrible thing he'd ever been engaged in. He survived it, and I think if I pressed him, he would have freely talked about it, but I never did. I know some people are pretty sensitive about their wartime experiences. I have a couple of cousins who were in that, and they just never talk about it too much. Paul told me that at some point he was in the Graves Registration Unit. Those are the guys that go around and collect the fallen soldiers, try to ID them, package them up and ship them back. Get 'em buried. Mainly I think it's just collecting dog tags and identifying these guys which is a pretty gruesome thing, but it has to be done."

"He was proud of our country and his participation in the war," says Fred Frees. "He related a story to me where once he was going between Allied and enemy lines, yelling in a German accent in one direction, and yelling in English in the other direction. He told me he had to carry the bodies of his friends on some occasions. Other than that, he didn't talk about it that much."

It was during the war that Paul got involved with Special Services, marking the beginning of his lifelong love affair with police work. He also met a future co-worker there.

"I was in the Invasion of Normandy," Frees later told radio historian John Dunning. "I was with the 35th Division as a combat infantryman. We landed at Omaha Beach and I went in, and then we were in a frontal attack on Saint-Lo. We were to replace the 29th Division. Instead of replacing them, they moved over and just made room for us. When we got there we found out none of us were getting out unless it was feet first, because we were there forever. The only way I got out was I became wounded.

"One day I'm out in a particular area in the front lines and I get trapped with five other guys in my outfit, stuck between the German and the American lines. The German artillery is shooting down on us from this hill and they're zeroing in on us. There was a forest area where the Germans were and there was an open side on the right where the Americans were. We ran between the two, and I'm yelling to the forest where the Germans were: 'Shustik come aben!' and then I turn to the Americans and say, 'Don't shoot, we're Americans!' And we got through.

We get back three, four, five blocks behind the German line and we hit a communications area of the 29th Division. We get there, exhausted and shaking, and there was a very nice guy, a 1st Lieutenant, who gave us some coffee and buns and biscuits or whatever it was instead of K-rations. We talked for a while then walked on back and got transportation back to our outfit.

"Now, seven years later I wind up at CBS and I'm doing shows like *Escape* on which Norman Macdonald was the CBS contact producer whose function it was to hold the stopwatch and have the notes for the producer and director. He was such a handsome guy, he should've been a star in motion pictures, that's how good looking Norm was. When we talked years later we found out that Norm Macdonald was the 1st Lieutenant who gave me the coffee in France when we got through that terrible escapade. We could never figure out where we knew each other from, yet both of us knew that somewhere in our past we had met. We finally figured it out."

Mom sees Paul off to war.

Wounded in the Normandy D-Day invasion at Saint-Lo, France, Frees received the Purple Heart; his leg was damaged enough to take him out of the war and send him back to recuperate in the States. His future wife Joy Terry stated, "He never spoke about his Purple Heart. It wasn't an issue one way or the other. And I found that was the way it was with most of the men who were in World War Two. They made no mind about it, they were very quiet about it."

Helen Frees: "I met Paul when I married Dave in 1940. I found Paul to be very sweet and friendly. We were living in the Wilshire district of Los Angeles at the time. It was lovely back then. Paul was not established yet as an actor. He volunteered into the Army in 1941. While in the service he did get shot in the leg and he was sent to the hospital. But his problems at this time were more than physical—the injury and effects of war affected him mentally as well. They told him that painting was a good way to relax and he took it up. This calmed him and he became a very good painter."

In his San Diego hospital bed, Frees painted to pass away the hours of his eight-month convalescence. While still in the service he had won third prize in a national art contest for a portrait, which was then shown in the National Gallery in Washington D.C. That had helped win him an art scholarship to Chouinard Art Institute in Los Angeles through the GI Bill. He hobbled

along to his weekly classes with the aid of a cane, while searching for a place to live. He was going to be an artist. A painter. But then came love.

While stationed in Ft. Rucker, Alabama, Paul met the lovely young Audrey Annelle McLeod (born November 14, 1924) who was working there. According to Audrey's sister, June Lewis, "One day Paul went into this place where she was working, saw her, and asked someone in there about her. The person knew a few things about her; she was, at the time, living with mother's father and two unmarried sisters in Slocomb, Alabama, which was nearer to Rucker. One of the aunt's names was Norma, which the person told Paul about and about her liv-

Artist and soldier.

ing with them. The next time he went in there he walked over to Annelle's desk and showed her he had handwritten 'Ann,' and told her he knew something about her. She questioned him as to what he meant and he said, 'I know your name is Audrey Annelle, you live in Slocomb with your Aunt Norma.' From that grew the relationship and it was not too much longer after they were married. I guess you could say it was one of those 'love at first sight's.'

June kept her sister's letters to and from Paul "Buddy" Frees, and they, quoted here, are the greatest first-hand chronicle we have into Paul's early years and first marriage. They trace Paul's war experiences, the couple's relationship before and after marriage, and the start of Paul's show business career, which began before he was released from the Army. Unfortunately, there is no dialogue of letters saved; there is a collection of Paul's letters first, then they are later wholly Annelle's.

[First saved letter, written on 137th Infantry, 35 Division stationery] "June 1, 1943. Dear Audrey: Well, here I am writing you as I promised I

Annelle and Paul.

would! I can't begin to tell you what a really delightful time I had in your town! And I do think the people I met there, were the nicest I have ever had the good fortune of meeting!! I have been terribly busy here at camp, as it is the end of the month, and all regimental business must be terminated & settled before the new month begins. I will be unable to see you on Thur. as I must remain in camp & do company duty. However, I want to take this written opportunity to wish you happiness, success, and a bright maturity, that you will find the world a place of wondrous treasures! But remember, to partake of the beauties, & pleasures you must also learn to endure the hardships & trials of our peculiar world------. (Please forgive the above philosophizing; it's just one of my peculiarities.)

"June 29, 1943. Audrey: Thank you for the lovely letter. I regret terribly that I have been unable to meet you at any occasion of the past couple of weeks, but I have been in the hospital, and am still in it!—I didn't deem it necessary to tell you before, but now that I am sure to be released in another day or two, it shouldn't harm to tell you—Aren't I the inflated ego to think that by not telling you I had spared you what concern you may have had for me—In so far as headaches is concerned I have quite a head on my shoulders? 7 3/8 to be exact—How long have you been working at

Paul goes to war.

the hat shop? Is it interesting and profitable?—I suppose you can hardly suppress the desire to know what my ailment is? Well, it was thought to be a form of ulcer or something. However it has proven to be nothing more than a gastric hyper acidity and few other things of reasonably little consequence. Please don't try to come & see me, because it is not bad, really—& besides, I am being held almost incommunicado—Well, guess I better close now, so write me a nice big letter, huh? Buddy

"July 8, 1943. Thursday. Dear Audrey: Thank you for the letter. I am now officially released from the hospital, and I hope I never see the place again… I feel as good as new however and I am grateful for the attention and treatment I received there…"

[Paul and Annelle were married on August 1, 1943.]

"November 22, 1943. My Dearest wife: To date I have received 4 of your letters and really honey, I don't think you could be any more unhappy than I am—I do miss you so much!!—I am in Lebanon (a small town nearby) to close our canteen account until next week—. I have been so busy, that I haven't even had a chance to eat a good meal for 2 days—(now, don't worry, baby, I'm o.k.)?. We go on our problem tomorrow & so I guess it will mean no rest for another 4 days—."

[The mail was slow and sometimes didn't arrive at all. Stationed near Nashville, TN:] "November 26, 1943. Honey, if I don't write to you as often as I should like to, it is merely because we are so busy that it is impossible! Let me explain the circumstances—you see, for 4 days (Mon. thru Thurs.) we are tactical which means no light of any kind at night & we are on the move & working all day!! During those 4 days, I don't do Special Service work at all, but instead I am on guard duty, and believe me, it is rough!! For a few hours during the day it is fairly warm but then… it starts getting cold &—ice cold! We all are suffering from frost bite here & there is no way of getting even slightly warm because fires aren't permitted! Speaking of free time. None of us have had a shave in a week or a bath, or even washed!! Even if we had time, there isn't any water so what the hell! Toujours gai!! Toujours gai!! We are having a few free minutes now, while we wait for trucks to take us to the front lines again. (Pardon the stationary, but it is some I kept in my pocket, hoping for a few free moments like this.)

"Honey Baby, I miss you, & all I can think about is when we'll be together again. No kidding, baby, I'll dream about you the first chance I get to sleep for awhile! You see, the weekends are the only time we get to sleep, & that's when I have to do Special Service work!! So between being on guard all week, I have to work on weekend rest periods also!! Oh well, maybe it will make the time go faster!!"

[Possibly December 1, 1943] "Honey, I know how much our being together at Christmas means to you, & it means a lot to me too, but, really, there isn't any way at all we could possibly be together! I know, baby, I hate to think that we have to wait almost 3 more months before we can see each other, but, for the present, that's the way it looks—. Darling, please don't worry about me, because I'll be o.k. I can take anything they give as long as I have you to think about—."

[Undated. The stationery header reads: Tennessee Maneuvers "Somewhere in Tennessee"] "About the radio show I was going to do, I won't be doing it, (yippee), mainly because I wasn't given any time & secondly because I can't be released from the company for the week it would take—. I'm not sad however, because all it was as far as I was concerned was another headache!! Gosh honey, I think all I've accomplished today is thinking of you, & that isn't work—it's a pleasure! Mud, mud & more mud right up to our ankles. Right now we are located on the near top of a large hill & the trucks can't get up here, because the mud is so slippery—.

"December 11, 1943. I got 3 of your letters today and, honey, I am so happy you are all better—. Darling, let me remind you, if you don't get a letter when you should from me, it is because I am so busy, or in a place where I can't write. This week has been a hectic affair! We keep moving constantly & what's more it has rained all week & the mud is actually up to our knees!! No kidding honey, it is so bad, we are sleeping half in it because there isn't a dry spot anywhere!! Darling, you mustn't worry about me, because honest, I haven't been sick a minute!!—. I feel fine, & my spirits are high even if it is cold & muddy!! Really, darling, I don't mind anything we do here one tenth as much as I feel about being away from you!!"

[They traded constant letters, and often tried to set up meetings together in North Carolina and the various camps to which he was moved, but more often than not, plans fell through. When they finally did meet, Paul sent this postcard to Annelle's parents on January 27, 1944. It was the last thing Paul wrote from these years that has been saved.]

"Tues. 8:30 p.m. Dear Mom & Dad: She has just arrived & we are doing nothing but looking fondly at each other. Thank you for keeping her so lovely. Buddy."

[In an undated letter to her mother, Annelle wrote:] "We do have a nice place through. Three rooms, a living room, bedroom, kitchen and private bath. We have a gas stove to cook on and a nice refrigerator. Buddy had already rented it when I got here. He just happened to find it the Sunday before. Everyone here is looking for rooms. They're begging for rooms at any price. One of the Capt.'s in Buddy's outfit is paying $175 per. month for an apartment. We're paying $42 plus half the gas, electricity and telephone bill and buying our own coal for fuel. If nothing happens Buddy and Charles get their furloughs Tuesday. I suppose all of us will stay here. We're afraid to turn the apartment loose and we can't keep paying for it and go anywhere on his furlough. This is a pretty town. It isn't much larger than Dothan, but there is so much more here. The only thing is that the weather is very changeable. When I got up this morning the sun was shining, now it's cloudy. One day it's freezing and the next day it's hot. Camp Butner [North Carolina] is fourteen miles from here. It takes twenty minutes to go out there. It's just a nickel to call. Buddy calls me about 5 or 6 times a day."

[January 1944] "Buddy was home Sunday and I like to have as much time with him as possible. Then Sunday night I was sick. Dr. Wilson, female specialist at Duke Hospital, said it was a cyst on one of my ovaries and had burst and one of my ovaries is enlarged. He says it isn't serious, but it can become serious. He told Buddy just what to do if I should have another attack. He also said it was possible that I'm pregnant, but I doubt it. If I am, he says I won't be able to carry it because it isn't in the womb, it's in the tube and it will burst very soon, but he says I have nothing to worry about. There were three doctors who examined me. Buddy leaves for maneuvers next week and then they'll have about two weeks here after they come back. I hate to see him go, but I know he has to.

"February 23, 1944. Buddy and I are all right. He's having to work rather hard. He had a show last night and will have one Thursday night, a quiz program Friday and a show for the prisoners in Raleigh Saturday. Then in about two weeks he goes on Virginia maneuvers for 18 days. They carry 120 lb. packs, climb 4400 ft. high and use mules for other equipment.

"March 1, 1944. Buddy went back to camp last night. It seemed like the time flew while we were on furlough. His outfit is going on maneuvers in Virginia next week. They'll be gone for three weeks, then they'll come back here and prepare for amphibious training, then I'm afraid they're going overseas. Buddy thinks so, too. I'm going to work as soon as I can.

When Buddy goes over, I suppose I'll be going to California to stay with Mother Frees and work in the defense plant.

"March 6, 1944. Buddy and I are fine. He is so tired though, he can't see. He worked all afternoon on some cartoons for the officers' party. He's sleeping now. I went out to camp today. The Under Secretary of War was out for a demonstration and we were planning to go, but Buddy had to draw all those cartoons. I don't think they had any men killed; several were hurt. I told you that Buddy did a show for the prisoners at Raleigh, didn't I? Anyway, he did and one of the boys sent him the most beautiful billfold I ever saw and he gave it to me. It is handmade with drawings on the outside and has his name cut in the leather on the inside. If it had been sold it would have sold for $15. He enclosed a card and told Buddy how much he appreciated and enjoyed the show.

"I went to see about the job at the hospital, but didn't take it because they wanted a girl who would be there permanently. I'm going Monday to see about a job at one of the tobacco plants. There isn't much news. Buddy's leaving next Friday for Virginia maneuvers. They'll be there until about the first of April. They come back here and stay until the 15th of April, then they'll be on their way overseas. Mother, it's the hardest thing I've ever had to face. Sometimes I feel as though I just can't bear to see him leave, but I know he has to go and I'll have to do the best I can. I know he'll get over just in time to be one of the first to go into the new invasion. If I just knew that he would come back just as he goes over, it wouldn't be so bad, but there's always the thought that he might be among the ones who don't come back. I'm getting so nervous, I can't talk about it anymore.

"March 7, 1944. I'm rather down in the dumps today. I've been walking the streets (until it started raining) looking for a job. I can't find anything. They wouldn't even take my application at the tobacco plant. With worrying about finding a job and the thought that Buddy will be leaving the 15th of April is driving me crazy. We're already two days late with the rent and it looks as though my check isn't coming. I have $46 in my purse and that's all the money we have. I suppose there is a way out. We have $50 in the bank, but that's part of my transportation money. Oh! well things will work out, I'm sure.

"March 17, 1944. I started working today at a cafeteria. It's a very nice place. I'll make $12.50 per week plus two meals a day. I'm so tired now though that I can't move.

"June 1, 1944. Today was ten months ago Buddy and I were married. It seems only yesterday. I wish it was and we could have all that time together again. No, I suppose that's wrong, but I'd sure give anything to see him. I'll try to write two or three times a week if I possibly can. If I don't, just don't worry about me. I'm usually rather tired when I get home from work and I just sit.

"July 6, 1944. Mother, I don't know why but everything seems so strange. It seems as though I've gone my last mile. I've felt all day as though I'm waiting for something that's bad news. There seems that I don't have any future to hope for any longer. I wish I could snap out of it, I'm so miserable, something I can't explain. So many people are being killed, within the past week, there's been three coal mine fires, two train accidents, a fire from a circus and so many killed over the 4th. I took a walk, trying to forget everything, but it's still there. I feel like crying my eyes out. Maybe it's because I miss Buddy so much. I've been hearing from him often but it seems that if I have to wait another day to see him, I'll go crazy. He's so sweet and good and nobody knows how I love him and to think they snatch him off into such!! Mother, it just hurts beyond words. If he was mean to me or did things he shouldn't maybe I could say he deserves it, but he doesn't. He never hurt anybody. He's too tender hearted!! I feel like dying, or something. I just don't have any desire to live while he's away!!"

[To take her mind off being alone, she was almost constantly in search of work. No one was hiring. Occasionally she got lucky.] "July 16, 1944. I started to work yesterday at Henshey's, the largest department store in Santa Monica. It's a very nice place to work. They don't pay but $24 plus a small bonus every month. I work in the Sportswear department from 9:30 to 5:30.

"July 23, 1944. I've been so worried for the past few days. I had a letter, in fact two letters from Buddy Friday and he is in France. Right in the thick of the fighting. The only thing I can do is to pray for his safety and I do every night with all my heart.

"August 28, 1944. Mother, if you can't read my writing in this letter, I'm rather upset. I had a letter from Buddy today. He is in England again in the hospital with a broken ankle.

"September 8, 1944. I had four letters from Buddy this week. He seems to be fine. They took his leg out of one cast and put it in another. He's very lonesome, you know he has so much time to think, but does some sketching and reads quite a bit.

"Sept. 17, 1944. He says, 'I'm doing something for the war effort, rolling bandages [while in the hospital]. I say there's nothing too good for our boys.' I had to cry when I read it for only God knows what he has been through. He never did tell me how he broke his ankle.

"September 21, 1944. Mother, Darling, If you can't read this letter, please forgive me but I have such a terrific stomach ache, I can hardly see. As a matter of fact I couldn't write a long letter to Buddy. I just took a Midol tablet, sure hope it relieves me. I had two letters from Buddy this week. He hasn't heard from me in about 6 weeks. I hope he hears soon. He is able to walk around now with the aid of a crutch.

"September 27, 1944. I had a letter from Buddy Monday. He said he would probably see Tokio before California. It didn't sound too good.

"October 2, 1944. I had a letter from Buddy today! Bless his heart, he's so faithful to write. He hasn't had but one letter from me in two months and I write every night. Somehow the letter I got from him today was almost too much for me. He told me that there are so many ugly and cruel pictures of war in his mind and it's so hard to try to forget them. He began by saying, 'Darling, I didn't get a letter from you today, but that is all right. I read your last one' (which made 50 times). Then he thinks I'm wonderful because I write and I'm true to him. Mother, I know that he is the most wonderful husband any girl ever had.

"October 30, 1944. Well, I had another letter from Buddy today. He is still in the hospital. He finally got all my letters. He got 65 at once. Bless his heart, he was so happy to get them.

"November 13, 1944. Mother, I knew that war does things to people. It has to Buddy. His letters are still wonderful, sweet and loving, but I know by some of the things he's tried to tell me. There are so many horrible pictures in his mind. If only I could help him.

"January 6, 1945. I'm writing this because I feel as though I haven't written anything since Buddy has been home because we were always going out. I just got back from the station after seeing Buddy off to the hospital again. The three weeks he was here were perfect. He is so nervous. He screamed at everyone when they said anything. He can't help it, but it just doesn't seem like him. He yelled at Mom so much that she got scared. He was wonderful to me, but still I worry about his condition. I think they will be able to do quite a bit for him at this hospital. They have every kind of recreation so he will be kept busy.

"You should see the medals Buddy is wearing! The one on the left is the purple heart, the center one is European theatre of war, the one on the right is a good conduct medal he got before going over. The big one on the bottom is the combat infantryman's badge. I think he looks good to have been through what he has. He doesn't limp very much.

"January 10, 1945. I had a letter from Buddy today. He is fine. I just finished a letter to him. He is 200 miles from here and will be able to come in rather often.

"January 13, 1945. Buddy came home Thursday night on a three day pass. He was very sick yesterday and last night, but feels better tonight. I think he has flu. He has a terrible cold and his head and stomach are bothering him. Bless his heart, he just isn't well. His leg is perfectly well. He only limps when it's damp. They sent him back here because of a nervous condition. I don't think he will go back overseas. It might be that he will get out. I do pray that he will. He was in the army three years the 8th of this month. I think he's had enough. He is sitting here beside me, talking to Mom and Pa about the things he did when he was a little boy.

"January 23, 1945. Yes, Mother, Buddy has been through so very much. I only pray to God to help me to know how to help him overcome that nervous condition. He tries so hard not to show it, but sometimes he can't hide it. Mother, he wasn't wounded, exactly. During a battle, he ran for his foxhole and stumbled on something and fell. He broke an ankle. They sent him to England to heal that as fast as possible so he could go back into action. While he was there, they noticed how nervous he was and investigated immediately and it wasn't long until he found out he was coming home. The doctor told him he should never have gone overseas. They say no actor should go over because they are all very nervous, anyway.

"January 31, 1945. Buddy is fine. He is beginning to relax now. He can sit through the newsreel and it doesn't bother him so much. The doctor told him that's the best way to overcome that feeling. He loves shows, so that's where we spend most of our leisure time. He gets home on weekends and it surely is nice to have him home. He is so wonderful to me. He does everything he can that he thinks will make my work easier. He's always bringing some little thing home for me.

"February 2, 1945. I had a letter from Buddy today. He is fine, but won't be able to come home this weekend. He asked me to send him money. He needed cigarettes and the little stinker plays cards at night. I can't say anything for that's about the only time he actually relaxes and to me that's worth a million dollars. He is beginning to be himself again. He is taking up commercial art and the instructor thinks he's terrific. His paintings are really marvelous. I'm very proud of him.

"February 25, 1945. Buddy just left about two hours ago. He comes home on Friday night and goes back on Sunday. It is so terribly lonesome after he leaves. Mother, he asked me to tell you that he wanted very much to write to you, but he doesn't do any writing. He's so nervous. He sends his love to all of you. Bless his heart, if it isn't one thing to upset him, it's another. They're trying to get him to become an art instructor at the hospital and he doesn't want to because it would kill all his chances of getting out of the Army. Just being there, waiting, is very bad for him. He's been in the hospital for over six months. Oh! I pray that he will get out very soon.

"March 5, 1945. You know Mother, I thought I was happy that Saturday morning in November when I got Buddy's telegram that he was back in the states and then when he came home I was so terribly happy, but it's nothing compared to the happiness I experienced Friday afternoon, when soon after I got home from work, Buddy walked in, and told me that he was discharged. Oh! Mother it's so, so wonderful to see him in civilian clothes. We went into the men's department at the store Saturday and bought him some clothes, we got part of his wardrobe but he has to have a few more suits and more underwear, if we can find any. He looks so sweet in his new clothes. For a coming home gift, I gave him a beautiful cigarette lighter, it's pure sterling silver, handmade and I had it monogrammed. It costs twenty-two dollars and I let him pay for it. Nice, aren't I?

"He won first prize at the art exhibit the day he left for the best painting. They gave him an oil paint set. Right now he's sitting beside me, making a painting for our bedroom. He's painting a face of an Arab. I'm still working and I like it very much. It will be a few months before Buddy can work. The doctor's made him promise he would rest for two or three months. I suppose he'll go into radio or go to art school.

"March 9, 1945. I suppose you got my letter, telling you about Buddy being out of the army. Bless his heart, he's already started out, looking for work. I wanted him to rest for at least a month, but I soon found out that I could just as well be talking to the ocean, because he's just about that still. He is in the living room, working on an oil painting, he just stopped to make a few monkey faces. I just pray that he can get started in something, for he wants to so much.

"March 19, 1945. We just heard Buddy's broadcast. Gee! he did a marvelous job! He will probably be home about eleven.

"March 30, 1945. Buddy had to go to Hollywood tonight for rehearsals, so I decided I better answer your letter while I have the chance. He has to go tomorrow also, it being Saturday night, we'll leave from the store, go into Hollywood for dinner and then he'll go for rehearsals. He's on the Lux Theatre program Monday night. He's only going to do radio during his spare time. He starts to art school Monday and will go for four years. They pay him $103 a month, plus all expenses. Then, the few shows he can do, will help out. He was paid $75 for the first show he did and I suppose he'll get about the same for this. We're trying to find an apartment, but it seems almost impossible. We want to save as much money as we can, so we can buy a house, someday. He goes to school 42 weeks a year, two and one half months for vacation. He's promised, the first vacation he gets, we're going to see you. Believe me, it can't be too soon. That's another reason we're trying to save money, to make the trip. It will cost us about $600.

"No, I've never met Rita Hayworth. She comes in the store quite often. Buddy did a show for the army yesterday with Edward G. Robinson and he drove Buddy home.

"April 16, 1945. Buddy did a show tonight. He was on "Sherlock Holmes." He did a terrific part! He's getting better all the time. He's still going to art school, but I think he's trying to do too much, but he can't keep still one minute so I suppose it's better he stays busy.

"May 3, 1945. Darling, about you coming out here. I wish there was a way. But, first, there is no place for you to stay. Mom has a small apartment. She and Pa have a bed, Mannie [Paul's eldest brother, Manny] is getting married and his wife will be here and Buddy and I have one bed. We just can't find an apartment. It's impossible. Second Darling, I don't have the money. It may sound funny to you, but it costs so much to live out here and Buddy and I are trying to save a little money to buy us a home. He goes to school and only gets $25 per week and I get $22 by the time they take out for income tax. It takes almost every penny for living expenses. The money he makes on the shows goes for his dues to the "Actor's Guild," a club he has to belong to so he can work on the radio. I know you work to pay your expenses back, but until we can find a place of our own, it seems almost impossible.

"May 5, 1945. Buddy and I are fine and especially happy tonight. We just found an apartment today. I got it through one of the men at the store. It isn't such a beautiful place, but reasonable. Gosh! I'm so happy about it!! We looked everywhere for one, but until today was unable to find anything. We're moving tomorrow. I'm sure you don't envy us that task. The address is 1155 11th St. Apt. B. Santa Monica, Calif. Buddy's doing very good in school. You should see some of his drawings. As soon as we get 'set up' in our new place, he will make a picture of me for you.

"May 8, 1945. Isn't it wonderful about the war in Europe being over?!! It's almost too good to be true. May God bless all those boys and bring them to a complete victory over Japan very soon, so they can very soon rejoin their beloved wives and mothers.

Paul's painting of Annelle.

"May 14, 1945. After such a long delay, I'll try to write you about some of the things we've been doing during the past week. First, last Monday, we went into Los Angeles and bought a few things we needed for our apartment. We spent quite a hectic afternoon, trying to shop. There were so many people we could hardly walk. Tuesday I washed and Wednesday I ironed. Thursday Buddy worked until 10:00, so I did part of my cleaning and Friday I finished that and a few more pieces of clothes I had to iron. Saturday we were so busy at the store. I had $185.00 on my book and was I tired. Buddy doesn't go to school on Saturday, so he made dinner for me. We went to the show Saturday night and Sunday we went over to Mom's for a few minutes and saw Mannie and his fiancée. They're going to be married June 3rd. Sunday night, Buddy had me pose for him about two hours. He's working on the painting now. It's an oil and it's good. Buddy still gets his head and stomach aches, but not quite so often. I hope in time, he will overcome them completely.

"June 4, 1945. We went to Mannie's wedding yesterday and it was nice, very simple and lovely. He has a nice wife. She's isn't too beautiful and not too young, in her 'thirties,' but a lovely person. That was the first Jewish wedding I've seen and I thought it was very nice. The Rabbi called them under the canapé about four times before they finally started the ceremony. It was beginning to get funny.

"Mother Darling, thank you so much for offering to send me some canned fruit, but I know you can use it and you work so hard to get it. I'll tell you something I'd like if you have it to spare, otherwise it's all right. That is, a small piece of bacon and a shoe stamp. Buddy needs shoes and he's already used all the [ration] stamps he has. I think I told you [agent] Phil Sherry is handling him for pictures and of course he has to have smart clothes when he goes in to see these producers. He has only two decent suits he can wear and I want him to have at least three or four more. Gee! but clothes are so terribly expensive out here. Gosh! you can easily spend two hundred dollars for one outright and have a fairly good looking suit.

"Buddy is doing a show from 10:00 - 10:15 tonight. I suppose it will be quite late when he gets home. Bless his heart, he works so hard. Say, when you see Uncle Al, please ask him if he knows where he can buy some cigarettes. If he can send us some, Buddy will pay him well. Buddy brought home about twelve cartoons when he got out of the army, but they are gone and it's almost impossible to find any out here.

"June 29, 1945. He goes to school every day and almost every night he has a rehearsal and gets home about midnight. He also has about three auditions a week and has to go to the different studios with Phil to try for pictures.

"July 4, 1945. I haven't felt so good today. I've been in bed. Nothing unusual, just my usual sickness. Dr. Pearson is going to start giving me shots next week so I won't have any pain. He gave Buddy some codeine pills for me to take this time. I'm lying in bed while I'm writing and my hands are so weak. It's because I gave blood to the Red Cross three weeks ago and I haven't had time to build it up yet.

"Poor little Buddy has been so busy today. We came home about twelve and then he walked five blocks to the market and while he was there, he called the doctor and then had the prescription filled and came home and made lunch, did the dishes and cleaned everything. Then he made dinner and cleaned the kitchen and he timed the pills I took and repeated them when it was time. Gosh! the one day I had off and I had to spend it in bed.

"July 10, 1945. I am going to the doctor Saturday to have a wart taken off my finger and I have to go next week to another doctor to take some shots for my monthly sickness. He thinks he can help me. I hope so. Gee! it seems everything comes up at once. I have to get something for Buddy for our anniversary and I just don't know what it will be. I'd like to buy a desk for him, but the only one I saw that I liked was $109.50 and I just can't pay that much.

"July 26, 1945. Buddy and I had already started planning on going home to see you when he gets his vacation, so naturally something had to happen. I hope to go to the hospital in a few weeks. It's nothing serious. Just a small tumor to be removed. I have a very good doctor, so there's nothing to worry about. The only thing I'm worried about is the money. It takes just about twice as much as we have saved. A few days ago Buddy went to Hollywood and bought a car, a '40 Chevrolet. He went to the ration board and got an 'A' and 'C' book and went back to the place to bring the car home and surprise me—so the first thing he did before he got out of the lot, he ran into a car and bent our car up. His nerves went to pieces so he had to take it back and now he has to pay about seventy-five dollars for damages. If anything else happens?!!!

"July 31, 1945. I went to another doctor since I wrote the last letter. He is just out of the Army and is a female specialist. His name is Koennecke and is supposed to be very good. He gave me a more thorough examination and found about the same as Dr. Mahoney. He also said that my blood was very low and he would have to build me up before the operation. I'm taking some iron capsules and little white tablets. I think I'll go to the hospital in about three weeks. He is much more reasonable than the other doctor. We won't have to go in debt this way, but it will take all we have and Buddy won't let me talk about going back to work within six weeks. I do have the insurance that will help quite a bit, though.

"We went to San Fernando Valley yesterday and it was beautiful out there. We spent the afternoon and evening with Buddy's agent, Phil Shelly. They are lovely people. Buddy is quite busy, just keeps going all the time. Bless his heart, he never gets any rest, but never complains. We celebrate our 2nd anniversary tomorrow. It's our first together and I think he has to work. Oh! well, such is life.

"August 4, 1945. We celebrated our second anniversary Wednesday night. Jeanne Beck and Lois Keen had dinner with us. Lois gave us a glass top coffee table which is very lovely. Jeanne is making chair covers and tablecloths to match. She didn't get it finished in time. I gave Buddy a shirt and four pairs of socks and he bought a typewriter for us. We couldn't afford to give anything expensive.

"I called Dr. Koennecke today and he hasn't been able to get a room for me yet, but he will know Monday when he can get one, so I don't know when I'll have my operation. I will be very happy when it's all over. I'm not afraid, but I want to feel good for a change.

"August 9, 1945. Mother please don't worry about me. As I told you before there is nothing to worry about. I'm sure that I will be all right. There isn't anything serious about the operation and it will only be a short time and I will be home, resting and taking it easy, which is the really important thing. I go to the hospital on the 21st and have the operation the next day.

"Buddy would write as I said before but bless his heart he is always working. Tonight he is rehearsing for the play. He hasn't been feeling too good for the past few days. His stomach is bothering him and he doesn't feel like doing anything but resting and relaxing when he is home. Talking about the fish he caught, he went fishing the other day and brought back seven bass that weighed about a pound each. He thought that the two of us could eat them for dinner. We finally gave them to our neighbors and they were very happy to get them. I sure didn't like to clean them and I told him he could just leave them at the boat next time.

"You wanted to know about how Buddy is getting along with pictures. Well, he has to lose a bit of weight before he can get into pictures so he is going to take reducing pills so his face will get thinner. Phil still takes him to the different studios and is doing everything for him that he can and I don't think it will be too long before he will get something, but he is quite busy with this play he is doing, but after that I'm sure that he will get something.

"August 16, 1945 [last letter]. Isn't it wonderful about V J Day? I was so happy when we heard the news over the radio that I cried and laughed at the same time. Everyone was in a dither and the customers were the same way. We closed the store a few minutes after we heard the news. No one could do anything. I went over to a girl friend's house and had dinner with her as Buddy wasn't home at the time. When we went out into the streets, everyone was throwing pennies and paper all over the streets and throwing anything else that they could find to throw. They started shooting firecrackers and a few other things. Bells were ringing and people were talking, laughing and crying. No one was hearing what the other was saying. We can sure say that we lived in the [most] historic time of all the world. What with the new Atomic bomb and everything else. If only we can keep our noses out of everybody's business but our own now, we will be all right. I just pray that this will be lasting peace.

"We celebrated that night. A couple of our friends came over in their car and took us out to the Valley to see Phil and his family. They were celebrating, too. We stayed until two in the morning. Oh, but it is wonderful. I can hardly believe it. Now the boys will come home to their wives, babies and sweethearts. The ones that have never seen their babies will be so happy to be home for keeps. God bless all of them for what they have [been] through and done and may they live in peace.

"Buddy just left for rehearsal and he will be gone until about midnight, so I think I will go over to Mom's and stay for a while. Gee, they sure got some of the things off ration lists fast. Gas and all canned goods. Buddy and I went shopping this morning and it was really a pleasure because we didn't have to fool with ration stamps except for meat."

Paul Frees had left his Army hospital bed in March or April of 1945. Alas, artists did not climb high on the pay scale. In order to make ends meet, Paul—no longer Buddy Green after the war—began a new career when fate spoke to him at CBS in Columbia Square in what is still known as "Gower Gulch" near the corner of Sunset & Gower. Earlier, he'd tried for two years to get work in radio. Then, because of the war, he found his way in.

The war had left Frees badly shaken. He later told Robert Cornthwaite ("Dr. Carrington" in Howard Hawks' *The Thing*) that he would stand on street corners, preparing to cross, and would have to force himself into doing it. Still walking with a cane, Paul also carried the Purple Heart insignia on his jacket. A small, rotund Irishman by the name of Ray Buffum noticed this and came up to him.

"Oh, I see you have the Purple Heart," he said. "I was a sergeant in World War I. I was in the Marines. Do you want to get in to see one of the shows?"

"Actually," Paul answered, "I'm hoping to get a job in radio so my wife won't have to be transferred out of the hospital."

He explained his need for an immediate $6,000. He didn't know what made him think he could get that kind of money out of radio, having had mostly "amateur hour" experience, but Frees was nothing if not confident.

"Well, what do you do?" Buffum asked.

"I can do about a hundred impersonations. I used to sing and dance but I don't dance anymore because I was shot in the leg."

"Do you do dialects?"

"Well, I can do three or four variations of every dialect there is."

"Can you do Australian?"

Paul answered him with an Aussie accent that impressed Buffum enough to land Frees his first radio work. He was now Digger Slade, the Australian Adventurer on *A Man Named Jordan*. Buffum was the writer-producer of the series, as well as his earlier hit, *Hawthorne House*. He would also write for *The Casebook of Gregory Hood*, *Rogue's Gallery*, and the short-lived dramatic anthology, *Twelve Players*.

A Man Named Jordan began as a fifteen-minute sustaining (not sponsored) adventure serial, becoming a weekly half-hour series after six months. Jack Moyles played Rocky Jordan, who ran the exotic Café Tambourine, an intimate restaurant in Istanbul that attracted enough mysterious characters to make a sequel to *Casablanca*. Like the best of the hard-boiled detectives (though this guy wasn't even a private dick), Jordan loved a buck and, with the aid of sidekick Ali (Frees in his best Peter Lorre voice) and girlfriend Toni Sherwood (played by Dorothy Lovett), he would find himself in the middle of any adventure that came his way.

When the thirty-minute version began on July 2, 1945, Jay Novello was added to the cast as Captain Sam Sabaaya of the Cairo police. Authenticity was foremost, with writers Larry Roman and Gomer Cool using Egyptian newspaper items for plots and real Cairo street names to give its mysterious Oriental flavor true excitement. Even Richard Aurandt's native score harkened an Eastern aura of intrigue and dangerous beauty over the popular action drama.

Most of Frees' known or existing work on this series came at the end of the '40s, after its name had been changed to *Rocky Jordan*; the show had returned in the Fall of 1948, the café having moved to Cairo.

While it was good to have some income he could count on in the mid-1940s, it wasn't nearly enough. Radio roles were small at first, but kept increasing to the point that Paul had to withdraw from art school in order to take on enough work to pay off his wife's hospital costs. Unfortunately, Annelle died on September 20, 1945, two months shy of her twenty-first birthday. Paul later wistfully recalled "that's how I am where I am today, all because of the worst tragedy of my life."

"Annelle had some difficult female problems," says Annelle's sister, June Lewis, "and, we think, was at one time pregnant. She lost the baby and continued to have the problems, so the doctor believed she needed surgery to correct some of her problems. She went through the surgery and was almost ready to come home, but developed peritonitis [an inflammation of the membrane which lines the inside of the abdomen and all of the internal organs] and died."

To forget, and survive, Frees plunged into radio work with an abandon few performers have equaled. He probably played every single great radio series, and though often uncredited, he could be heard throughout the later 1940s on such stellar network series as *Escape, Suspense, The Whistler*, and even comedy favorites such as *Maxwell House Coffee Time*, with George Burns and Gracie Allen.

In a 1982 radio interview Frees explained that the very first radio show he did was *The Burns and Allen Show*, as an impersonator. Jack Benny heard him on it and asked him to be on his show. "I'd never seen eleven cents at one time in my life. I was writing songs with a guy at night and we were at the piano at his home, trying to get started. I didn't have a job of any kind. I'd done the Burns and Allen show but it's hard to live on one check."

He subscribed to an answering service, as all actors did at the time, which called up saying Jack Benny wanted to talk with him. He thought it was an obvious joke. Adopting Jack's voice to answer the phone, Paul soon realized that this was the *real* Benny requesting an interview with him. He started shaking, as Jack was an idol to the young actor. He took a cab to Jack's home, and was ushered upstairs by wife Mary Livingston to his bedroom, where the great man was lying in bed in a pair of shorts. That casual interview led to several freelance jobs on Jack's popular program, sparking more interest in Frees' mimicking skills. "I have never known a more generous man in the industry. Jack Benny was the one person on whose show you never had to make a deal, because you would get more from him than you would ever ask for."

In another interview Paul claimed his first radio job was on April 2, 1945 in *Lux Radio Theater*'s production of "Swanee River" with Al Jolson. "They gave me one line, about twenty miles off-mike."

It took more than bit parts to live, and "radio actors didn't have agents," so Paul knocked on doors and had a business card made up: The Versatile Paul Frees. When asked what he did, many directors and producers couldn't comprehend his three or four variations of every dialect or his three-and-a-half octave singing voice. Finally, a friend told him, "Look, when you go to see someone who has a gangster show, just tell them you do a Brooklyn gangster." Bit by bit he built up a solid reputation as a voice who could handle anything "and I worked in radio right up to the point where the industry left me."

From 1946 his work in radio was as constant as it is now hard to find. He did an average of 35 shows a week at his height. Even Frees would not remember the thousands of credits he would amass years later. He established himself quickly, winning the *Radio Life* Award in 1948.

Frees became a semi-regular on the high-quality dramatic series *Escape*, and was the narrator of a number of episodes beginning in August of 1947. Before the show returned for the Fall lineup, he was given a voice audition by CBS for the announcer role on September 18, 1947. His world-weary, cynical delivery was unmistakable. "Tired of the everyday grind? (Pause) Ever dream of the life of romantic adventure? (Pause) Wanna get away from it all? (Pause) We offer you...(Dramatic musical chord) Escape!" More music. Then the commercial announcer, Frank Goss, would interject, "Escape. Designed to free you from the four walls of today—for a half-hour of high adventure!"

Paul recalled later: "Billy (William Conrad) and I would trade off doing that opening. If I starred on *Escape*, Bill would do the opening, in the same voice. If Bill was doing another voice or couldn't make it, I would do the opening. So we covered for each other, and nobody ever knew the difference."

Directed toward the listener in present tense, the opening narration, this example from the "Judgement Day at Crippled Deer" episode, was intended to titillate thrill seekers. "You are one of four people trapped in an isolated trading post somewhere in the Yukon territory. The blizzard outside making escape impossible. And you know that before the spring thaws release you—before you can leave this cabin behind you, one of your companions, by consent of the others, will be killed."

Though he was too busy performing on radio shows to listen to them, he did have his favorites. For *Escape*, it was "Evening Primrose," broadcast on November 5, 1947. He also remembered having won a radio award for "Country of the Blind," which he heard for the first time in 1979 when a radio station sent him a copy they were re-broadcasting.

One of his better leads on *Escape* came on October 1, 1947 when "The Most Dangerous Game" shot Frees into the narrative guise of the big game hunter who becomes the hunted. The exposition was heavy, but tense, anxious and, like a classic adventure short story, ran swiftly into action, gaining momentum as Frees scored point after point, finally winning the game by murdering the evil General Zaroff (Hans Conried).

Being a part of *Suspense* was probably Frees' greatest personal achievement and, more often than not, it would be the first series he would list when rattling off his many radio credits. He had auditioned against sixteen other actors for the job.

The widely popular mystery series began on July 22, 1940 with a show called "The Lodger," directed by Alfred Hitchcock. Many famous stories were adapted for the program, with probably the most famous episode being "Sorry, Wrong Number" by Lucille Fletcher, starring Agnes Moorehead. Paul Frees' first appearance came in "Easy Money" on November 7, 1946, supporting Jack Carson in the role of the greedy husband who wanted to kill his nagging wife, played by Cathy Lewis. He also performed alongside friend William Conrad in the first hour-long show, on January 3, 1948 in "The Black Curtain." But it wasn't until the July 8th episode that he became the show's announcer, a job he valued even more than starring in the episodes. He would continue the ominous introduction of "a tale well-calculated to keep you in…Suspense" until December 29, 1949 when "The Bullet" aired. Joseph Kearns took over Frees' signature voice on *Suspense* beginning on January 5, 1950.

Paul Frees and Dorothy Lamour.

The top stars—everyone from Humphrey Bogart to Judy Garland—appeared on that chilling program. Among the many unsung supporting actors were Paul's future *Bullwinkle* cohorts Hans Conried, Daws Butler and Walter Tetley who made numerous appearances. Frees would irregularly appear on the series throughout the 1950s, last appearing on August 16, 1959 in the episode "Like Man, Somebody Dig Me," starring Dennis Day and Lillian Buyeff. Oddly, this was also at the same time that Frees was filming his own cool cat tale, *The Beatniks*.

"The real pros were in radio," Paul Frees told an interviewer. "There was no room for fakeries. Appearance didn't mean a thing. If you didn't have the ability, you didn't survive. We—people like Jack Webb, Frank Lovejoy, Stacy Harris, Raymond Burr and Charles McGraw—weren't actors. We were insurance policies. When we were called, they knew they would get what they wanted.

"There was a ring of about twenty of us who did all the work. Bill Conrad, Hans Conried, Frank Lovejoy, and we worked all the shows. We couldn't hear the shows we were on because we worked seven days a week. We would do a read through, a second run on some shows, a dress rehearsal, then a show for the East, then we'd come back three hours later for the West coast. It was all live. It was pretty hairy at times. I have lumps on my head still because Conreid or whoever would hit me on the head with a script because you get to the very last line of the show and blow the line. There's no way to go back. I miss that pressure, but not that much."

Radio actor Harry Bartell recalled, "In radio, freelance actors worked with different people every day and sometimes in the same day. There was a relatively small group of actors involved and they all knew each other primarily from working contacts. Naturally, they got to know some better than others, but usually the contacts, while 'friendly,' were hardly intimate.

"My knowledge of Paul falls somewhere in between. I have no recollection of where or when we met but I am certain it was in a studio. Paul was easy to remember. He was always immaculately dressed, usually *a la* Brooks Brothers.

"It was somewhat of a shock to hear him speak. He wasn't a big man but possessed a very big voice which he could use with tremendous skill. He was capable of myriad character voices, a lot of dialects but, in my opinion, had more difficulty in portraying characters closer to the real Paul Frees.

"Paul gave the impression of being chubby although he was not fat. And he had an air of innocence which sometimes made him the butt of jokes. But he was a gentleman and I liked him. He was also a skilled draftsman and a sensitive person.

"I can't recall now whether the loss of his first wife was due to her death or divorce but I know that it really shattered him and I remember spending time with him trying to help him find his feet again.

"Asking what shows we worked on is like my asking you what you had for breakfast on August 13, 1984. I can recall *Escape* and *Sherlock*

Suspense, "The Morrison Affair" with Madeleine Carroll, Paul Frees, and director Jack Johnstone.

Holmes, but there were many others including the deservedly short-lived *Green Lama.* It was on *Sherlock* that Paul created one of the greatest bloopers of all time. He had an impossible line that ran something like, 'Dr. Sanderson was Miss Eustace's allergist.' We went live to the East coast at 5 p.m. and Paul got tangled up in the sibilants. He sounded like a leaky steam pipe with all the S's. When we did the West coast repeat at 8, he backed up very carefully to that line, said it perfectly, took a bow toward the control booth, and booted his next line. Ah! Live radio!"

Veteran voice actor John Stephenson (later known as Fred Flintstone's boss, Mr. Slate) recalls his radio work with Frees: "We were both radio actors working freelance in the late 40s, early 50s. Everything from *Suspense* to *Escape* to *Lux Radio Theater.* I was also a poker playing buddy of his, we played usually at his house. He organized the game and invited some friends.

"I was working on a radio show with him once, with Douglas Fairbanks Jr., on one of the foreign intrigue shows [*The Silent Men*] that was around in those days. I remember the director throwing up the key and

saying, 'I can't tell who's talking!!' Paul had that ability and didn't even know he was picking up Douglas Fairbanks' rhythm, voice, pitch and everything else, and before long they were both sounding the same. Fairbanks didn't even realize it.

"I also remember being at an audition for a Peter Lorre voice once, and when Paul Frees came out, he said to the rest of the people waiting around to audition, 'You can all leave! *I* do Peter Lorre!' He was half-kidding, half-serious. You never knew if he was serious or kidding about a lot of things. He was putting on the world."

As much as he loved to perform for the microphone, he loved joking and ragging on his fellow actors, a trait that would almost define his studio character. In 1989, prolific radio actor Larry Dobkin recalled that Frees, with his constantly mischievous ways, was a highly popular target for retaliation. "We all played jokes on Paul Frees. And he was never, ever at a loss. During *Murder and Mr. Malone*, we'd set fire to his script, or we 'pantsed' him [removed his pants while he was acting a scene]. We even tied him to a stool one day, when we were live on air. It was a stool with wheels. We pushed the stool under him while he was reading his lines; one of us held his script for him so he could keep reading, and he never dropped a line! And he had a lot to do that day. Then we tied his hands behind his back. Then we tied his legs. By the time he finished the show, he was tied to this stool. The organ theme came up, and the show was over. We were off the air. Then Bill Conrad and Frank Lovejoy wheeled him out to the lobby at ABC, where there were phones for the actors to call their service for messages. Someone was using the phone, and as he hung up, he said, 'Oh, by the way, Paul, someone's looking for you.' And Frees, without missing a beat, came back with, 'I can't take the call. Just tell 'em I'm all tied up.'"

Bill Conrad related the exact same incident in 1991, when interviewed by Keith Scott; Conrad added that he was furious about the fact that Frees was unruffled by the practical joke. Conrad said, "When he came up with that line about being all tied up, I said, 'You smart-ass son of a bitch. You want the last word—well, okay, fine!' And we all walked off and left him there, struggling in the lobby, tied to the chair. He was yelling, 'Hey, fellas, come back!' We never knew when he finally found someone to untie him."

Joy Terry Frees: "The boys used to play practical jokes on him in the early radio days. You would sit around at a table before you went to the microphone. Sometimes they would tie his feet together so he couldn't get there! One time when they were on the air, they were burning his script. They put it on fire!"

Paul had met Joy Terry during his second marriage, to a girl named June. Not much is known about June except for a small article in *Radio Mirror* magazine in 1948, that also tells of a special award CBS had received from the National Conference of Christians and Jews for the network's Memorial Day Broadcast of 1948's *For This We Live*, in which Frees appeared. In their San Fernando Valley home Frees would sketch pictures of June and their Doberman pup, Belle Frees McPherson, and also drew caricatures of his fellow radio actors on the scripts he was sent. He also continued his oil and water color painting. But it was not a happy home life at the time.

Joy Terry Frees: "I had come out here from New York, because I had worked in radio. I started working in radio in New York when I was 5 years old, and appeared on shows like *Coast to Coast on a Bus, Young Doctor Malone,* and *Your Family and Mine.* I was sent to do the ingenue lead on a little epic called *Chandu the Magician* [which went to air in June of 1948]. So while I was working, that's how I met Paul, who was divorcing his second wife who was an alcoholic."

It was while dating in the late 1940s that Joy noticed something... odd about the great voice man.

"He was extraordinarily psychic, in every way. When we were dating in the summertime in Hollywood—this is a time when nothing happens, no weather, nothing—I was living on a street lined with big oak trees. He drove me home, pulled over to the side of the curb, and I got out of the car. All of a sudden his voice went down twenty notches to the lowest depth. He was staring at the wheel, and in that low voice he said, 'Don't walk down that street.' And I said, 'What do you mean?' And he said, 'A tree is going to fall down.' The next morning he rings my bell, I was on the third floor, and he said, 'Come on down. I want you to see something.' So I went down. Not in front of us where we were parked, but behind us, in the middle of the night a tree had fallen down and the fire department was picking it up.

"He used to scare himself with this gift. He could always find anything. In fact, I would even call him at work, 'Quick, where's my ring? Where are my keys?' And they'd be just where he said they were.

"One time I was getting dressed in our huge bedroom and he was on the other side of the room when he said, 'You know, I wonder whatever happened to Joe Shaftell?' Dingalingaling goes the phone. 'Oh, hello, Joe. It's Paul.' And Joe said, 'I don't even know why I'm calling you. I was phoning the Beverly Hills Hotel.'

"Sometimes he would scare himself to death because he would be laying in bed and would see himself looking in his own eye, and he didn't know how to bring himself back. Neither of us had a clue about any of this. But he didn't know how to advance it. We all have the ability, it's just that some have it more than others. But Paul wasn't sure what to do about it. So we didn't make it a big deal. I would just call him if I'd lose things. But if he thought about using the ability, he couldn't do it. It had to be spontaneous.

"I remember we'd go to restaurants and they'd have these psychics walking around, for amusement, and I'll never forget it when one of them sat down next to Paul and looked at him and said, 'You should be doing what I'm doing.'"

Fred Frees: "Dad was able to 'sense' things which, had I not witnessed them for myself, I would have considered dubious. He would sometimes answer the telephone before it rang, knowing exactly who was calling. He would 'hear' a knock at the door seconds before there was one. Whenever we would lose something (such as my mother's wedding ring), we would call dad and he would give a not precise but indeed accurate description of its location. He could predict what playing cards would be turned over in a deck. He could predict the outcome of many horse races. Things like that. He said he could see through his own eye sockets, as if he was somehow miniaturized inside his own head. It happened all the time."

When Paul met Spike Jones' drummer Eddie Brandt in 1946, the two almost immediately began writing songs together; music by Brandt, lyrics by Frees. They would release several songs in the next decade, including "The Skin Diver," about which a 1959 newspaper review wrote: "A gimmicky novelty, this is the adventure of a skin diver who finds a mermaid. It's light, upbeat and fresh. Cute material that can attract spins." It *was* an enchanting two-minute novelty record about a skin diver who falls for a slippery dish, but:

> "He wooed her and pursued her across the ocean floor.
>   She said 'You'll never hook me 'cause I've heard that line before.'"

The smitten swimmer would not be put off. Frees *gargled* the chorus:

> "I love you, I love you—he gurgled tenderly (sang the harmonizing backing singers)
>   —I love you, I love you, say that you love meeeeeee."

Fred: "This picture was taken in 1963 by me in the Doheny house where Sabrina was born."

The flip side of the single was "I'm Ready," which the same review called "a blues chanted adequately by Frees. Material can't match the flip, however." It was released on the Cascade label.

Through the Brandt connection, Paul met Spike Jones who first used him for the comedy recording "Popcorn Sack," a festive, close harmony (by The Sportsmen) song that parodied the evils of sitting in a theatre, trying to watch the film, with a variety of noisy popcorn eaters interrupting the viewers and the viewed both. Released on July 25, 1947, Paul got to play a variety of voices in such a short space of time: a Charles Boyer-type lover in the balcony, Edward G. Robinson and Katharine Hepburn on screen (forever annoyed by the rattling audience), and a croaking Al Jolson. Alternate takes from the same session had Paul ending his part of the gig with a pleasant Bing Crosby (rather than Jolson) imitation, crooning as someone in the audience bites into their husky popcorn.

His most famous Spike Jones record was, of course, the brilliant "My Old Flame," which began as a serious enough song, sung by crooning tenor Paul Judson who speaks of getting back a long-lost love. After a few verses of this, the usual Spike craziness zooms in, via a cranked-up fire engine siren, honks and other anarchic sounds. It is when Paul Frees, in the vocal guise of Peter Lorre, comes on the scene that the parody becomes a classic.

> My old flame
> I—I can't even think of her name…
> WHAT—WHAT WAS HER NAME?!
> DORIS, LAURA, CHLOE, MANNY, MOE, JACK!
> No…it couldn't have been Moe…
> I—I CAN'T STAND IT, I TELL YOU! THIS IS
> DRIVING ME SANE!

Spike originally wanted him to do the entire set of lyrics as Peter Lorre, but during rehearsals Paul started ad-libbing, adding new lines to the already written masterpiece. The original demo disc done in 1946 was pretty close to the final October 7, 1947 release.

"My Old Flame" was performed on CBS's *Spotlight Revue* on Halloween, 1947, and the crowd went crazy for it. Jones, Lorre and Frees also did the song a year later on *The Spike Jones Show*. In his dressing room Lorre had to practice his own voice since, after Frees' extravagant caricature, he didn't think he sounded like himself anymore.

Paul Frees: "Pete would come on doing an imitation of *my* doing an imitation of him doing 'My Old Flame.' Few people know that Peter Lorre, who looked like such a terror, was the most gentle, sweetest, lovable person you have ever met in your life. When we'd do the public appearances, he would say to me (in voice), 'You know something, Paul, you're a difficult man to follow. I'm not going to work with you again, you're too good.' The reason he said this was because the way I did him was an exaggerated version of what he did, so he came out trying to do 'My Old Flame' and it came out flat. He didn't sound like him compared to the way I sounded. People remember the imitation, not the real."

"When Paul came to Chicago," recalled Eddie Brandt, "the funniest thing happened. We were doing the Peter Lorre thing on radio, which went out on a Saturday night. We went out on the town, a real honky-tonk town right on the border of Chicago and Indiana. We were there for three or four days, and it's a town of nothing but nightclubs, which Paul always enjoyed. Working in them the way he did, he developed a taste for them, I guess. But in one particular club we ran into a friend of mine. His name was Buddy Green. Paul says, 'Well, that's funny. That was my name!' And they got to know each other. It was like they were related or something."

"The Skin Diver." (*Laura Wagner*)

Back in the studio, usually the master of voice would only require a short amount of time for laying down his vocal tracks. "But I would work several hours with Spike, or maybe half a day. He was very picky. He knew exactly what he wanted and how he wanted it—and he worked until he got it. He was very much the perfectionist.

"I also did 'Too Young' and 'Deep Purple' with Spike. I did 'Deep Purple' as Billy Eckstein, falling asleep during it, which was my idea. Billy was a very relaxed singer; the gag was that he was so relaxed, he fell asleep during the song."

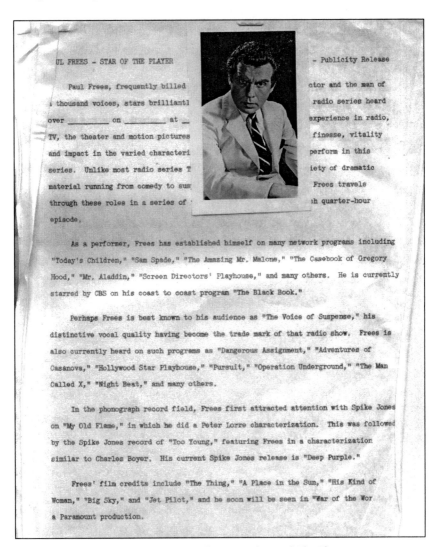

Picture stapled to Paul's press release of *The Player*.

But it was the ever-increasing radio work that was paying the bills and buying the newest suits and the oldest pocket watches. By 1948 his reputation as master impersonator led to a lot of stand-in jobs for stars or guest stars. He once replaced Humphrey Bogart when the star couldn't make it to his half-hour radio program. Orson Welles was another. Even into the 1980s Frees would be brought in to dub, redub or replace the portly Welles if the great actor was too difficult to reach or simply too difficult.

In the 1948 film *The Lady from Shanghai*, he handled just such a job. "Welles had a line that came out exactly like Peter Lorre," said Frees. "He's lying in [Rita Hayworth's] lap and says, 'Do all rich women play games like this?' So I had to redo the line to make Orson sound like Orson."

He did the same thing for Van Johnson, but as Frees himself asked at the time: "How do you loop for Van Johnson?" He also stated in an interview that he looped "two songs and lead-ins" for Ray Milland in *Let's Do It Again* in 1953.

Filling in for radio performances was much easier than looping (dubbing) for films, which requires imitating an actor and matching his line *exactly* with a line in the soundtrack. Sometimes (but rarely) Frees would only have the soundtrack to go by; no film would be played for him to match his words to the actor's mouth, so his timing and rhythm had to be faultless. He was good at it, but it was his least favorite chore.

In the late 1940's Frees reached the pinnacle of his radio career by playing *all* characters in the 15-minute syndicated series, *The Player* (a revival of *Nightcap Yarns*, which had featured the 1940s Man of a Thousand Voices, Frank Graham, also playing all the roles). Under contract to the sponsoring Capitol Records, he performed in 130 episodes, some of which were continuing shows with continuing characters. "During my high point in radio I was doing 35 or 40 separate shows a week," Frees recalled. "When I went into the studio for *The Player* I would record five or six separate stories at once. I would have to remember the continuing voice of the character I may have done the week before, so that by the time I got through with six or seven shows, I would be doing 35 or 40 different characters in that one sitting within the space of about two hours. I had to remember who it was and what they sounded like, and that was difficult. We didn't have tape to refer back to. They were open-ended shows, sold everywhere, so stations put their own commercials in." The original title of the series was *Studio X*. Gary Goodwin was the announcer.

Peter Lorre.

Starting with an oddly tropical instrumental theme, *The Player* recited an interesting hook to lure listeners before the announcer began: "And so begins another story by—The Player, America's most versatile actor, Mr. Paul Frees. And here, before we begin, is your announcer." Over the continuing music, stations broadcast their own pitches for products, after which the announcer introduced Frees against a more urgent musical vamp. It was one of the best solo vehicles Paul had on radio for trying out new voices and impressions. In the English manor story "The Red Macaw," the butler

Paul Frees, Spike Jones and Peter Lorre. (*Jordan R. Young*)

Nivens was an early cockney template for his Inspector Fenwick voice. This comical thriller involved Nivens stealing money from the household budget to bet on the horses. When a Red Macaw bird starts blabbing like a parrot that he'd stolen a hundred pounds from the household funds, the manservant chases it all over the house, and kills it. Desperate to get that money back after his horse loses, Nivens' face turns red with rage after reading an item in the paper: Lost—Red Macaw. Reward: 100 pounds.

Jeff Regan, Investigator starred Jack Webb, sounding almost nothing like his rushed, clipped delivery in *Dragnet*. "My name's Jeff Regan. I get ten a day, plus expenses, from a detective bureau run by a guy named Anthony J. Lyon. They call me the lion's eye." It was a hardboiled detective series along the lines of *Sam Spade* and the like, spouting tough guy lines like "My car was as full of holes as a cancelled check." Paul could be heard on several shows in character parts, though he was often hard to spot. He once played a cop named Granger; another time he was a weight-lifting undertaker, slow on the take but quick on the temper. It was a zesty CBS series for Paul and Jack both, full of dialogue always trying to top itself with a witty comeback. Regan might try to get information out of a dame with, "Light up, lady, I don't like the dark!" or "Come on, lady, this is a fat blister, let's break it!"

Frees was also heard as Ludwig Von Drake-like Dr. Honeger on *The Private Practice of Dr. Dana*, starring Ira Grossel (later known as Jeff Chandler).

Along with Hal Gerard, Virginia Gregg, Michael Hayes and others, Frees was a regular cast member on ABC's *California Caravan*, an adventurous tale of the gold rush days of the forty-niners. It was a sustaining series airing on the Mutual network.

On March 6, 1949 Paul was heard on *The Prudential Family Hour of Stars'* episode "Impact"; one of his all-time favorite performances, and one of the few specific episodes he would fondly remember thirty years later. "Each week," began the announcer over a rather ethereal chorus of voices and music, "the Prudential Insurance Company of America brings you one of its family of six great Hollywood stars: Bette Davis, Ray Milland, Gregory Peck, Ginger Rogers, Barbara Stanwyck and Robert Taylor, in a series of radio plays by Hollywood's finest writers. With the music of Carmen Dragon." Gregory Peck played Father Michael, the padre who dared to stand up against the rough South American dictator, Colonel Mendosa (Frees). Peck was the hero, but Frees was the star of this two-man show. It was a powerful three-act morality play dealing with Mendosa's terror at knowing of an assassination plot against him that would occur at 1:42 p.m. He'd sent for Father Michael, needing to vent and debate against someone until the time passed. Worked into a frenzy as the last seconds tick down, Mendosa is overjoyed when the fatal minute arrives—but it makes him accidentally knock his pistol off his desk, mortally wounding him. The least the hated leader can do is deny it was the priest who killed him.

Don Quinn, famed writer of *Fibber McGee and Molly*, wrote the episode. Paul Frees was only credited a single time, at the end, by Peck himself.

One of his best starring vehicles was in the supernatural action series, *The Green Lama*, which began over CBS on June 5, 1949. Frees portrayed wealthy young writer Jethro Dumont who, having mastered "strange, secret powers" after ten years in Tibet, fights crime as the enigmatic Green Lama. Aided by his trusted Tibetan servant Tulku (Ben Wright) and Sergeant Whalen (Herb Vigran), Dumont's voice was pretty much Frees' regular voice, steeped with confidence in a slightly lower register.

Georgia Ellis, Laurette Filbrandt, Jack Kruschen, Paul McVey, and Charles Russell could be heard in supporting roles, with music again by Richard Aurandt. Larry Thor, sometimes easy to mistake for Frees, announced. The sustaining series filled a programming gap for the vacationing

Broadway Is My Beat, and was later moved for the same reason when *The Spike Jones Show* was canceled.

Through the eerie, dreamy music comes Frees chanting his Tibetan, "O Ma-Ne Pad-Me Hum. The Green Lama strikes for justice!" Eastern music continues, then the booming voice again. "It is truly written that the man with no future is dangerous. There were one hundred such men in…The Adventure of the Perfect Prisoner. All of them with guns." So began the final show in the series. The announcer: "From the mystery of the Far East, from the mountain peaks of a Shangri La, come the exciting adventures of Jethro Dumont. Jethro Dumont, the wealthy American who, after ten years in Tibet returned—as the Green Lama, to carry on a single-handed fight against injustice and crime." Dumont chose the color green, which symbolized justice, as it was one of the six sacred colors of Tibet. Tulku spoke in precise English with an Oriental accent.

This final show, "The Adventure of the Perfect Prisoner," involves murder and a riot at a prison, with Bill Conrad as the main guard, Summers. Dumont risks his life walking alone into the felons' section to talk the prisoners into giving up their arms and the riot. He does, then solves the murder by going into the "path of concentration taught to him by the High Lamas of Tibet." Summers turns out to be the murderer and initiator of the rioters getting guns, in order to eventually get the warden's job.

This "superhero" was a highly moral character, much akin to The Shadow. "If I were to carry a gun," said the Green Lama once, "to shoot even a *criminal*, then I too would be guilty of the evil I fight." The scripts were dotted with cryptic, mystic sayings, giving a spiritual air to the series that would make it quite distinct from Frees' other radio work. "Darkness hides all things…except evil."

Though the series ended on August 20, 1949, it received great reviews. One stated, "As 'Jethro Dumont,' a romantic figure known also as 'The Green Lama,' Paul Frees is cutting a dashing swatch on KNX, 2:30 p.m. Sundays. Frees, the possessor of one of the most intriguing voices in Hollywood radio, makes an ideal hero in the best melodramatic tradition.

"Script is on the fanciful side, but it manages to be fun, too. Many out-of-this-world characters pop up in each script and Jack Kruschen has been particularly good in a variety of roles, including a recent snappy Chinese private eye.

"Though the 'Lama' operates out of New York, he seems to be able to appear in a variety of locales with great ease. And it's always explainable."

Another review wrote: "It's all an unpretentious, low-budget 30 minutes that sustains interest pretty well to the end. Ken Crossen and William Froug have prepared the script skillfully, with the appropriate interspersal of Confucianism considered par for a whodunit with Asiatic overtones. Paul Frees' voice as Dumont is authoritatively suitable, as are Ben Wright's as Tulku, and others of the small cast. Norman Macdonnell's direction was effective and Richard Aurandt's music supported the action smoothly. This one should have a fair share of the Summer audience."

Crime Correspondent was a brief CBS sustaining series in 1949, produced by Gordon T. Hughes, and starring and co-written by Frees. It was just one of many shows he was writing and pitching to network executives, in between radio work, a budding film career and the start of voicing cartoons.

Debuting in November, the series only lasted through the next month, but it was a notable start as a professional writer. Even though he was not credited as writer on the audition show.

Paul Frees with Paul Dubov (seated), Ben Wright (as Tulku) and Nestor Paiva on *The Green Lama.*

The opening show began with a long beep, then: "Time! (*Another beep*) Time for your *crime correspondent*! (*Morse code beeps follow. Music.*)" Frees' higher-registered voice begins in earnest: "Good evening, citizens, this is Larry Mitchell with the latest news of the world. The underworld!" Energetically pitched in radio documentary style, Frees reads the events of a solved crime, interspersed with "realistically-sounding" interviews with cops and the people involved in the cases. Eventually the narration breaks away, revealing the way in which Mitchell, who becomes part of the plot, assembles the story and solves the puzzle.

The audition show on October 21, 1949 had Mitchell in a race against time. "Yes, citizens, last night, somewhere in your city, a bomb had been planted. A bomb that would blow up an entire city block. Only one man knew where it was—Dino Saroty, cop killer. But he wouldn't, couldn't talk for a *very* good reason: he was stretched out on a marble slab at the morgue. Why had he planted that time bomb? That was the very *big*, big question. And there was another very important question—would your police find it in time?"

Variety's November 9, 1949 review was fairly complimentary. "Another addition to the catalog of private detectives, newspapermen and amateur sleuths, who beat the police in tracking down criminals and solving mysteries, *Crime Correspondent* stands as an average entry. Revolving around a radio commentator, who personally investigates criminal cases, program is strictly a formula item that should satisfy the whodunit fans.

"As indicated by the initial airer, show has its title character undergoing the regular run-ins with law enforcement officers, unearthing clues, getting into what looks like inescapable situations and eventually becoming the hero of the evening. Preem broadcast title 'The Chair for Dino' had moments of excitement, but as the plot developed its threadbareness showed through. Program followed the crime correspondent as he progressed in solving a murder and preventing a large-scale disaster.

"Paul Frees handles the lead role capably and direction and production by Gordon T. Hughes fills the bill. Marlin Skyles' work provides the proper musical background."

Frees would sometimes give his services to charitable broadcasts. On October 15, 1948 he received a thank you letter from Mrs. Benjamin Miller, Los Angeles Chapter President of Hadassah for so generously giving his time to *Stars Over Israel* on the preceding evening. "The affair

The Green Lama with Paul Frees, Herb Vigran, Paul Dubov, and
Ben Wright (partially hidden).

was a complete success," she wrote. "You have helped us to send urgently
needed medical supplies to Israel and you have given new life and hope
to those who have finally achieved freedom from the DP camps."

He even donated his May 17, 1949 paycheck of $34.40 for his
performance on *The Best Things in Life*, a variety series sponsored by
the American Federation of Labor, to purchase CARE (Cooperative for
American Remittances to Europe) packages.

Parley Baer and Paul Frees in *Crime Correspondent*.

Now that the jobs were coming to *him*, he could afford it. *Box 13, Richard Diamond, Dragnet, The New Adventures of Philip Marlowe, Screen Director's Playhouse, NBC University Theatre, Dangerous Assignment*—his radio list went on and on, continuing well into the late '50s.

He had a lot of laughs playing with Dick Powell and William Conrad on *Front Page*, an ABC series based on the classic Ben Hecht/Charles MacArthur play. He was joined by future Stan Freberg alumni June Foray and Peter Leeds, and a host of other top supporting talent.

On *Romance*, a CBS sustaining series, Frees joined Harry Bartell, Herb Butterfield, John Dehner, Larry Dobkin, and just about everyone else in radiodom to give life to romantic stories, from the sappy to the adventurous. The Voice of Romance (Kaye Brinker, then later Doris Dalton) narrated the series, which began on April 18, 1943.

As every other actor did, Frees kept several scrapbooks during his lengthy career. In one of those was a letter from Charles Chaplin dated February 18, 1949. He had worked for the great silent clown on a show earlier that year, and now Chaplin wanted Frees back to be a part of *Newsweek Looks Ahead* when it came back, though no one was sure when that would be.

Director Gordon T. Hughes and Paul Frees in *Crime Correspondent.*

Though there were few lead articles on Frees in his early radio years, many of the smaller blurbs contained interesting references: In 1949 he was hired by Roy Del Ruth to play a bellhop in the George Raft film *Red Light*, after having won *Life* magazine's award as the most promising radio actor.

Eventually, Frees called radio his favorite medium, especially late in life when he was feeling pangs of nostalgia for the close community of actors that he was no longer enjoying in the '70s. In various radio interviews he would reminisce fondly.

Frees on *Dr. Kildare*: "Oh, the terrible things I used to do to Lionel Barrymore. He was in a wheelchair and outside of NBC at the corner of Sunset and Vine across the way there was a place called The Key Club we used to go to. I would wheel the old man behind there, and I would start running and I would wheel his wheelchair so fast down the ramp. I'd be wheeling him at 30, 40, 50 miles an hour and he'd be shouting, 'You sonofabitch, if you don't stop this chair...!'"

Another time, Frees was embraced by a white-haired old gentleman from the audience after a radio performance. He began speaking Austrian incessantly until Paul surprised the man by replying in English, "I'm

Howard Hawks and his cast (including Frees, upper right) behind the scenes.
Photo courtesy of Laura Wagner.

sorry, sir, I don't speak your language." The man from Vienna, having just witnessed Paul's perfect Austrian accent in the show, was amazed and wondered how he could have executed it so perfectly.

"I was doing Arthur Godfrey's show," Frees told John Dunning in 1982, "and Arthur Godfrey in the East would be selling Premium Crackers, but they weren't Premium Crackers on the West Coast. On the West Coast, we had Snowflake Crackers. So at a given time, at a quarter to three in the afternoon on the West Coast, he would start in the East talking about Premium Crackers, and I would continue [speaking in an excellent Arthur Godfrey imitation] with Snowflake Crackers on the West Coast. (The contact producer from the agency was a man named Neil Reagan, who is Ronnie Reagan's older brother.) And this went on for five years in Studio 6 at Columbia Square, five days a week. We would do that for that one minute, leave, and then Steve Allen would come on and supposedly say, 'This is Steve Allen, for the Columbia Broadcasting System.' Well, it just so happens that Steve had this nutty mind of his, even then. He would get up there and say, 'This is CBS, the Columbia Broadchasing System,' and he got fired. He would always come up with little things like that, or

Paul Frees and Don Diamond.

he would come up with (Does high pitched laugh), and they said, 'We've gotta get rid of this nut.' Nobody ever caught on when I'd continue on as Steve Allen."

It has been wrongly attributed to Paul Frees that he voiced the slick con-man, or con-crow, character in Columbia Pictures' *The Fox and the Crow* cartoon series. As it was a wartime series that originated in 1941 and lasted through the decade, it's impossible that Corporal Frees had had the opportunity of playing this half a world away. Mel Blanc, then Frank Graham through the series' end, collectively take that honor.

But by the end of the 1940s Paul began moving into films, ever so slowly. He was a bit player at first, seen briefly as an elevator operator who speaks to John Garfield in *Force of Evil* (1948). Gradually he moved into more important, though usually still small, on-screen appearances.

And lots and lots and *lots* of cartoon work.

The Millionaire
The 1950s

"**I'M PREPARING FOR TELEVISION** by going into pictures," Frees said around 1950. "I would like to do some video now, but I'm not exactly warm to the idea of doing it 'just for the experience.' I already have a good seventeen years experience—in vaudeville, clubs and the theatre, besides radio and pictures. It's because of my background on the stage that doing television appeals to me. It's back to my old medium, the visual. However, I'm not decided on which course I'd like to take television-wise, since before assuming dramatic roles in radio, I was a singer and emcee, and always did comedy."

Frees' older sister Rose recalled that the sudden, imminent death of network radio scared her brother so much that he almost had a nervous breakdown. It caused him to undergo something of a reinvention of his public persona. Rose said, "He was shaking, and he was constantly panicked by all the talk in his industry about how radio was going to die at any moment, and be completely replaced by television. At that time, and this was around 1949, he was very spooked; he thought that every radio show was going to disappear overnight. I don't know who exactly got him into that Church of Religious Science group, but he joined that because it was like a self-help group, and the leader used to tell Paul, 'Be confident. Realize that you and you alone are the world's best.' That was the beginning of what people called his big ego behavior. It wasn't really ego - he was actually very scared! But to any outsider, it suddenly appeared as if Paul had this giant ego. Arrogant! I remember getting very angry with him once, and yelling at him, 'Solly! You weren't brought up to act so high and mighty. What do you think you're playing at with all these airs, putting on that pompous voice?' And he said, 'But we were told to act confidently.' That's where all that stemmed from."

Quizreel, circa 1951. Unknown woman, Paul Frees, Joy Terry Frees.

Recording *Quizreel*.

He called his new objective in life "pom"—peace of mind. "I guess it can be summed up this way—it's just a matter of never losing sight of the fact that we're only here for a limited stay. I'm still working hard and enjoying it more than ever, but I make it a point to keep myself open for other activities. In other words, I want to make a living, but I want to live at the same time. I'm a 'square' now, but I've never had more fun. I take the

time to do all the 'corny' things like spending a day at the zoo, or going off to the mountains, or taking a real tourist's look at the city. It's a new perspective on life, worked out during the last war when I came to the easy decision that anything is better than sitting in a foxhole being shot at all day."

The 1950s was the only decade to showcase Paul Frees in every medium. He was literally everywhere, not the least of which was on screen in some very major motion pictures.

For *The Toast of New Orleans* in 1950 Paul begins the film with narration in a blithe French accent. He's rhapsodic about the blessing of the fishing fleet festival. "Boats were scrubbed and painted for this occasion. Flowers gathered from the buyou." The musical starred Kathryn Grayson and Mario Lanza, and included arias from *Madame Butterfly, Aida* and *La Boheme*.

Hunt the Man Down had to do with a man named Richard Kinkaid (played by James Anderson) who had been wrongly accused of a murder twelve years before the start of this plot. But he had escaped, and was now caught again, after he'd foiled a robbery at his workplace. A new murder trial was then set, and it was up to the public defender's office to find the old truth of the matter. One of the men public defender Paul Bennett (Gig Young) comes across is Packy Collins, played too briefly by Paul Frees. Packy's smooth, smiling gangster personae lightened the mood of the film and would've benefited the plot more, especially since his 'boys' try to knock off the PD and his father/helper, for some reason. The RKO film was released the day after Christmas, 1950.

Hunt the Man Down, 1950, RKO

It was the next year that Frees had his most memorable movies. The most artistically applauded film of his career was certainly *A Place in the Sun*. Called for an interview with director George Stevens just forty minutes before airtime of a *Screen Director's Playhouse* episode, Frees raced to grab a cab, drove to Stevens' office on the Paramount lot, got the job and got back to NBC in time for his radio show. "Stevens is a great man, and it was thrilling to do my first major picture for him, but my interview with him had its disconcerting moments. Knowing I was being considered for the part of a priest, I was doing my best to be serious. But it wasn't easy—with Stevens sitting across from me wearing one of those trick bow ties that he kept lighting up!"

Based on Theodore Dreiser's *An American Tragedy*, about a poor relation who is accused of murdering his pregnant girlfriend in order to marry the rich and beautiful woman he loves, the film went on to win six Academy Awards, including Best Director, Best Score for Franz Waxman, and Best Screenplay for Michael Wilson and Harry Brown.

Paul has the all-important role of Reverend Morrison in the end scene, asking the difficult question of the convicted George: *who* he was thinking of while trying to save his girlfriend from drowning. "I don't *believe* I'm guilty of all this," says George Eastman (Montgomery Clift). "But I

Hunt the Man Down, RKO, 1950.

don't *know*. I wish I knew." When George realizes that he was thinking of Angela (Elizabeth Taylor) at that moment when he could have saved Alice (Shelley Winters), Morrison admits then that there was truly murder in his heart. For the first time George knows that he is guilty, and deserves his punishment. Priest Frees gives him last rites as he is called down that long prison hallway to his death, and follows George into the final shot of the film.

When the film was screened for Charlie Chaplin, he called it the best American film he'd ever seen, which made for a lot of great publicity. *The New York Times* named it "a work of beauty, tenderness, power and insight."

Paul Frees' most beloved sci-fi film is probably *The Thing from Another World*, an RKO picture from 1951, starring Kenneth Tobey. Based on the story "Who Goes There?" by John W. Campbell, Jr., the picture's title burns into being before the credits begin in such a memorable way that John Carpenter used the same device in his more graphic 1982 remake. The lavish Dimitri Tiomkin score (with occasional Theremin) heightened Howard Hawks' A-movie production.

It was an ensemble picture, with some of the group dialogues spoken with an almost rushed, Jack Webb-type conversation speed. It gave the lines a more natural feel. Frees as Dr. Voorhees is first seen in the plane with Noble-prize-winning scientist Dr. Carrington (Robert Cornthwaite) as they speed through the frozen arctic to uncover The Thing. Outside, it sounds as if the men are dubbing themselves, so clear are their voices above the snow. Once The Thing melts from its block of ice, it loses an arm in a fight with the sled dogs. Studying the arm, the scientists find that The Thing, a monster ultimately played by the mammoth James Arness, is biologically composed like a vegetable, most likely a carrot. Dr. Vorhees then opens a box revealing a dead sled dog; The Thing lives on the blood of animal life. In order to experiment on the plant tissue taken from the dog, it is planted and fed blood. The new plants thrive on it…

In later life Frees recounted that Hawks and the others didn't tell him that there was a stuffed dog in the box; he almost had a heart attack. "Everybody was in on it but me. Those dirty rats all stood around. Mr. Hawks was *always* doing that to me—*always*." But he had his revenge: according to Cornthwaite, Frees did a great "Japanese fag" character and would crack up the cast with it in between takes.

He also related that everyone was allowed to rewrite lines as they went along, to feel more comfortable with their characters.

The film was perhaps Frees' most revered on-screen role, and came at an important time in his life. Joy Terry: "We got engaged during *The Thing*, and were married in February of 1951. Most of the cast was there at the wedding. We dated for a year because we had to wait for his divorce to become final from June. We shared an agent [Mitchell Hamilburg] when we dated and were first married.

"The filming for that movie went on forever and ever. The scene where they form a circle around the spaceship on the snow was actually the last scene shot. It was shot in Montana and they were waiting for it to snow. So Howard Hawks kept everybody on salary. Paul was waiting to do other work. He was on the movie for 28 weeks, a long time for a film back then, but they were able to do other work in the meantime. But it was costing them too much money so they decided to shoot that last scene on the backlot of Columbia Studios. And wouldn't you know it, the day they shot it was the day it snowed! We went to see a screening of it, and I was petrified."

The film went on to become one of science fiction's most notable classics, helping to pave the way for many similar alien movies, some of

The Thing, 1951, RKO.

Harry Shannon prevents Paul Frees from breaking up a murder trial in RKO's *Seven Witnesses*. The officer is Charles Phillips.

which Frees would slightly be involved in. That same year he was heard as the President in the Oscar-winning (special effects) film, *When Worlds Collide*. But such roles did little to spark a fire under his live-action career.

Walt Kraemer, who would record many of Frees' commercial and other later sessions, recalled: "Paul told me one time that after filming *The Thing* he should have become a leading actor but Hollywood or studio

Paul Frees, Joe Granby and Robert Mitchum in *His Kind of Woman*, RKO, 1951.

politics prevented this from happening. He told me this with a straight face and I'm sure he believed it."

After that, he appeared in *His Kind of Woman* and *Seven Witnesses*. "My roles are brief," said Paul at the time, "but I'm lucky because in the sequences in which I appear, the characters I play dominate the scene." It was sometimes true, but already he was finding out that in cartoons he could be King for life.

In the late 1930s MGM had sponsored the development of the character of a slow-witted, sympathetic-natured bear by the name of Barney, which would give Paul Frees his first animated series.

Barney Bear, created by Rudolf Ising at MGM, was a take-off on the slow-burning, slow-learning Wallace Beery. The character was redesigned in the late 40s by Preston Blair and Michael Lah, who also directed the series when Rudolf Ising (also the Bear's first voice) left in 1943. Frees' first known utterance for the character came in 1952 with *Busybody Bear*, doubling as Buck Beaver, as well.

Meanwhile in radio, for one CBS season (1951) Frees was heard as the magical investigator, *Mr. Aladdin*. The half-hour mystery drama featured music by Marlin Skiles, and often included Joy Terry Frees who, it was then reported, was currently studying voice with famed teacher Luigi Rosselli.

"Once upon a time," began the announcer (Bill Anders), "being the year nineteen hundred and fifty-one, a young man walked down the streets of an island—the island called Manhattan. And if some of the feats he performed had a feeling of magic, it's not surprising. His name was Aladdin. (Music) Mr. Aladdin—a wonderful new adventure series, starring Paul Frees." Frees' happy-go-lucky voice was modeled after and reminiscent of the optimistic side of Jack Benny. With the aid of his secretary Jeannie Mobly, Robert Aladdin advertised himself as the man who could do anything. In the last show of the series, "Miracle of the Four-Legged Husband," Aladdin was employed to "get rid" of a woman's husband, Arthur, who had died three years previously but kept an eye on her night and day through the family dog, "that's his spirit's control." It was a clever, well-produced comedy, produced and directed by Elliot Lewis, written by Frees' old friend, Richard Powell. Sylvia Simms appeared as Ms. Mobly. The series was suggested by a book by Carlos Drake.

October of 1950 had seen the release of his Capitol Records 45" "Space Girl," in which, like "Skin Diver," Paul tells of meeting a "special" girl, this time an alien. "I'll never forget that night I first saw Space Girl. She looked so cute standing there with that little antenna growing out of the back of her head. She could get eight television stations, and that's hard to do without a set!" The novelty doo-wop number was released by The Earthboys and written by Jack Marshall, with gag input from Frees.

The next year saw a hilarious reunion of Frees and Spike Jones, with the lush ballad "Too Young." Naturally, the Disney-like orchestration falls apart when Paul begins his deep French accent, speak-singing like Charles Boyer: "They try to tell us we're too young" at which point the singular Sara Berner (one of the eminent switchboard operators on Jack Benny's radio show) begins laughing like a knowing schoolgirl. Paul clears his throat and tries again, and again is nipped in the romantic bud by the New York-accented Berner answering, "Oh, this is so sudden, Tyrone." She can't seem to latch onto the guy's name, calling him everything from Cary to Mario. She upsets him so much he almost launches into a Ludwig Von Drake tirade—but controls himself. As he tries to whisper sweet "nothings" in her ear, the ol' Jones band starts up with horns and loud music aplenty, making the poor "young" girl cry out "What?" at every slight, noiseless pause. After which, as she would on Jack Benny's show, Sara tries to sing

Paul and Joy Terry, 1951.

the song properly, sounding more like a high-pitched goose than a real woman. Frenchie Paul has his revenge by calling her every sex symbol's first name he can think of, but she loves it. He finally calls her Trigger, and she runs away like a horse—into a train. Pure Spike Jones.

One interesting Spike Jones clone that had been recorded around 1950 was *The Hollywood Babysitter*, a soundtrack for a TV pilot which was never broadcast. The visuals were to be built around the recording, performed by Eddie Brandt and His Hollywood Hicks, so there's a heavy influence of Spike there. The song begins with close harmony singing to the tune of "Braham's Lullaby" as the singers describe the Hollywood Babysitter. Frees appears as a baby Peter Lorre: "I just love his technique! I go *MAD* when we play that game of hide and shriek…" It was an admirable little gig for Paul, who also got to conjecture what a three-year-old Larry Parks would sound like (Al Jolson), and ditto for little Humphrey Bogart. Between imitations there was the usual loud, brassy Spike sound. Then back to a single "Yup!" from wee Gary Cooper; tiny Charles Boyer who romances by pitching a little goo; and a baby Ronald Colman.

For "Too Young" Paul had received a one-time payment of $600 for all rights to the song, with an additional $150 promised if more than 300,000 copies of the record sold. But he was required not to make *any* other recordings for a period of six months from the date of the contract, July 20, 1951.

Spike and Paul had met in Las Vegas earlier that year to discuss possible songs to record, including a few with lyrics by Frees. He would have sung them himself, but Spike passed on this latest batch.

Building somethin' in the '50s.

Paul Frees, the artist.

"The Collector's Item" had Paul in Bela Lugosi voice asking if he's crazy just because he collects bats...? The three-minute "Rigoletto" was an epic for a trio of voices (Bette Davis, Humphrey Bogart and Peter Lorre) in which Bogie scours the city to locate the four-foot missing person (Lorre) he was hired to find. "Barber of Seville" involved a girl coming to see a psychiatrist and ultimately getting a shot in the arm as a cure. They weren't Frees' best works, but no doubt would have been interesting with City Slickers treatment.

In the letter accompanying the lyrics, Paul wrote: "Incidentally, Joyce and I bought a house out in the Valley in North Hollywood. It is 18 years old, but it is nice and solid and will be a comfortable place to store babies in (starting next year)."

"We had the longest marriage," says Joy Terry Frees, "and the best one, for him. No doubt about it.

"He was extraordinarily talented, whatever he touched was good. Whatever he did, he did well. And it came very easily to him. Excellent draftsman, excellent painter, and sketch artist. His paintings are divine. He also made furniture. He was extraordinarily handy - he could do whatever he wanted to do. In our apartment he made a spice rack, which I still have on the wall. And when we moved into our first home, he paneled the dining room. And when he was finished with the wood, he made a beautiful desk that Fred has out of the spare lumber. Then he made a beautiful coffee table, which Fred also has. There's not a nail in it, he just doweled the four ends.

"He also wrote special material for *The Donald O'Connor Show*, with Ruby Raksin. Ruby's brother was David Raksin who wrote 'Laura.' Ruby wrote the music, and Paul wrote the lyrics, for Donald, and a couple of other people in Vegas. I think it bothered Paul that nobody outside the business knew who he was. I really think that.

"I once heard him make an outrageous voice deal on the phone, and when he hung up, he laughed and said, 'Don't they know I love it so much I'd do it for nothing?' And he meant it."

He lived to work. On November 2, 1951 Paul rehearsed an audition show for CBS called *The Perfect Crime*. "This is The Man in Black. A year ago tonight, an innocent man was murdered in a small New England village." Clyde Ross, the narrator (Frees again), had told his story of killing his rich Sexton friend to The Man in Black just before he was executed. Like *The Player*, all voices were done by Frees, though it was read more like a short story.

The Man in Black (later *The Black Book*) audition show was done the following year on February 2nd. "The Price of the Head" by John Russell began with the dramatic opening: "Come with me down the long corridor. Through the shadows. To the secluded study of the famous—teller of tales." As the door opens, a voice like Disneyland's Ghost Host bids you, "Welcome. I—am The Man in Black." He sits surrounded by a fantastic collection of books containing the great unusual stories of the world, from which he takes each week's episode. The premiere show, also starring John Dehner, was more action-oriented, less narrative than *The Perfect Crime*.

"I have another story to tell you today," speaks the playfully confident Frees in the opening moment of Nelson's Bond's "On Schedule" on *The Black Book*. "This one is about a crime in which nature, not man, trapped a murderer. Do you want to hear it?" Trumpets herald the sinister music, at which point the announcer says, "Now, starring Paul Frees as your teller of tales, another story from The Black Book." It was the story of an employee who, having been caught embezzling $300, is given a chance to steal a much larger amount with the help of his crooked boss. When the employee is caught and offered a lighter sentence to give state's evidence, the employer knows he has to kill him. He rehearses the killing many times, but is undone when sudden light shows him killing in the dark train car. Unfortunately, the employer had only rehearsed the dark deed while traveling on night trains; he did not expect sudden daylight to show from an air shaft as they traveled through the tunnel. Frees narrated and portrayed the murderous boss, who would get the chair for this crime. John Dehner was on hand to play the thieving employee. The show was directed by Paul's old friend Norman Macdonald.

The fifteen-minute sustaining series only ran for three broadcasts in February, 1952, with music by Leith Stevens and Clarence Cassell announcing.

The previous year he supported G-Man Steve Mitchell (Brian Donlevy) in the popular adventure drama, *Dangerous Assignment*. Slightly taller than Paul, Donlevy once loaned Frees his five-inch lifts to wear at the microphone.

In the summer and fall of that year Paul was heard in several episodes of *The Whisperer*, a thrilling action-mystery series starring Carleton Young as Philip Gault, the brilliant young man who could only speak in whispers after having his vocal chords crushed in a car accident. Once his voice had been restored through surgery, Gault cleaned up the crime of Central City through the mere thirteen episodes the series lasted.

As radio slowly disintegrated in favor of television, Paul continued to fill his off-time with more painting and writing. One magazine reported that he would sometimes paint professionally on commission and "warm up his long-neglected bowling arm." But it was his writing that he pursued rigorously and commercially.

He had begun writing spec scripts for radio in the late 1940s, but with television he was far more prolific. Though many of his scripts are undated, these were most certainly from the early to mid '50s.

You're the Boss was an original game show for television, and a very heady idea in which each contestant had the opportunity to win the business of his dreams. He is loaned $15,000 and has to make a profit, having to log in with a CPA to make sure things are progressing positively. He's also given the opportunity of answering questions, the correct answers of which would raise or lower his bank account.

Partners in Crime (Jeremiah Shade, Esq.) was a mystery-comedy series that involved Jerimiah Shade and his sister Jennifer as fun-loving, adventurous private eyes. Paul's five-page treatment of the idea only gave a brief overview of what the series could be. He would later give the idea to William N. Robson and pay him to create a pilot television script with it. Paul had worked for Bill Robson on radio, but as Frees told author Keith Scott later, "He ended up coming to me one day, flat broke, couldn't get a job, had nothing. I had a little production company and I was putting scripts together, so I gave him a job putting together some of my stuff. He fell in love with my secretary and married her."

Frees collaborated with Jack Connell on the radio idea *The Curio Shop*, which may have been written in the late '40s or early '50s. Much like *The Black Museum* starring Orson Welles, this show dealt with an elderly antiques dealer and the customers who would come into his shop in the French Quarter of New Orleans to buy, sell or browse. Each object in the musty store held a curious story, which the old man would begin to relate…

Down to Earth was a fanciful idea about "the below average son of an average family, who live on an average street, in an average town…on the planet Mars!" The twelve-page treatment, co-written with Leonard Burns, involved son Zeemor's exploits to Earth by way of a runaway rocket he was testing for speed. Trapped there, he has to figure out how to get home.

Also written with Leonard Burns was *Miss Matrimony*, a light comedy about a retired, romantic old lady who has set up shop as matchmaker by way of ads in the local paper. Miss Hobbs delights in bringing new strangers together every week and leading them to the altar. The title role was written with Marion Lorne or Elsa Lanchester in mind. A treatment and first episode had been scribed, but more often than not, Paul found it difficult to get anywhere with his scripts. Yet, he would continue to write projects and hire others to flesh out his ideas, and accept cold submissions from friends and other writers until the early 1970s.

Who Knows? was a television panel show created by Frees and Sam Pierce. Essentially an interview/improv show, the idea, however, was writ-

On the set of *The Big Sky*, 1952, RKO

ten in script form in 1956 in order to give producers a sense of the structure of this very odd "talk show." Each episode would take an unexplained event—flying saucers, missing people or things, etc.—and toss it at four guests, experts in everything from entertainment to science, in order to come up with a sensible, working hypothesis for the viewer. The origin show that Frees and Pierce wrote put the problem of the disappearance of the British freight and passenger ship, the *Waratah*, before Professor Yale Mintz, author Donald Keyhoe, director George Pal, and comedy writer Jack Douglas. They were more than likely all personal friends of the authors who agreed to do the pilot.

A collaboration between Paul and George (last name unknown) resulted in the unlikely television project, *The Legend of Barnacle Bill*. The short treatment began with the song:

> He'll fight and swear and chew and smoke,
> That's Barnacle Bill the Sailor.
> But he can't swim a bloomin' stroke,
> That's Barnacle Bill the Sailor.
> He'll spin you yarns and tell you lies,
> That's Barnacle Bill the Sailor.
> He'll kiss girls' cheeks and black their eyes,
> That's Barnacle Bill the Sailor.

Burly and confident though Bill might have been, it's doubtful whether a series based around such a loose-living, hard-hitting seaman would have made it past 1950s censors.

Frank Sinatra, Paul Frees and Christopher Dark in *Suddenly*, 1954, United Artists.

Nancy Gates, Paul Frees, Frank Sinatra, Christopher Dark,
James Gleason in *Suddenly*.

Paul's most ambitious writing project was probably the bulging sci-fi screenplay, *The Demon from Dimension X*. Having recently played in several top science fiction classics, he knew exactly what to write and the proper formula for the B movie genre. The story involved two scientists who intentionally crack into another dimension of space and time that they label X, through a series of secret experiments. Unfortunately the unknown planet they tap into brings a horrible monster through, which kills one of the scientists with a deadly ray before going on a murderous rampage through the country!

Frees gave Bert I. Gordon an exclusive 6-month option on two of his screenplays: *The Demon from Dimension X* and *The Crawlers*. He was to arrange financing and production, serving as producer. Paul was to receive 33.3% "of all the proceeds" received from the film, with screenplay credit and screen credit of "Produced by Bert I. Gordon in association with Paul Frees Enterprises."

He wrote at least one more sci-fi/horror screenplay: a story about piranhas.

Among the spec scripts Frees received from others was a first draft of *Best Laid Plans* (written in the early '70s), from his old friend, Ray Buffum, with whom he had written a lost script called *The Reluctant Sleuth*. "Imagine Peter Ustinov as Billy," stated Buffum, "Joey Heatherton as Miss Means, Jack Lemmon as Davis, Suzanne Pleshette as Jane, Goldie Hawn as Carol and Lyle Waggoner as Pat. As written now it would be rated R I suppose, which is the most desirable rating for the box office." Frees was given first crack at producing it, but was far too busy with other projects, including an idea for an album of love poems for Paul to read to music, called "The Deep Frees."

Once *Mr. Aladdin* had finished, Frees shipped out to Jackson Hole, Wyoming to shoot the lavish Howard Hawks western, *The Big Sky*. The part was no bigger than a cameo, though he was playing the important role of Louis McMasters, an ornate, limping dandy responsible for giving Kirk Douglas and Dewey Martin much of their traveling trouble through Blackfoot Indian territory. Russell Harlan, who shot the beautiful landscapes, certainly earned his Best Cinematography Oscar nomination for its sprawling epic look. Frees himself was so taken with the location that he took a number of snapshots of the area and his surrounding cast. He seems to have spent more time doing that than acting in front of the camera.

Riot in Cell Block 11, 1954, Monogram/Allied Artists.

Another good *noir* crime drama came in 1952. *The Las Vegas Story* had buxom Jane Russell married to Vincent Price, an on-the-rocks business man who decides to try his luck at some gambling before the world collapses in on him. There were a few admirable songs by the co-author of "Stardust," Hoagy Carmichael, and an interesting mystery of 'who stole the necklace,' but alas it was just another one-scene film for Frees who plays the district attorney who decides to lock up Price. His role was almost unnecessary. But played so straight, the audience could do with more of him.

The film parts that followed were not much bigger. In 1952 he was briefly seen as the bandleader in *Million Dollar Mermaid*, but he did have a significant scene as writer Richard Stanley talking to Bette Davis at the end of *The Star*.

It was his brief on-camera work as the reporter in the brilliant *The War of the Worlds* that many fans still remember, along with *The Thing*, above

Goodies and baddies socialize off the set of *Riot in Cell Block 11*.

all his other in-person roles. The H.G. Wells classic science fiction story starring Gene Barry won a richly deserved Oscar for Gordon Jennings' fantastic special effects and still holds up well fifty years later.

He followed that up with another on-screen role as the guard Monroe in the tense prison drama *Riot in Cell Block 11*, starring Neville Brand and Emille Meyer. That same year, 1954, brought Frees possibly his largest live-action role.

Suddenly starred Frank Sinatra as John Baron, leader of a gang of assassins who take over Pop Benson's (James Gleason) house in order to get a clear shot at the President of the United States who's arriving by train. Frees is seen as the nervous Benny Conklin who is sent out to scout around, and is ultimately shot by suspicious cops. As an added bonus, he is also heard as the voice of the TV announcer in the house, giving the gang the news of what is happening on the outside.

Frees and Sinatra had begun a friendship in radio (on the *Rocky Fortune* series) that would last throughout the 70s, when Paul moved to Tiburon. Sinatra would also use him as a dubber on several later films.

He wasn't through with radio, however much television and feature films were eating into his time. During NBC's 1953-54 season Frees starred as Richard A. McGee, director of the California State Department of Corrections, in *Confession*. The series had an edge: Frees was moonlighting as an agent for the US Department of Justice, Bureau of Narcotics & Dangerous Drugs at 1340 West 6th St., Los Angeles, California 90017. He had been given an office to use, and, along with an official ID from

Joy Terry, Fred and Paul Frees.

the government, had business cards printed up that he could leave with associates. He was listed in the Corrections' contact list of government employees, but little is known about his duties. In any event, that connection helped the realistic slant of *Confession*, since the CSDC cooperated with making the series believable.

Along with still more Barney Bear (and other) cartoons, he found time to perform with June Foray for thirteen weeks on *Carson's Cellar*, Johnny Carson's first TV show on KNXT, Los Angeles, in 1953. It was reported that he also appeared at least once on Jack Benny's TV show. On September 14, 1953 *Variety* wrote, "Narrator Paul Frees intoned that the sea plays strange tricks and Benny's next call for Marilyn brought out Miss Mmmm." It was Marilyn Monroe's first TV appearance.

He also showed up as Marie Wilson's boyfriend on TV's *My Friend Irma*. He even had his own late-night talk show, *Frees on 2*, in the mid-50s on KNXT. It was a CBS series, broadcast from Studio D at 1313 North Vine Street in Hollywood, Monday through Friday from eleven to midnight. One show's ticket read: "Paul Frees, M.C. Guests Joe Venuti, Tony Romano. Also audience participation. Music! Games! Prizes!" Disney animator Floyd Norman recalled, "I loved the show, which featured Paul roaming the TV stage interviewing guests, doing comic bits, and joking with the musicians. The show was fun and free-wheeling, the perfect example of how much fun live television could be back in the fifties."

Of his work in the early 50's, Frees said, "I'd be doing two or three live television shows back to back at the same time. I can't visualize now how I ever did *any* of it without dropping dead."

As radio pickings became slim, Paul put feelers out for more on-camera work, though his heart was moving more toward faceless jobs. Joy Terry Frees: "Paul was always very self-conscious about his appearance. He was handsome and didn't have that crazy mustache he grew later." Yet his dress was always immaculate: full suit with handkerchief and tie, complete with jewelry and pocket watches and fobs (chain or ribbon attached to the watch). To those who knew about it, his fob collection was impressive:

Large bell-shaped fob with Cornelian crest bottom
Large ornate fob with black onyx bottom and soldier on crest
Large fob with 24-carat amethyst in bottom

Large fob crest in shape of shield
Medium-sized Masonic Ball fob that opens into a cross
Large ornate fob that looks like a crown
Round gold fob that opens for photos
Alexander the Great museum-quality fob
10 ornate shield crest, solid gold fobs

His ring collection was equally snazzy:

Gold insignia ring (PHF)
Large sovereign ring in large-square raised setting with
    cufflinks to match
Gold sovereign ring: Victorian on round raised setting with cuf-
    flinks to match
Victorian solid gold sovereign cufflinks
Large antique square gold ring with Cornelian crest
Large antique square gold ring with crest of soldier in seal
Very large solid gold antique ring with embossed crest
Small antique gold pocket watch with 2 birds in rubies and dia-
    monds on front, opening at front and back
18-carat gold pocket watch with ornate gold face, with Roman
    numerals and two 18-carat gold keys for winding
Large gold antique pocket watch: Victorian white enamel, with
    Roman numerals face, opening at back and front
Solid gold antique metal on ribbon, ornate and signed
Ten or more gold tie pins, all antique: 1 ruby, 1 diamond, 1 horse-
    shoe diamond, 1 ruby and diamond, 1 gold shield, 1 large
    cultured pearl, 1 amethyst, 1 amethyst and diamond, 1 gold
    cloverleaf, 1 head of man in suit of armor, 1 coat of arms

He could afford the lifestyle, and more. He, Joy and son Fred Frees, born on July 21, 1953, were living in style. Joy: "Sometimes he'd get checks in the mail, residuals, and he didn't know where the hell they were coming from, because he didn't remember doing the work. He handled our money beautifully. I was never in want.

"After radio stopped he went into real estate because he could not be without work. He wasn't about to sit on his hands, and he didn't do a 'woe is me.' His work ethic was very, very strong at that time. He went out with

| International Bank of Goodwill | №181318 |
| SILVERSTONE, U.S.A. | |

PAY TO THE ORDER OF _____ $1,000,000.00

AMOUNT __One Million Dollars Worth of Good Luck__

CASHIER'S CHECK   "MICHAEL ANTHONY"

From the hand of *The Millionaire*
(*Thousand Oaks (California) Library's Special Collections*)

his little satchel to real estate school three times a week and got his real estate license, which I thought was great, I still do. He worked for Monty Vanton, an Englishman. It didn't last long though, just a couple months. They sent him out to an open house on a Sunday, it was his first time out, and he sold it! He sold private homes in the Valley and Hollywood.

"But he preferred being an actor, that was his life. Every day, you contact agents, you contact directors. Right after that he got *The Millionaire*. I think that was his big moment in time."

By 1955 Paul Frees was in every way *The Millionaire*. But now his chance to shine in the unseen role of wealthy John Beresford Tipton completed his mastery of every medium. This popular anthology television series starred Marvin Miller as Michael Anthony, who began each episode explaining that he had once been executive secretary to the now late Mr. Tipton at Silverstone, a 60,000 acre estate where Tipton had retired from high finance. Miller had each case history in a bound folder and narrated for a moment directly to camera, at the beginning and end of each show. In a flashback, he then received the million-dollar check (typed up during the show's opening credits) from Tipton's hand. John Beresford Tipton, sitting in a large leather chair, was never seen on camera, though Frees did sit in that chair and hand Miller the check, at least in its early days. Miller/ Anthony would then take that check and pass it on to the disbelieving guest star of the night's episode. The only rules for receiving the check were that the gift's exact amount could never be revealed to anyone, except to a spouse, and that the donor had to remain anonymous. The rest of the show would follow the resulting magic that a million can bring.

It wasn't much work for Miller or Frees, but the series was enough of a hit to still be held in esteem fifty years later. For the Tipton role, Paul Frees altered his voice into that of an older, more tired man, a little higher than that of Miller, whose own vocal range ran dangerously close to Paul's anyway.

The series was much like the 1932 film *If I Had a Million* in which a dying tycoon gives away a million bucks each to eight people picked from the phone book. Sponsored by Singer sewing machines and Colgate toothpaste, *The Millionaire* was another kind of *Twilight Zone* that boasted great actors, actresses and directors—from Agnes Moorehead to Robert Altman. It debuted on January 19, 1955. Though Paul never got screen credit, his character, John Beresford Tipton, always received last billing in the cast's end credits.

"Marvin Miller got stuck with an exclusive," said Frees, "since he was seen on camera, but I had conflicting sponsors. I was able to work for them because I wasn't using a regular voice. I was using my John Beresford Tipton, which was exclusive to that show. I would go in for about four hours once every five weeks and on one stage we would have five partials (parts of a set), and these would be the openings for five separate shows."

He would read the script with his left hand while his right hand was being filmed. "But you never saw my head. That was always my hand. One time on the set we had to close it after Marvin broke up. I was sitting in the chair and had a gorgeous extra in my lap; she did make-up. Marvin came in and said, 'You sent for me, sir?' I said, 'No, go away.' The cameras were rolling when he tried again and again, but he just couldn't say the line again." Frees may also have played in some of the episodes in other roles.

Recalling his co-star, Marvin Miller remarked in 1976, "Well, he always has to be 'on!' He makes so much money on commercials now that he thinks he's a big guy, but he's a very little man. You had to always be prepared for the fact that Paul was always 'on.' On *The Millionaire* he was pretty dependable—of course he never learned a line. He always found a place to prop up a script so that his lines were within reading distance. On the earlier shows you saw more of him; the old man Tipton character had more to do. In one show, we opened with him dressed in a fishing outfit, with a creel. I come up an exterior path saying, 'You sent for me, sir?' And he had a line, but at the same time he had to swing in a fish that he's just caught, remove it from the hook, and deposit it in the creel. But no one realized that Paul hated the touch of anything wet and slimy—he took a lot of takes that day. He was certainly a character, but we got along fine."

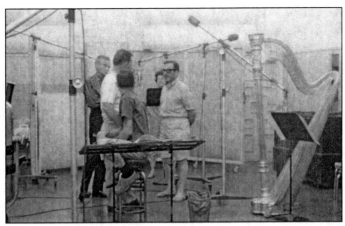

Paul Frees, Spike Jones and others at a record session.

Because of this role, in 1958 Frees was given a similar bit on the unaired *Joan of Arkansas*, written and directed by Philip Rapp, starring Joan Davis as a dental assistant who is drafted into the United States' astronaut training program by the world's smartest computer. Frees was heard and his faceless body seen (though it was more than likely a simple voice dub) giving a pep talk to Joan near the end. Unfortunately, the 30-minute comedy pilot failed to sell.

In 1956-57 Hans Conried, Walter Tetley, and Paul Frees could be heard in a few segments of UPA's *The Gerald McBoingBoing Show*. Bill Scott was assistant producer on the show. Future Bullwinkle directors Bill Hurtz, Lew Keller, and Ted Parmelee were also involved.

Back in films, Paul had the fleeting, yet important, on-screen scene in Humphrey Bogart's last picture, *The Harder They Fall*, a hard-hitting exposé on the crooked fight game, based on Budd Schulberg's 1947 book. Again a priest, Frees has received an urgent letter from the fighter's mother, who wants her son (played by the towering Mike Lane) to come home, and not to hurt/kill anyone else in the ring; she's in mourning for the man who was killed by her son (though he was basically dead from his last fight). So the fighter wants to go home, right now, placing publicity guy Bogart in a very difficult position with the mob.

"I did the short scene because Bogie asked me to," said Frees. "We used to do a radio show together (*Bold Venture*), with Bogie and Betty Bacall. In fact, I did Bogie for Bogie many times, on the show, and at Columbia. I looped for Bogie many times, but I can't remember any of the titles."

This was to be Bogart's last picture. His voice sounded husky due to throat cancer, so it's quite possible that Paul was called in again to loop some of the star's lines. "I've never really been fond of looping. That was always a bread and butter type of job that you did. I was expert at it, though."

Also in 1956 he had the all-important role of "alien voice" in Ray Harryhausen's classic sci-fi film, *Earth vs. the Flying Saucers*, containing the famous scene of a flying saucer crashing into the Capitol building. Said Frees: "We are speaking to you through the translating device above your head," a glowing paper-flower looking thing. The evil aliens had contacted Dr. Marvin (Hugh Marlowe) the previous day by sound that was too high-pitched to be heard. It was to be unfortunate for the entire planet that that message went unheard… The whirling of the saucers, the pre-Frees "talk," was actually the partial sound of sewage going through pipes at the Los Angeles sewer plant where scenes in the first half of the picture were shot.

Later that year Frees rejoined Spike Jones for a bit in a song called "Little Child (Daddy Dear)," actually a quite beautiful ballad of high-pitched questions from George Rock aimed at "daddy dear," who turns out to be Frees doing a Finnegan-type voice (Charlie Cantor, the dumb "duh" guy from *Duffy's Tavern*). Daddy tries to answer the difficult question, "Is the world really round?" but, struggling, admits it's a tricky category. Another version of the song, unused, had Frees doing a croaky Frankie Fontaine voice.

He followed this up by narrating an album called *Exploring the Unknown*, a mono recording composed, conducted and arranged by Leith Stevens, famous for his soundtracks to *The Interns, The Wild One, Private Hell 36*, and many TV shows.

The opening track, "Preparation and Blast Off," in which "your" (the listener's) rocket blasts off after countdown, is reminiscent of Paul's later narrative to Disney's *Adventure Thru Inner Space*, but with orchestral and vocal backing. As the journey continues, Frees describes the wonders of outer space, in a straight voice of incredulity and reserve. The music and chorus are much like those done for Disney by Buddy Baker, *et al* on *The Wonderful World of Disney*.

Meanwhile, he was still busy working on his *own* songs, with Eddie Brandt. "You know, he was so busy," says Brandt. "He worked from seven in the morning until midnight at night every day. Running from studio to studio. I went with him a couple of times all day. Sixteen hours of different jobs. He worked for everybody.

Fred Frees and friend at Disneyland.

"More than anything else, he loved to write songs. So we started writing songs every Saturday because he never worked on Saturday. We wrote a lot of tunes together over the years. We had a big tune with Teresa Brewer that's still big in Europe, a tune called 'I'm Drowning in My Sorrows.'" (It was released on January 20, 1957 and reached #24 on the charts.) "It's still big in Europe. It just goes on and on and on. I get a check for maybe $15,000 every six months. It's strange because they don't play it here. It's sold over a million copies in thirty years.

"He was probably the best guy I ever wrote pop songs with because we connected. It was one of those things where we bounced ideas off each other. I wrote with a whole lot of different people, but Paul was the easiest to write with. We both thought the same way, I think.

"I didn't have the kind of money like he had. What really got us together was songwriting. He had great friends, very intellectual friends. He had great actor friends, like Everett Sloane. Sloane wanted to write with me. He had poetry, tons of poetry, he wanted me to put music to. It was so funny, here were these great actors, these guys were making tons of money, and they wanted to write songs!

"Paul didn't play an instrument. I would play the piano, and he would sing them. We would record them. I wish I had the recordings because we wrote tunes with two melodies, counter-melodies where I'd do one part, and he'd do the other at the same time. He liked to do those, but they are very hard to do."

Amazingly Frees still found time for friends, a family, and more painting. Joy Terry Frees: "The business he was in, we were in, was just a business to us. It wasn't an ooh and an ahh. Paul and Lorne Green, whom he met in 1954, had businessmen's heads. When they got together, they weren't talking showbiz, they were talking investments, orange groves and real estate and things. And Paul out boomed Lorne. Put Paul in a room, he *owned* the room." (Helen Frees stated that when Lorne Greene was a struggling actor, Paul took him in for two or three months until he found a job. Exaggeration, or truth?)

"For years we fed Lorne and his wife Nancy, long before he got *Bonanza*. So finally Lorne got *Bonanza*, and he was able to buy a second hand car. He was very proud of it. And Paul and I only had the finest and the best. He lived on Hillside, and took Paul down to look at the car. Paul walked around and looked at it, looked at it, looked at it, and said, 'Well… you can always make it a planter.'

"He was crazy. When we played poker in the early days for a nickel, a dime, and a quarter, Paul would be playing a trumpet in his mouth, or banging on the table like he was playing a drum."

John Stephenson recalled those poker games. "There would be maybe a Bob Hope writer, people like that. The stakes weren't small, but it was a group thing. Paul liked the camaraderie. This was in the '50s, early '60s. The games would last three to five hours. Sometimes if you're losing, it seems longer.

Fred: "My mother said that he often would cross his eyes for photos in those days."

Joy Terry, Fred and Paul Frees.

"You enjoyed his personality. I considered him a friend. He was more of a voice man than an actor playing an emotion. Assuming a character was his forte. At the games, he always had a nice greeting and a smile and a good story to tell in a booming voice. He also did work of a secretive nature, though why he confided in me, I don't know. I can't imagine Paul putting his shoulder to a locked door!"

Joy: "Then there was Lenny. He lived in the house with us, and was best man at our wedding. It was the three of us, constantly. His real name was Leonard Bernstein. Going out to dinner, Paul would always pay the bill, but would slip the money underneath the table to Lenny so the ladies would think he was paying. He always had a gorgeous woman on his arm. Never worked, but was one of the funniest men who ever lived. He was a fantastic dresser, as was Paul who wore only Brooks Brothers suits."

Fred Frees recalls his home-life at the time. "It was a mixed bag. My parents were happy together until I was six years old, though their problems probably began before that. Living with Dad at that time was happy for me, too. I most remember the 'family' portraits taken of us. I also remem-

Paul snaps while Fred golfs.

ber badgering my father to take me to Disneyland (just an idea that suddenly hit me). After a while, he relented, and we were on our way there.

"After the divorce, my father moved out and I was only able to see him every-other weekend. Those were usually happy times for me as I always wanted to be with him. But there was a lot of animosity between my mother, who married someone my father could not stand, and my father, who remarried, and remarried, and remarried (which my mother could not stand). I felt caught in the middle, being the only child (my sister is ten years younger than I am, so she was not around then).

A rare test for a TV commercial in the 1950s.

"We would always end our weekend visits at Ah Fong's, a Chinese restaurant owned by his friend, the actor Benson Fong. Dad loved to eat... almost anything! We would order practically one of everything (or was that two of everything?). He loved the spareribs. I suppose Chinese was his favorite. By the way, Dad never called a napkin a 'napkin.' He always referred to them as 'serviettes.' Always. When he lived in L.A. he used to pick me up himself and later had his driver pick me up. He never visited me at my mom's house, which was originally his house. I would stay with him from Saturday morning to Sunday evening, regularly twice a month.

"As to the 'voice' aspects of living with Dad, well, he basically didn't take his work home with him. If I had a friend over for a visit, I would try to get him to do some voices, but he always tried not to. But I always convinced him to, and then he seemed to enjoy it after all.

"There's one story I remember. When my parents were still living together (I must have been five or six), in the late 1950s, I was going to go for a swim in the pool. Floating in the water was a giant tarantula. By the time I got Dad to come outside, it had found its way to the side of the pool and began climbing down under the water in the deep end. Eventually it walked all the way to the bottom of the deep end (why, we never knew). My mother was in a panic, of course, and Dad wasn't too calm, either. But in usual Paul Frees fashion, he took control of the situation.

"He took the long pole with the leaf-net (the net that skims the leaves out of the water) attached to it, and worked it down the deep end until he 'scooped' up the tarantula, pulled it out of the pool and laid it down on the nearby slope of our backyard. (Our backyard was hilly.) Before the tarantula had a chance to climb its way out of the net, into the comforting surroundings of the nearby hillside, my father took his shotgun, and at close range, fired several times, blasting the poor thing into oblivion. Now that's taking action!

"I suppose he was always enamored with firearms, although unlike the stories you hear of tragic accidents happening when a child finds their parents' guns, I never knew (or was interested in) where he kept his. Other than the tarantula incident, I don't recall Dad displaying or mentioning his weapons until I was a teenager.

"I felt more 'normal' with my mother. I felt somewhat differently when I was with my dad. Then things were not exactly 'normal,' but rather 'super-normal.' Although, the closest thing to 'normal' would probably have been the time when my parents were still together.

"Outings between father and son would be movies mostly. He liked movies, all kinds. I remember seeing war movies, horror movies, comedy movies, and sci-fi movies with him. Not too many musicals, though. He liked bonbons, popcorn, and all that stuff. Occasionally, we'd do some miniature golf, and sometimes bowling. He once threw his back out trying to impress me in a batting cage, but he never did that again. After that, we always went to restaurants.

"Oh, yes, I always looked forward to being with Dad. Although, I had some difficulty because I always felt he had expectations of me that I could never fulfill. But that was manifested more when I was older. But no matter what, I always loved my dad, always felt it was a privilege to be his son, and always wanted to spend time with him.

"Our times together were never planned. We would just 'play it by ear.' Sometimes, he was simply not feeling well enough to go out, and that was fine, too. As long as we were together. And even then, we weren't always in the same room all the time. I might watch TV in my own room and then see him later in the day. But if he was up to it, we'd spend as much time as we could doing something. We had a family motto, which Dad would repeat quite often: 'We are the Freeses and we do as we pleases.' Amen.

"He did not have 'work hours.' In his line of work, you work as long (or as short) as required. It always fluctuated. But he rarely worked on the weekends, so it didn't interfere with personal time. But there were times when I went with him to work, so either I am mistaken about the weekends, or I was with him during the week on occasion. I can't really remember which. Neither can I remember him talking too much about films he was proud of or didn't like (that he participated in). To him, a job was a job."

As for Paul the artist, Joy Terry Frees remarked, "He never gave an exhibition. Sid Caesar has a lot of his paintings. They became friends after my time with Paul. The paintings were really, really good."

Helen Frees: "Years after the war we had dinner at his home and I saw a painting of his that I wanted very much. I asked him for the painting and he said, 'No!' I continued on saying, 'Come on, Paul, you have so many, couldn't you give me one?' and so on. He continued to say absolutely not. That is one of the strange things about Paul. If you asked him for anything he would not give it to you, but out of the blue, for no reason at all he could be extremely generous and give you the most wonderful present. But when you asked him for something it was 'absolutely not'—it had to come from him, not because you wanted it. But on this particular evening when we were going back and forth for three or four hours—my husband, Dave, finally said, 'Good night, Paul' and put the painting under his arm and we walked out with it—in plain view of Paul. You see—he loved Dave and Dave didn't ask for the painting—he just took it and that was alright with Paul! In many ways, as I say, Paul was a strange fellow."

"He painted in our house," recalled Fred Frees. "There was a guest room on a higher level than the master bedroom, and he used that as his painting room. He seemed to take months to complete a painting, but I was too young to actually pay attention to the exact time it took. My favorite of Dad's paintings, which I have, is a painter holding a pallet of paint in one hand, and a paintbrush in the other. He is facing you, as if you are what he is about to paint. It's totally different from all his other paintings.

"He never had people sit for him, except maybe his wives. He mainly painted from memory or his own imagination. I watched him paint. He used oils but occasionally used a black pastel pencil. He did not sketch first. He would just 'go for it.' He mostly painted people. He definitely had his own style, and some portrayals were not particularly flattering. I would call his painting 'stylized' as opposed to realistic, though he was capable of painting any way he chose to."

He gave several pictures to friends, such as Telly Savalas, Vincent Price and actress Marilyn Nash, best known for her role in Chaplin's *Monsieur*

Fred: "This one features Alan Hale, Jr. standing behind him. And Dad's eyes are crossed in this one, too!"

Verdoux. She was given the painting of a horse race.

Sometime in the 1950s Paul relieved some tension by privately recording a few commercial parodies, occasionally aided by Shep Menken. One of his solo brainchilds was as the voice of a punchy boxer spieling the fab qualities of Boxer Beer. "Do you belch like a canary? Drink Boxer and watch the difference! You'll belch like a tiger!" Another had him as an energetic announcer for Johnson's Six-Way Tool. "Now how many men do you know that can hold his head up and say…" Another voice then shyly boasts, "I have a six-way tool…" Frees: "You can open cans with it, swat flies with it, you can scrape paint with it, it will not bend, it will not rust"—and other lewd, but helpful wonders.

Another "commercial"—"You too can know a thrill, by buying a car from idiot Phil." He *was* an idiot, not being able to pronounce or understand half of what he was saying. "My cars is *good* cars." He told the story of the beaut of an automobile that was only owned by one li'l old lady from Pasadena. She had committed suicide in it.

A few of Paul's paintings. Photos courtesy of Gerald D'Onofrio.

1957 was a busy year. Frees played the bailiff in *The Sword*, a thirty-minute adventure series that sold to CBS, airing on May 31, 1957. The pilot episode, written by Fenton Earnshaw and produced & directed by Richard Irving, involved Paul De La Force, a swashbuckler in the 17th century who aided those in trouble, saving Cyrano de Bergerac from the guillotine after being accused of being a spy.

Also that year Jay Ward had been prepared to hire Paul, Peter Leeds, Hans Conreid, Mel Blanc and others for *Phineas T. Phox, Adventurer*, a series about a detective fox which was really another version of *Crusader Rabbit* and a takeoff on Sam Spade. Unfortunately, there were differences between Ward and animator/studio owner Shamus Culhane which ultimately resulted in the series dying the next year before any real production began.

The 27th Day, released in 1957, was a thought-provoking preach-piece for peace during the Cold War. An alien—who calls himself The Alien—from another world usurps five seemingly random people to represent the human race. Aboard a flying saucer he gives each of them a small box containing three capsules which have enough radiation power to destroy all human (and only human) life on the earth. When the world finds out about this power, the hunt is on to find these people so that global supremacy can be assured to either the USSR or the USA. The USSR menace is of course the bad guy here, and is ultimately foiled by the one scientist in the world, who was given his own box of capsules, genius enough to figure out a peaceful solution to the problem; though as newscaster Ward Mason (Frees) states, "I know it's unbelievable. Fantastic. But the rays appeared to have killed *every* person throughout the world known to have been a confirmed enemy of human freedom."

Paul only has one brief on-camera scene, as he sits smoking before a wall-sized map with clocks of all time zones behind him. His newscaster's voice, however, is the most important non-character role heard throughout the film, giving (cheaply for a sci-fi film of this budget) a concise account of the turmoil that spread for the 26 days leading up to the rather heavy-handed conclusion. Yet it was a very imaginative idea for a science fiction film, written by John Mantley, based on his novel. The saucer effects were done by an uncredited Ray Harryhausen who would crop up more than once in Frees' career.

Also that year he did some dubbing for *Beginning of the End*, a low-cost picture about the world being in danger from radioactive mutant

Spacemaster X-7, with Paul Frees and Lyn Thomas, 1958, 20th Century-Fox.

locusts. Directed by Bert I. Gordon (famously known for his big animal horror flicks), much of the more expensive scenes (the army, crowd scenes, and so forth) relied on stock footage. Paul was first heard in a Dudley Do-Right narrator-type voice over the short wave radio, telling the army that all traffic was being rerouted around the Ludlow area (where the grasshoppers first struck). Though he was also heard on the plane coming back from Washington, DC, his main work was dubbing the helicopter pilot in various scenes, especially the "exciting" finale when all heroes are trying to drive the locusts into Chicago's bay. It was so typical of Hollywood monster movies of the 1950s that *Mystery Science Theatre 3000* gave it a good going over on their series. It would not be the last *MST3K* version of a Frees film.

In 1957, *The Snow Queen*, an animated feature film originally from a Soviet Union studio, was filled with the American voices of Sandra Dee, Tommy Kirk, Patty McCormack, June Foray, Paul Frees, Joy Terry Frees and others. Even though the Cold War was on, *The New York Times* liked it. "So much is this a picture in the manner of a classic Disney cartoon that we wouldn't be surprised if the Russians will soon be claiming that they invented the Disney style." It was a hopeful fairy tale based on the much-loved Hans Christian Andersen story. An original soundtrack album, narrated by Frees, was released on Decca Records in 1960. He gave a warm performance as a caring old man who delighted in the storytelling. "The golden chariot was shining in the sun as they speeded clippity-clop past beautiful cherry orchards."

Frees was also getting into commercials heavily by this point. Joy Terry Frees: "Right after he got *The Millionaire*, that started the television thing going, and that's what started the commercials going. He was doing commercials long before everyone else did."

Sometimes exhaustion got the better of him, but he had a way to steal some moments for himself. "He could fall asleep with his eyes open," said JTF. "And I knew when he was gone. Certain people would talk to him, and his eyes would glaze over. He'd be gone.

"Paul was a funny, funny man. He did change vitally, but in the early days, he was absolutely hysterical. We would go out and he would wear a cape with red lining, and he would assume a dialect, and he would be the Duke and I'd be the Duchess, and he'd get away with it! In the restaurant, absolutely outrageous!

"He never would read. I was a big reader. When *From Here to Eternity* came out, in the early '50s, I said you've got to read this book, since he was in World War II and everything. We were in our first apartment, and I said you're GOT to read this book, and he'd say, 'I'm not going to read this book, I'm going to write one!' So I went to bed; the bedroom was upstairs, and you could look from the top of the stairs down into the living room. There were two chairs in front of the fireplace. It was two o'clock in the morning and he hadn't come to bed yet, and I thought, what is he doing? So I went down, and he was sitting in front of the fireplace, with the book in his lap, and of course he was fast asleep. He was sitting in his army jacket, with the Purple Heart, and he wouldn't give it up; even asleep, he was doing schtick!

"Nobody else in his family had the talent. He was the only one. But Fred has his dad's talent and his dad's voice."

"I liked all my dad's voices, but I guess I was most amused by Peter Peachfuzz for some reason.

"No matter what my father did, he was still 'Dad.' I was very proud of him and very proud to be his son. I knew he was the best in the business. In spite of kids boasting that their dads are the best at what they do, to me, it was a matter of indisputable fact. I was born into my

Boris (Paul Frees) and Bullwinkle (Bill Scott), September 1961. (*Keith Scott*)

father's talent, and I went with him to sessions often enough to, perhaps occasionally, take it for granted. Sometimes they would take all day, and to a youngster, that can seem very long and tedious. Don't forget, even doing the Bullwinkle sessions, they would repeat the same lines over and over again. Besides, my father was always impressing into me the need for absolute professionalism. That translates into an attitude. Add that to the repetition, and the 'awe' is sorely lacking. The 'process' entailed elements of fun, but you could always tell that it boiled down to hard work.

"Through my father, I even accepted his fellow actors, many of them 'name stars,' as ordinary people (although with extraordinary abilities). I was particularly fond of Michael Rennie and Lorne Greene. As far as cartoons go, I think I watched every single one, especially on weekends. Dad always encouraged me to watch television—what kid can say that about his parents? It was always fun to watch the shows that Dad did, especially when I wasn't with him. It was like he was there with me. I felt more pride and love than awe. That I left to others."

In 1958 Erich Maria Remarque's 1954 novel *A Time to Love and a Time to Die* received a big budget film treatment from Universal-International. It was a well-done and beautifully photographed film of 1944 disillusionment from the German soldier's point of view, starring John Gavin and other American-sounding actors mixed in with the German voices. Many of those were from Paul Frees' throat throughout the picture. In fact, he is the first voice heard in the film, as the German sergeant shouting roll call to the freezing troops at the Russian-German front. His other overdubs include: the man calling out the train stop, man digging, agreeable man in the air raid shelter, man digging the Pax grave, doctor at restaurant bombing, the one-eyed man in the Justice of the Peace office, a workman in front of the professor's house, Heini, the bald Nazi pianist, the superior officer who says no to Ernst Graeber's (Gavin) extended furlough, and perhaps the man in the train who wishes his little boy hadn't come to say goodbye.

"I had done so many pictures," said Frees, "with Bob Arthur (producer) that he knew my versatility when it came to looping. Douglas Sirk (director) would find beautiful characters in Europe, but they couldn't speak English." The director wanted to use them, so Arthur told him to go ahead: Paul Frees would just loop them back at Universal. He ended up doing sixteen different characters in German dialect.

In *Last of the Fast Guns*, also released that year, he looped for a number of the Mexican actors in the western, which featured old friend Lorne Greene.

Back on camera, Frees was hired to save the earth from *Spacemaster X-7*, released in 1958 and directed by Edward "The Three Stooges Meet Hercules" Bernds. Spacemaster X-7 is the name of a satellite which returns to earth containing samples of a Martian fungus. A scientist (Frees) experimenting on the fungus accidentally exposes it to human blood, changing it into evil, ever-expanding "blood rust." The one woman (Lyn Thomas) carrying the virus hides out from the scientists seeking her, thinking she is wanted for murder, as she is responsible for her husband's viral death. The film is interesting in that scientist Frees is, for a change, not likeable and rather negative, unlike most brilliant minds of '50s sci-fi. It also gave a rare dramatic role to Moe Howard as cab driver Retlinger. In 1983, Fox Video Games even made an Atari-like video game of the same name, but it had little to do with the plot, though 20th Century-Fox's logo adorned the cartridge cover.

Paul's first major sale to television was to executive producer Herbert B. Leonard at Screen Gems in 1958. He created (with George Draine) and narrated the series *Rescue 8*, initially called *Dial 1116*. The syndicated show

The faces behind the voices
(clockwise):
Akim Tomiroff (Boris),
Eric Blore (Inspector Fenwick),
Ed Wynn (Captain Peachfuzz),
Boris & Natasha.
Courtesy of Ward Productions, Inc.

ran for two full seasons (1958-59), starring Lang Jeffries and Jim Davis as the adventurous paramedics who were always rescuing young ladies and children from dangerous situations in a variety of exotic locations. It was an exciting series with beautiful location photography. Adventurous music comparable to "The Peter Gunn Theme" crept over Frees' voice: "You are watching a rescue team in action. One of twenty-seven such teams attached to the first department of Los Angeles County. Five-and-a-half million people in this area are dependent on their ability to act swiftly and efficiently in any emergency. This program is dedicated to rescue teams throughout the United States. And to the men who risk their lives daily to save others. We will be back in a moment to bring you the story behind this exciting rescue."

Another popular syndicated cartoon series for Frees came from Larry Harmon Productions who had taken the ever-popular Capitol Records' creation of the 1940s, and turned out 156 five-minute *Bozo the Clown* cartoons. Harmon himself voiced Bozo and Butchy Boy, with just about all other voices falling onto Paul's plate. 20 were made in 1958, 84 in 1959 and 52 in 1962, filling a massive need for more animated product in late 1950s television.

Paul Frees' first work for Jay Ward's arm of animation was to be for the incredibly successful *Rocky and His Friends*, the saga of the plucky, optimistic squirrel and his dumb-sounding cohort in crime-fighting, the quick-quipping moose Bullwinkle. The sharp satire of the scripts easily made up for the crudeness of the animation, swiftly gaining an adult audience of die-hard fans. As everyone knows by now, Paul voiced that dastardly arch-villain from Pottsylvania, Boris Badenov, whose deep, jovial Russian sound would very seldom be reused later in the Frees canon. Boris was a squat, pudgy, no-neck no-goodnik who, with the aid of lanky female spy Natasha Fatale (voiced by June Foray), was always under the thumb of Fearless Leader (voiced by the ever-versatile Bill Scott) to destroy the heroes of the show, Bullwinkle J. Moose (Scott also) and Rocky, the flying squirrel (again, June Foray, in her most innocent boyish voice). He always dressed in black, often even when trying to vaguely disguise himself, and wore a two-triangle hat, perpetually downcast eyebrows and an immodest array of white teeth.

Naturally, Boris was foiled at every turn, often shouting "Raskolnikov!" (the murderer in Dostoyevski's *Crime and Punishment*) or growling at the unseen narrator at a frustrating moment. The voice was partially based on Akim Tamiroff, a Balkan actor who gained Oscar nominations for *The General Died at Dawn* (lead role) and *For Whom the Bell Tolls*. Because of this, the series irked the Russians a bit, but everyone else ate it up every time Boris yelled at Natasha to "Sharrup yo' mout'!"

The first four weeks of recording *Rocky and His Friends* had been completed by mid-1959, with the show's prime-time debut occurring in November of that year. By the time he'd finished with Jay Ward Productions (which never really seemed to end, thanks to a steady stream of Cap'n Crunch commercials), Frees had put a voice to 325 episodes of *Rocky and His Friends*, 91 *Peabody's Improbable History*s, 39 *Dudley Do-Right of the Mounties*, 100 *Hoppity Hoopers*, and countless commercials. He also substituted for Bill Scott in five *Fractured Fairy Tales* when the great moose voice had a cold.

Frees was also heard as Captain Peter Peachfuzz, the rattled Ed Wynn soundalike who often got directions, instructions and the world mixed up. Peachfuzz had actually originated in the first Bullwinkle story, "Jet Fuel Formula," but was voiced very differently by Bill Scott. Frees claimed the character in the third adventure, "Upsidaisium," about the moose's antigravity mine on Mount Flatten.

The perpetual satire of the series is what keeps it a popular show to this day. The Cold War backdrop of the main Rocky and Bullwinkle segments was just one of many "adult jokes" of the time, making the scripts and in-jokes intelligent enough for the kiddies to grow into and love even more as they got older. The clever writing team came up with some of the most memorable and beloved, although sometimes very cheap-looking, animated situations in television cartoon history. When Rocky and Bullwinkle were on the playing field of Wossamotta U, watching their inadequate football team being murdered (not quite literally) by Badenov's huge brawlers in disguise, the squirrel asked, "Do you think we'll win, Bullwinkle?" To which the moose honestly replied, "We'll be lucky to *lose*."

Stalwart Jay Ward writer Chris Hayward remembered Frees vividly. "He was a little bit ashamed of his size. He wore big boots with tall heels. The voice was in the chest, it was extraordinarily bombastic. He had great command. I don't think anything ever threw him. At a cold reading, he was bar none. I've never seen anything like that. Other people would have to rehearse. Not Paul. He'd done it so often, he knew it as he read it.

"Whenever I view the end of *A Place in the Sun* I think: he really could've inherited the mantle of Edward G. Robinson. Who was also short, but commanding. I also thought it was a shame he never got into really serious acting. But it wasn't worth his time. He got such easy money doing things like voices.

"I was just so glad my life-path crossed his. It's something I really look back on with great fondness. His sense of humor was endless. He took great sport at laughing at himself and at life in general.

"Jay Ward was a sweet man and he had a great sense of humor. He barely rewrote anything that I ever wrote for him, which is remarkable. I had a great time. But he was so cheap. He would take you to a golf match rather than give you money to live on."

A later component of the series was *Dudley Do-Right of the Mounties*, inspired by the Nelson Eddy-Jeanette MacDonald Mountie musical, *Rose Marie*. The high-pitched, ever-loyal idiot Do-Right was a Canadian Mountie whose greatest crime was once eating peas with a knife. His girl, Nell, who loved his horse more than he, was again voiced by the only woman on the Jay Ward team, June Foray. Paul Frees' droll impression of British actor Eric Blore was heard as Inspector Fenwick, one of Paul's highest-pitched voices. Hans Conried regularly stole the show as the pernicious Snidely Whiplash, he of the cape, tall hat and curling mustache, who came straight out of old silent movie melodramas. In fact, the entire look and tinkling piano music of the series was based on this quick-visual medium, with Frees narrating in true *March of Time* style. A dud, live-action, major motion picture was made of the cartoon in 1999, starring Brendan Fraser and Sarah Jessica Parker, with Robert Prosky taking the Fenwick role. Except for *George of the Jungle* (with John Cleese in Frees' erudite gorilla role), Jay Ward cartoons have had bad luck breaking box office records as live-action films.

The Jay Ward recording sessions were a scream. Luckily Ward kept the reels running throughout, recording some of the funniest outtakes and hilarity ever captured on tape. Frees dominated the scene, telling story after story, joke after endless joke, ragging on poor old friend William Conrad who would often be reduced to tears or have to leave the room altogether, so hard was his laughing. Sometimes Conrad started it, joking on Paul about something, but no one could out-zing the master.

"They are like my *family*," Paul later said of the Bullwinkle clan. "We still are. I just absolutely love them, and they are *so* incredible in their talent, as well as being marvelous personal people. I would drive Bill Conrad absolutely crazy. He would just go out of his mind. The Ward work was one of the high points of my life. The things that we did were so clever and so beautifully done and written, done with such a light heart…I would've paid to go and do that." In the early 1980s he said he would give his eye teeth to work with the Jay Ward organization again—the cast in its heyday, though he was still doing the Cap'n Crunch commercials; they would send his lines to him in Tiburon, California and he would recite them and send them back by post. He vastly preferred the Ward work to his time with Hanna-Barbera, which he considered the opposite end of the spectrum. "They are devoid of imagination. Single-handedly they've made a million dollars, but they no longer do what Bill Hanna and Joe Barbera created at MGM. When they worked for themselves, in the beginning it was fine, but then they became a mill, turning out product. I quit that years before I moved here (Tiburon). It was laborious working there, because it was *work*. They would do a sentence at a time, over and over again. Then they would fit them together. There was nothing funny about it. Very dumb subjects. Fine for kids. Though I don't know why dumb subjects should be fine for kids. The quality of their stuff is *very* inferior to Jay Ward and Disney. The only ones I'll work for outside of Jay Ward is Rankin/Bass. I love them equally."

Frees was also constantly heard as various historical celebrities on the *Peabody's Improbable History* segment, often imitating the actors of yesterday. He joined dog Peabody (Bill Scott) and his boy Sherman, voiced by radio actor Walter Tetley, as the two traveled through time in the WABAC Machine, righting timelines that have gone awry. In 1960 the segment caused some hot collars at ABC and sponsor General Mills when they feared ethnic groups might be offended by some of the voices given by Frees to Confucius, Lord Francis Douglas and others. They also wanted to stop making fun of American heroes, but Jay Ward held his ground and the irreverence continued.

168 half-hour *Rocky* shows were completed before the series wound down in 1963. There was talk for years about reviving the series, and scripts were prepared, but according to Bill Scott, the humor just couldn't plow through the layers and layers of studio executives required to make those "artistic" decisions. That was a tragedy, especially for the fans who have kept the beloved series a cult legacy for 40+ years. Finally, in 2000 a feature film, *The Adventures of Rocky and Bullwinkle*, was produced with an all-star cast. It was a combination live-action and cartoon film, along the same lines as *Who Framed Roger Rabbit?*, and was nominated for

At a party in 1959.

several sci-fi awards. June Foray again strapped on her goggles to provide the voice for the cartoon Rocky, while author of the ultimate Jay Ward biography, *The Moose That Roared*, Keith Scott, took on the heavy task of voicing Bullwinkle, the narrator, the cartoon Boris, and the cartoon Fearless Leader. The live-action Boris Badenov was attempted by *Seinfeld*'s Jason Alexander, while Rene Russo did likewise with sexy Natasha Fatale's role. Robert DeNiro produced the film through his production company (Tribeca) and also played the "real" Fearless Leader. Other celebrities such as Carl Reiner, Jonathan Winters and John Goodman appeared throughout the film, but it did not gross back its cost of $76 million, and definitely lacked the Frees presence.

In 1960 Paul's voice was all over the Golden LP *Rocky and His Friends*, even as the energetic Conrad-type narrator. "From the stratosphere to the now and here, from the vaulted blue direct to *you*—it's Rocky, the flying squirrel!" It was a delightful album filled with songs, sound effects and all the other silliness that made the series such a hit. June Foray opens up the frivolity with the fun march, "I Was Born To Be Airborne." When Bullwinkle recites "Tom, Tom, the Piper's Son" Frees appears as one of the deadpan detectives to ask what Tom has in the bag. "You got a permit to pack a pig?" They take the pig away as evidence, after finally asking Tom if he's got an apple. Paul is immediately heard in the next poem as Peter Piker who scolds Bullwinkle for getting all his P's wrong. "You've got a bad case of pookles there, fella," he says, admitting to being out of the pickle business because he couldn't say it either. Now he's helping his sister Suzie sell sea shells at the seashore. When Mr. Peabody and Sherman visit Ponce de Leon, Frees voices the famed Fountain of Youth discoverer. The poor guy is now washing out diapers for all his thirsty men who had turned to babies after discovering the Fountain. Searching for one of the lost men/babies, Frees again appears in the woods as one of the Seminoles in an "ugh" voice.

Finally Boris Badenov shows up. He's stopped the elevator in Bullwinkle's building and is charging everyone $100 to get out. He and Natasha sing a weird song introducing their evil natures, but he's glad when side one ends, because what he says next "is off the record." On the second side, Frees again provides voices for the meeting of Stanley and Livingston on another Mr. Peabody adventure. One of his best bits comes from reprising his Moon Man voice of Cloyd in the Latin-flavored "Moon Men Mambo." Immediately after, Boris gets a solo song to explain why he's there. "You Got To Having A Crook," because after all, "if there's no one who is bad, then how do you know who is good? Huh?" With goodbyes from all the cast, save for a "badbye" from Boris, the little album ends.

The previous year Paul was part of Jay Ward's pet project, a puppet show along the lines of *The Muppet Show* meets Daws Butler's *Time for Beany*, called *The Watts Gnu Show*. The lead character was, of course, a gnu, voiced by Bill Scott, and featured a variety show format with songs and comedy bits by Leon Pober and Forman Brown. In the unsold pilot

Frees revamps his Peter Lorre impression for a duet with Bill Scott as Boris Karloff on the inadequacies of then-modern horror films. He also has a great song as he simmers in a cannibal's stewpot, lamenting "Never Raise Your Son to Be an Explorer." The satirical TV show was shot over three days on an expensive soundstage, but failed to gain network interest.

One of the main reasons Paul Frees found these recording sessions the most invigorating of his career was that he had known most of the people involved for years, ever since his early days in radio. And he would work with many of them again and again for the rest of his life.

At some point Paul and Daws Butler worked for Bing Crosby Enterprises on a syndicated television series: a takeoff on Sherlock Holmes and Dr. Watson with chimpanzees. Twenty-six episodes were made, but an unfortunate accident in Thousand Oaks, California burned up all remaining prints. "I was [the voice of] Sherlock Holmes," Frees stated, "and he [Daws] was Dr. Watson plus the other characters. They had little sets built to size for the little chimps."

Don (son of Daws) Butler recalled the love/hate relationship between these two top voices: "I remember Dad on the telephone saying, 'I get up in the morning and the first thing I do is get down on my knees and thank God I am not Paul Frees.' He and Dad did a pilot that we called *The Babysitter,* but it was to be the pilot of a whole series called *Nice Try, Virgil.* Dad played a character called Virgil, and the idea was that he'd be trying different occupations, but it never got further than the first film which dealt with him as a babysitter. My older brother David played the kid that he was babysitting, and my younger brother Paul was a baby at the time, so he was in the film, too. The narrator was Paul Frees. It was made around 1949 or '50."

Frees was happily grabbing every job that came his way. He gave a very brief introduction to the Disney classic, *The Shaggy Dog,* in 1959. His clipped, newsreel-style narration introduced poor Wilson Daniels (played by Fred MacMurray) who hated dogs, being a retired mailman. Alas, his son, Wilby (Tommy Kirk), becomes a dog after reading the inscription on a ring belonging to the Borgia family. When Wilby, as the dog, overhears part of a spy plot, Wilson does his duty by reporting it to the police. Unfortunately, when he has to tell how he knows this information, he's labeled crazy, and sent to Dr. Paul Frees to discuss the situation. The scene finally gave Paul a chance to shine, however briefly, in a live-action comic role, after a whole decade of playing the heavy or bit parts in dramatic features. It was a great way to say goodbye to his on-camera appearances. And it was a marvelous introduction to a superb career with Disney.

It wasn't his first outing with Disney Studios, however. His distinctive tones were heard at least three years earlier voicing a few characters in "Boys of the Western Sea" on *The Mickey Mouse Club* in 1956. He had done voices for *Your Host, Donald Duck*, and narrated *Mars and Beyond*, both for television in 1957. He had even auditioned for a role in 1951's *Alice in Wonderland*. But 1959 was his breakthrough year with Disney.

The Shaggy Dog record album, released the same year as the film, literally trumpets its opening before Paul Frees speaks his introductory words: "I'm—a dawg." He gives a slow, big, dumb and lovable performance as the low-sounding Shaggy Dog who sings his way through the lavish production of songs and comedy. The lively "Did You Ever Hear a Dog Talking?" begins the musical journey, followed by Dog having the non-speaking Fred MacMurray playing his saxophone—something he did not get to do in the film. Honking like a sax out of *The Goon Show*, Dog ruminates, "Didn't ask 'im to play it in the picture…I wonder why…" and then launches into his poem, "Ode to a Dawg," while the music continues to be murdered. Borrowing the sax, Dog tries it out and blows that thing the way it should be played. After which, a real '50s song begins: "The Shaggy Dog Shag," doo-doo'd by a group of young guys who really swing it to the youngsters out there.

Even cute Roberta Shore (French girl owner of the dog in the film) gets in on the act with an up-tempo pop song called "C'est Chifon" (the name of the dog). One of the catchiest songs has to be "It's a Dog, Dog-gone It, It's a Dog" which Paul sings, backed up by a group of girls who alternate singing the title in answer to his questions, such as "Who's the head of the German police?"

Side Two began with the bouncing bobbysox number, "Shaggy Dog" sung with verve by a girl keen to be a teen idol, complete with lively beat, yakety sax and lines from dog Frees. The coolest, brassiest number came next: "Flat Foot Floogie," in which Paul sheds his fur for a few minutes to coolly state "Floy doy, floy doy, floy doy, floy doy" at the repetitious but strategic moment, between whispered mentions of the title from a male singing group. After, Paul is given an energetic cha-cha-cha number all his own, with lots of Latin punch by way of steamy brass. While there was little continuity to the album, nothing could be less important. The songs shone, as well as any of the day, and gave 1959 some hot novelty properties. When The Four Hounddogs howled something akin to "How Dry I Am," it was obvious there was a demented genius at work on this oft-neglected release.

After Dog gives us the advice to "Be nice to your dawg. The leg he bites—could be yours," the record swings into one final sax-inspired twirl of "Shaggy Dog," and abruptly ends.

It was such a rich sound, with humor that still holds up today, that it's hard to believe it's been out of print for 40 years and has never been released on CD (as of 2003). Perhaps it was merely built as a promotional piece for the film—indeed, elements of it are thrown in throughout the record—but the production values and catchy (though dated) tunes make it much more than that.

Frederic Grimes, Special Projects Producer for Capitol Records also used Paul for a stereo demonstration record called *Hystereo!* in 1959. "Since none of the other A&R types, being too busy with their own stables, wanted to do it, I got the assignment," says Grimes. "I thought about it and worried out a script. Capitol at that time had a studio tour in their new tower on Vine Street, and one of the features was a demonstration of the startling realism of stereo. One major effect was the sound of a bowling ball clattering down the alley and concluding with a strike. That idea, the instant cliché effect of a bowling ball in action, was the basis for my script. That went up through the approval ladder and was okayed.

"I then approached a dear friend, the very talented and capable arranger, Bill Loose. Bill 'ghosted' for most of the 'star' arrangers in town—Billy May, Percy Faith, lots of folk. I told him what I wanted and when those wheels started to turn, I cornered Paul Frees (who was in the studio doing voices for a Bozo the Clown album) and confirmed him as my narrator. I had written the script with him in mind, and it would have been embarrassing if he had turned me down! There was nobody in town who could do so many voices so distinctly. He bridled at my chintzy price ($1,000 flat, no royalties), but I showed him the script and he gave me a break.

"There were three live recording sessions for the album—one had the large orchestra (38 folk), one had a small band (like ten people), and the one where Paul did the voices.

"The large orchestra was typical of the all-star congregation available in Hollywood in those days. The players included Paul Smith, Larry Bunker, Willie Schwartz, Shorty Sherock, Ted Nash, Shelly Manne—it was an awe-inspiring aggregation. The big-band date ran half an hour overtime. We needed musicians of that caliber to cut music that quirky within one session. I think they did right well. Oh, and June Foray was the voice of the lady bowler!

"After that it was into an edit room with miles of half-inch tape and some very competent help and many, many hours of splicing things together, overdubbing, pan-potting, remixing, re-equalizing, and praying a lot. When I finally put the master to bed, I was quite pleased with the product, since the whole thing was my baby. When the Repertoire vice president, Lloyd Dunn, my boss two layers up, told me he had decided not to release the thing I was damn near destroyed. His reasoning, he told me, was that it was too sophisticated and he had too many reservations about it. Being job-dependent, I nodded bravely and skulked off. I remained at the label for one more album and three singles and was then invited to leave. My next career move was into aerospace, where my degree got me hired as a technical writer on the Apollo program.

"Mr. Dunn admired Meredith Willson inordinately, which resulted in the soundtrack of *The Music Man* on Capitol's label, along with other memorably Broadway turkeys (*Tenderloin, Fiorello*). He also thought Stan Freberg was incredibly clever (an instance in which I agree), and (this is where I am completely without substantiation) Dunn played *Hystereo!* for Freberg, and Freberg pointed out, legitimately, that he considered himself Capitol's comic-in-residence. My basis for this opinion (and the non-release of my baby) is Dunn's comments to me—a 'sophisticated' audience had, in addition to the too-hip flavor of the thing, objected to the 'fag' bandleader, and in general he felt that my effort didn't 'fit,' whatever the hell that meant." (*Hystereo!* has at last been released on the BearManor Music label.)

Frees also worked on the cartoon soundtrack of *Noah's Ark* this year with Jerome Courtland and singers, released later on a 45 record as "Building the Ark" with a flipside of "The Maiden Cruise of Noah's Ark." The tracks were later put on an album called *Pecos Bill*, a Disneyland Record from 1965. The *Noah's Ark* soundtrack was a hip pop score, with Paul spilling lines through "Building the Ark" in a nasally barker way between snatches of vocals and loud, brassy jazz.

On June 26, 1959 Disney released one of Paul's best and most lasting cartoons. *Donald in Mathmagic Land* is still heralded as one of the single best pieces of learning material ever animated. Even the Motion Picture

Academy thought so, as it was nominated for an Oscar the following year for Best Short Subject. In the guise of the True Spirit of Adventure, Paul gave Donald Duck, clad in hunter's clothes, a lesson in the heavy side of math. It was a brilliant work, using a wealth of adroit gags (such as trees with square roots) and illustrative live-action film (i.e. a billiard player who uses the diamonds on the side of a pool table to plot his shot trajectories). Paul was first heard as the circle-square-rectangle bird who kept reciting the precise number of Pi. His narrating tone for the rest of the short was straight-forward and helped make this the Disney classic it is still. And of course Clarence Nash, the original voice of Donald Duck for 50 years, was on hand with his usual superbly quacking delivery.

1959 was very good to Paul Frees, and paved the way into his busiest decade. In *Operation Petticoat* he could be heard as the voice of Sgt. Ramone Galado, the guy with the stolen cigars, the man chasing the bus at the end, and others. He also directed the American dubbing of the Japanese sci-fi film, *Bijo to Ekitainingen*, renamed *The H Man* for American release the following year.

And, of course, there was the infamous dubbing in Billy Wilder's hit drag comedy, *Some Like It Hot*. First, he is the voice of the funeral director: "Good evening, sir. I am Mr. Mozerella, what can I do for you?" The funeral parlor fronts the hidden entertainment (a band and dancing) and drinks club. Among other scenes, he is also heard briefly as the waiter who takes a cop's (Pat O'Brien) order in the speakeasy.

It wasn't until years after the film's release that it was learned that Tony Curtis did not do his own Josephine voice. "We had a voice coach to help us pitch our voices higher," Curtis claimed in his autobiography. When he recreated a scene from the film, with Rich Little playing the Jack Lemmon part, on *The Kopykats* television show, Josephine was without "her" subtle masculine boom. In *Some Like It Hot* Billy Wilder himself thought Curtis' efforts left something to be desired. Though the performance is obviously dubbed, it was yet another work of profundity by Frees.

He also did a two-day session (January 20-21, 1959) as the wildly happy announcer introducing "Late Late Movies" for Spike Jones. Films like *The Flying Tigers Meet Lassie* and *Death Takes a Holiday, Cha-Cha-Cha* had only a few lines to emote before being interrupted by wacky commercials. Paul plays in the commercials, too, at one point interviewing a garbage collector who eats fire for a hobby. What does *he* smoke? "Why, isn't it obvious? I smoke the cigarette with the stinking man's filter and the smoking man's taste." It was an entire album of TV parodies first called *The Late Late Late Movies*, then retitled *Omnibust* when the master tapes were sold to Liberty Records. Every show from Captain Kangaroo to Lawrence Welk was sent up.

Around that time he also recorded for the new *Spike Jones in Hi-Fi* (AKA *Spike Jones in Stereo* or *Spooktacular*) for Warner Brothers. Paul was allowed to ad-lib his lips off on this one. Carl (no relation to Eddie) Brandt did the arrangements: "The 'Spooktacular' was a complicated album. Spike had a million voice tracks. We finally broke it down and ended up scoring it like a movie, because it had to be done in bits and pieces. Nothing was ever done in haste; it took a lot of thinking. But we knew what we wanted and we knew how to do it. I made conductor sheets: which side the stereo was supposed to come from, and all the effects. It was like it was a regular score."

Smokin' Paul Frees.

The first voice heard on *Spike Jones in Hi-Fi* was Jeeves, an Inspector Fenwick soundalike who introduces the awaiting Invisible Man to Count Dracula (Frees again), but the butler is rebuked: "Well, tell him I can't see him." But with the Invisible Man is Vampira, and being the cold-blooded lover that he is, he bids her welcome. Thus starts the musical album, corrupting popular songs with a spooky arrangement and Addams Family-flavored lyrical pallor. "I Only Have Eyes For You" is up first, an eerie duet between the two, ending with "I just wanna neck (sucking and popping sounds inserted) with you..." The ambitious album was engaging, creepy fun, dotted with some ingenious lines and lyrics. Vampira (voiced by Loulie Jean Norman): "All of a sudden my heart sings, when I remember little things. Your razor blade against my wrist, the very first time we kissed."

It might as well have been called *Paul Frees in Hi-Fi*, so dominant was his presence. He was in every scene—it made a great demo tape for his impressions. He was heard as Alfred Hitchcock giving the interviewer from *Poison to Poison* a tour around his pad, showing off weirdo treasures like the armchair made from real arms. "Alfred, why did you shoot that canary?" "Because he was just plain *yellow.*"

He enunciates Frankenstein's Monster (*a la* Boris Karloff) singing "Everything Happens to Me," then goes right into an announcer introducing "This Is Your Death," with host, Edward Ralph. Dr. Von Steiner, with a voice somewhere between Boris Badenov and Ludwig Von Drake, is the subject of the television homage show. All the creatures Steiner created for films (Phantom of the Opera, King Kong and others) are brought into the studio. Another highlight of the album includes a hilarious expanded version of "My Old Flame" (worth the price of admission), minus the crooner.

Frees: "Spike supervised the 'Spooktacular' LP, but he gave me more or less a free hand. A great deal of it was ad-libbed by me, like Orson Welles' 'Down here with the werewolves.' He had respect for my judgement."

"During that album," recalled Eddie Brandt, "we went out on the town a lot. He was a very fun person. We worked on the album for weeks. He would come one night and two days later, he'd be there for three hours. He did a lot of overdubbing. Spike liked him very much, and he liked Spike. He was tough to deal with because Spike was so cheap, and Paul was beyond that price range. All the rest of us were not making big money, and our only job at the time was writing some songs, but Spike wanted to cut in. He'd cut in on everything that everybody wrote. But Paul said, 'No. I don't work that way,' and Spike let it go, because he needed Paul. Paul was just the type of guy he needed for his recording studio. He could do so many things. Everything else I've got, Spike's got his name on it, too. But not the stuff with Paul. Paul, that was *his* material."

With few exceptions, with the close of the 1950s, Paul Frees put his on-screen persona to bed. It was too lucrative to keep taking the straight voice work, and the hours, per job, were infinitely shorter. That gave him the time to take more jobs. And more jobs. And more, many more than we may ever truly know. His work ethic at this point in his career was larger than life, prompting Frees to post the following poem in his study:

LIFE IS NOT A DRESS REHEARSAL!!

I would rather be ASHES than dust.
I would rather my SPARK should burn out in a brilliant blaze
than it should be stifled in dry-rot.
I would rather be a superb METEOR,
every atom of me in magnificent glow,
than a sleepy & permanent planet.

Man's chief purpose is to LIVE, not to exist.
I shall not waste my days trying to prolong them.
I shall use my time.
– Jack London (1876-1916)

I'm Spartacus!
The 1960s

PAUL FREES *OWNED* THE 1960'S. It was by far his most prolific time, with twelve-hour days increasing at a swift pace as he moved from commercial session to cartoon recording to narration gig. Later, he would wonder when he found time to sleep during this intense period.

He now refused all offers of regular film roles. A decade later he recounted to a fan the disillusionment he felt with on-camera work. "It's all right, but it's too long and involved. You sit on a set all day, waiting for cameras to be set up, and lights to be set up, whereas off-camera, I go into a studio, and I record, and ten minutes later, I'm out! Twenty minutes later, I'm gone, and doing what *I* want to do." When asked at the time if he minded having a hidden face, Paul replied, "Sometimes it creates an ego problem, but nothing so serious I can't overcome it when I look at the bank balance."

Now that things were financially fantastic, with a driver and Rolls Royce to take him to more and more sessions, Paul decided to lash out some of his growing wealth by writing and directing his *own* film, complete with songs by Frees and Brandt. Thus was born the incomparable youth film, *The Beatniks*.

It told the story of aging teen Eddie Crane (Tony Travis) and his climb to would-be stardom as a singer crooning "What a Look," "Love Is a Thief" and other tuneful '50s-type Frees songs. But the rough crowd Eddie hangs out with doesn't mix well with the "establishment" trying to give him his big chance, and ultimately leads him off to jail and away from the arms of lovely Helen Tracy (Joy Terry Frees). If "beatniks" are thought to be Teddy Boys in leather jackets or poetry-spouting, unsociable intellectuals, the film was poorly named, but engaging as a movie of its day.

Paul is heard briefly as the announcer who introduces Eddie Crane to TV audiences for the first time. Eddie croons "Anything Your Little Heart Desires" to a "Theme from A Summer Place"-like piano rhythm.

The opening robbery in *The Beatniks*, 1960. (*Photofest*)

Paul also overdubs the driver who pulls up to Charlie's after the "beatniks" have assaulted the barkeep, as well as for the cop in the hospital, who keeps his face mostly hidden from the camera.

The film, released in 1960, failed to make any kind of box office impact. Eddie Brandt: "It was so bad his ex-wife, Joy, disowned it. We did, too, just about. There was one guy who is still going: Peter Breck. Nothing happened with anybody else in the cast. The picture was so bad when we went to see it. They sneak previewed it in a little theater, and all the streamlines got laughs. Paul hung his head real low when we snuck out of the back of the theater twenty minutes into the thing. And now it's a cult thing. It was so bad it was a cult. It's like all the worst pictures are a cult thing. But that's funny because Paul couldn't direct. Directing's a tough thing. I wouldn't know how to direct. He directed it and we wrote it, and we wrote all the songs.

"The original title of that picture was *Sideburns and Sympathy*, a takeoff on *Tea and Sympathy*, which was a big picture, but it was too crazy. It ended up *The Beatniks* because the Beatniks were very plausible at that time. And we did all rock and roll songs for it, which were terrible. When I listen to it now, it's terrible. It sounds like we wrote it like you would do

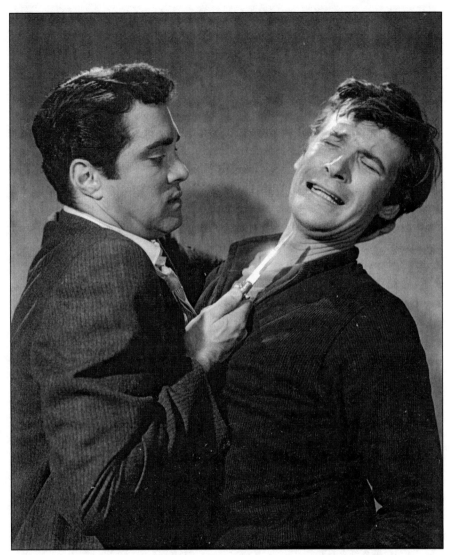

Tony Travis and Peter Breck in *The Beatniks*, 1960 (*Photofest*)

a painting by the numbers. It was exactly copying the style of music of the day. It was nothing original or anything because we didn't know. We were already too old to write rock and roll.

"Paul had a lot of trouble with the guy, Kenny Herts, who produced this under the name Hertz-Lion International. There was a lot of trouble. They went broke or something, so Paul put a couple hundred grand in the film. And they did two or three other movies, using the same sets a lot. Many small companies did that. And, of course, we didn't have the right editor, either. If we could have gotten the right editor, we probably could have turned the picture around and made it better. Editors come in sometimes and save the picture because they know how to cut it down and do this and move this scene here. But we didn't have it. But—now it's a cult."

When this author mentioned *The Beatniks* to Joy Terry Frees, she warned, "You don't want to watch it. No, no, no, no, no! I think we had a blind photographer and a deaf sound man. Paul just didn't say much. As a director, he just sat there. It was terrible! And he wrote it, too. It could've been something very fun, but it was god-awful. And the people he had around him, they took such advantage of him. You name it, they did it. Paul put too much of his own money in it, and he let everyone walk all over him. Naturally I didn't say anything to him on the set, and I *certainly* didn't say anything to him when we got home!

"He would have meetings in the house with the co-producer, Kenny Herts, and others; they'd be there for lunch. I don't know why, but they all wanted tomato soup for some strange reason…Anyhow, we had German Shepherds, they were our other 'children,' and Kenny liked to eat dog biscuits. So the whole thing was nuts. I think it was a five- or six-day shoot. It's not even good enough to be cult. It's just *bad.*

"I did another film when I was three months pregnant with Fred called *The Neanderthal Man.* Now *that* should be a cult, it wasn't bad."

The film was so "bad," the satirical sci-fi show *Mystery Science Theatre 3000* latched onto it in 1992 for a jovial scoffing session, preambled with "You have no clue what you're about to endure…" As if watching *The Rocky Horror Picture Show*, one man and several robots made fun of the eighty-minute film from their theater seats, yelling out quips like "Oh, no, they're gonna do Kabuki theatre!" as the gang put on masks for the opening robbery. During a break in the film, the viewers, released from the screening room, let out a collective sigh and rant, "Who are we tryin' to kid? These kids are no more beatniks…! They're not even Boatniks! Beatnik guys *don't* wear sensible Sears windbreakers! *Carousel* had more beatniks than this movie!" They then give a hilarious list of how to identify yourself as *not* a beatnik.

But even with the horrendous experience of *The Beatniks* behind him, Frees continued to seek out film and TV scripts, and to write his own. He'd been cured of wanting to produce or direct, but as a writer the 1960s were just as wildly creative for him as the previous decade had been. Encouraged by the sale and broadcast of *Rescue 8*, he continued to pitch

Scenes from *The Beatniks*

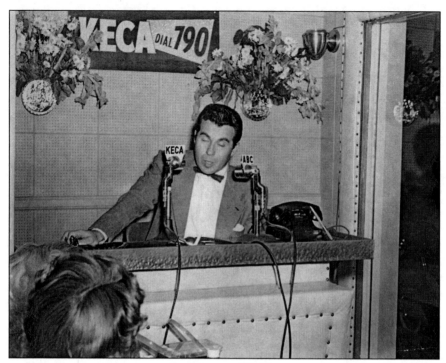

Paul Frees on KECA.

his ideas to television brass. At the same time that he was serving as a disc jockey on ABC radio's KECA Dial 790 between 11 p.m. and 2 a.m., he was also writing extensively with Danny Arnold, who later created the hit series, *Barney Miller*.

Freddy, "a warm human comedy series," was originally titled *Our Little Egghead*. It concerned an innocent, brilliant boy, Freddy, who was always getting into difficulties with the "aid" of his Baron Munchausen-type grandfather, who claimed to know everything and to have accomplished everything. The pilot script Frees wrote was a charming, though slightly scientific, sitcom, which again failed to sell, even though he had already lined up Ed Wynn to play Grandpop Charlie.

What he did not have time to write himself he handed off to others. William N. Robson, Paul's old director/producer/writer friend from the *Escape* days, had been contracted to write pilot TV scripts for his company, Hark, Inc. For writing *Cabrini, Partners in Crime, Tour de Force*, and *The Private World of Keyhole Kelly* Robson was to receive no interest in the scripts or shows, but $500 for each delivered script, plus $2000 on the first day of shooting, and 15% of whatever percentage Hark, Inc. took in.

On November 14, 1960 Leonard Burns signed over all rights to the properties *Never Say Love* and *For the Birds*, having been paid to write them already, and was to receive screen credit.

Either written by or for Frees, *Border Incident* was a film treatment completed in January of 1961. It followed the exploits of poor seaman Davy Douglas, who is robbed and beaten up in Tiajuana, but finally finds the strength to turn his life around when he's helped by an innocent young call girl named Josefina.

Frankie Vendetta, "written by Paul Frees Enterprises," had private investigator Frankie Vendetta killing off all the mobsters in town who had taken part in killing his sister, Lucia. Each episode would strike another no good crumb off the list, while Frankie ditches the pleas of Father Brophy and evades the clutches of his unknowing friend, Lt. Sal di Donato. "The keynote of this series is Realism. The stories take place *today*."

Paul's philosophy for writing was the same as his formula for life. "You cannot start at a climax. If you do a story, you start out in establishing it. And this is a good lesson for all you young listeners: don't expect it to happen all at once. And don't be afraid of the mishaps. Live through those and experience them and be strengthened by them and don't let anybody put you down. If you want to do something, if it's show business, if it's any other pursuit, if you have the feeling that you want to do it, and that becomes such a big, burning, obsessive thing, then nothing can stand in your way. There is no failure. There are only mistakes."

"He was incredibly creative," remarked Joy Terry Frees. "When he wasn't writing, he was painting; when he wasn't painting, he was making furniture. When all that stopped, he changed. He was around 40. Part of the reason I think was because a lot of the work that was coming in was just too easy, and he needed a challenge. Around 35 he grew that mustache. For the first eight years of our marriage he was a lot of fun around the house. Extraordinarily handy, he could fix anything."

Fred Frees: "My mother knew him in the 'early' days, I didn't. To me, he was always Dad. His demeanor and attitudes toward me and towards life seemed rather consistent. Anybody can grow a mustache, or a beard, or gain weight, or lose it, or whatever. You are still the same person. And so was he. I remember joking with him about having a mustache when he was thin, and then having a mustache when he was heavy and not having his mustache when he was thin (and heavy).

"I think he was more carefree in those days. I believe success was more of a burden than anyone realized. His health was worse as he got older as well. That can take the steam out of anyone, but he was still 'good ole Dad' to me. In fact, I used to tell him that GOD really stood for 'Good Ole Dad.'

"My father was not outwardly religious, although he was born into a Jewish family (his birth name was Solomon, with a brother named David, and his father was Abraham.)

"Around the time of my birth, my mother and father were members of the Church of Religious Science, which is neither a church and has little to do with science. The founders, Ernest Holmes and William Hornaday, were my Godparents, and I have two middle names, one for each of them. Other than that, though, my father hardly set foot into a temple, and showed absolutely no interest in things religious."

In George Pal's most famous feature film, *The Time Machine*, Paul spoke the all-important role of "The Talking Rings" which gave time traveler Rod Taylor the low down on Earth's history in his travels from the late 1800s to the far, *far* distant future. Frees spoke with a slightly lower Inspector Fenwick inflection, a semi-superior English accent, as he explained the hopelessness of earlier history: "The war between the East and West which is now in its 326th year has at last come to an end. There is nothing left to fight with and few of us left to fight." The incredible stop-motion special effects won Gene Warren and Tim Barr the Oscar.

Frees had also won a few awards around this time. Nine in fact, at the 1960 Commercial Film Festival. He would assemble many more for commercial work through the years.

"For fifty weeks of the year, Ft. Lauderdale, Florida is a small corner of tropical heaven," said narrator Frees at the beginning of the teen comedy *Where the Boys Are*. But when the teenagers descend upon its beaches by the thousands during their Easter vacation (Spring Break), it's like one giant Love Boat on land. Love and sex and infatuation are the themes of this vivacious beach comedy, involving three girls played by Dolores Hart, Paula Prentiss and, in her film debut, singer Connie Francis. Aside from the brief intro, Paul Frees is also heard in at least one overdub, that of the policeman telling the guys to get a car out of the street near the beach. Released on December 28, 1960, the film, based on Glendon Swarthout's book, won several comedy awards and spawned the hit title song sung by Connie.

Paul's long association with UPA's *Mister Magoo* series also began in 1960, with fecund millionaire voice Jim Backus in the lead role. Frees portrayed Tycoon Magoo and others, while the rest of cartoondom's voices came along for the syndicated ride throughout its three seasons: Daws Butler, June Foray, Mel Blanc, Richard Crenna, etc. The intensely nearsighted, lavishly wealthy, stubborn cackler soon became UPA's most valuable property, spawning many more series and TV specials. It had all begun in 1949 with a UPA short called *Ragtime Bear*, in which nephew Waldo was the star, but his blind, bombastic uncle easily stole the show with his farcical hallucinations (mistaking Waldo for a bear, for instance). The cartoon shorts ultimately won two Oscars in the 1950s, but the 130 five-minute color cartoons of 1960-62, done in quick, sometimes sloppy limited animation, were the start of Magoo's television empire.

Frees would move effortlessly from TV to films to cartoons to narrator with astonishing speed. In Stanley Kubrick's lavish slave epic *Spartacus*, he is heard more than a few times: "Get up, Spartacus, ya Thracian dog!" shouts the Roman guard at the Libyan salt mines. As a Roman soldier trying to weed out the real Spartacus from the fakes, he warns the uncooperative slaves about the terrible penalty of crucifixion.

The next year, he narrated the nudie exploitation film, *Not Tonight Henry*, a silent comedy starring funny man Hank Henry who found himself surrounded by beautiful, barely dressed women at every turn. Frees half-improvised his spiel in a German dialect.

He followed that up with radio spots for the American release of Mario Bava's *La Maschera del demonio*, known in the United States as *Black Sunday*. "The sound you hear is dripping blood..."

It's still a mystery exactly how much work he did in European cinema and for the vast number of trailers its industry consumed. Between 1961 and 1963, Frees again provided his jack-of-all-voices talent to supporting Larry Harmon in the lead role of *Tintin*, a fearless teenage reporter. First seen in Belgium's *Le Vingtieme* in 1929, the comic strip had been translated into thirty languages, as well as launching cartoons, a stage play, illustrated novels, and more. Though the cartoons were produced in France and Belgium, the voice work was recorded in Los Angeles. Unfortunately, though *Tintin*'s reputation was huge in Europe, National Telefilm Associates made few syndicated sales until 1971 when more UHF stations were hungry for color product.

Dallas McKennon, who worked with Frees on the series, recalled that not all the characters were cartoons. "We were under the same tutelage of the Jack Wormser Agency. One of Paul's most memorable traits for many of us was his making sure that every producer walking down the hallways of either NBC, CBS, or ABC would see his name on the on-call machine controlled by agents throughout the industry; and would make sure that when they were calling at a certain time, his name would be paged, so that the producer he was aiming for would be sure to see it. It greatly irritated many of us, but we could do nothing about it. It was his own designed manner of flaunting his name and abilities to the proper producers.

"I don't know how many times we all had to put up with this, but one day on the *Tintin* session which was done at Radio Recorders, I was doing the character 'Tintin' and the dog, and Paul would do assorted varieties of deeper voices than mine. But on this one occasion, we were right in the middle of the session, when the phone rings. The engineer calls out, 'Paul Frees, your agency's calling.' He would have this done purposely to bolster his presence with the recording session, where he was trying to make his point. And this time, I had had it! Even though the engineer was calling through the mike at the same time, the line was open at the other end. I called the engineer and asked who was calling. And was told it was my own agent. If he wanted to get a hold of Paul, he could have easily said it in a manner that anybody in the studio could have heard. And I felt this was an affront to my time, the engineer's, and everybody else's. He was just publicizing himself to any potential producer.

"Well, this time there was nobody in the studio but myself. I blew my stack! The great Paul Frees was being affronted by a little dog-barking kid! He then turned around and 'bellered' back at me, 'Well, who are you to stop this session?' And I said, 'Who are you to make it stop by a phony phone call?' And we went to it!

"Then as I was getting ready to leave, he called me back and said, 'Dallas…I may appear to you as somebody you don't want to work with, but I want to tell you something. You are one of the luckiest men I know. Why? Because you have a happy family and wonderful kids that appreciate what you're doing for them…I have nobody who cares about me or any part of my life.' [Paul and Joy Terry would divorce in 1962.]

"And then I turned around, shook his hand, and thanked him for his honesty. And from that day forward, all of the other sessions with him were a pure joy."

"This was unfortunately a recurring theme with my father," says Fred Frees. "When he said these things to Dallas McKennon, I was eight years old, and I loved my dad. I always cared about him. But, he didn't always acknowledge it. That was very hard for me. At that time, I was beginning what was to be a ten-year hell with my step-father living in the house my dad left behind. There was nothing I'd rather do than be with my real dad. But, I could only see him twice a month. My mother was always saying that the ten years with her were the best years of marriage my father had. But, obviously, things were going bad a long time before the ten years had passed. She said he changed over the years. And, perhaps that's true. But, to me, he was always my dad, and my feelings about him never changed.

"I don't really know why my parents divorced, since neither of them ever sought fit to tell me. But it was obvious that they blamed each other. Neither my dad or my mom shouldered any responsibility for their break-up. I do know that my mother had met my step-father before she met my dad, and his presence was always a thorn in my dad's side. My mother accused my dad of having an affair with one her best friends, and it was rumored that my mother once had an affair with Anthony Quinn of all people. But neither rumor was ever substantiated.

"The only thing they had in common was that they both kept telling me that the divorce had nothing to do with me. My dad always told me that my mother loved me, and my mother always told me that my dad loved me. And, to this day, I know that was true."

Paul was supposed to do the voice of the talking duck in 1961's *Everything's Ducky* starring Buddy Hackett and Mickey Rooney, but was replaced by Walker Edmiston, who recalls his brief times with Paul: "In *Everything's Ducky* with Mickey Rooney there was a talking duck. Paul had done the voice and for some reason they just weren't really satisfied with that. So they held auditions, and I came in and did a variation of the Hans Conried crackly voice. So it was a little awkward, my having replaced him. We weren't close, we didn't see each other socially or anything, but from time to time when he was busy, he would suggest me for parts. I don't know why he couldn't do it, since he did a great Orson Welles, but he suggested me for a film called *Start the Revolution Without Me* with Gene Wilder, so I did the narration for that. He also turned me on to a Lugosi-type commercial which he didn't have time for.

"Once, he was thinking of buying a Rolls-Royce and I had been in-volved with the Rolls-Royce Club. So he called me and I met him and we drove one. He was driving it kind of cautiously, carefully and I told him these are really hot rods, so we took it over on Sepulveda Blvd., and I opened it up at about 100. He bought the car and had a phone put in it, so they could reach him at any time, because he was always on call.

"He put on a front, but if you got behind it, he was a really nice guy.

"When I was doing some voice directing at Mattel, I brought him in because in those days there were about thirty of us who covered all the voice work. Paul was always 'one take and I've got to go. Next session in 20 minutes, gotta go.' We were working on one of those Mattel things where you pull the string, so timing was very critical. One or two ticks of a micrometer and you were over! Paul said, 'Well, that's all I can do, gotta go. So I said, 'Well, go on, you know I can match any voice you do anyway.' 'Well, listen…' he said. 'I can give you another 15 minutes or so.' I think he stayed another good 45 minutes. As soon as he thought he had some competition, things changed. But really, there was no competition. We could all do each other's voices, but not the way he did them. There's something that each of us has that's unique. You could essentially match some of the things, but there was only one Paul Frees."

Yet with all the work he amassed, he must have been cloned at *some* point. September 27, 1961 saw the release of Hanna-Barbera's answer to the hit series *Sgt. Bilko*, with their own wheeler-dealer *Top Cat*, voiced in Phil Silvers "homage" by Arnold Stang. Hanna-Barbera was reaping such primetime profits with their *Honeymooners* copy *The Flintstones* that they lifted *Bilko*'s situations perfectly for the scheming Top Cat (T.C. to his friends), whose animal cohorts boasted voices from Leo de Lyon, Marvin Kaplan, John Stephenson, Paul Frees, Daws Butler, Don Messick, Bea Benaderet, film tough guy Allen Jenkins and others. Hoagy's Alley in New York City was the place, among the junk, warehouses and garbage cans, just a little way from the docks. Officer Dibble (Jenkins) walked his beat to make sure the cats didn't break too many laws in their mere 30 primetime episodes. Like most HB efforts, the series lasted *much* longer in syndicated reruns, and is probably on TV somewhere right now.

Frees also recorded the pun-filled soundtrack to a pilot for animator Bob Clampett in 1961 called *The Edgar Bergen Show*, with June Foray and Bergen himself. The cartoon series was to have shown the Bergen family "at home," sprawling the adventures of Charlie McCarthy, Mortimer Snerd and Bergen into a colorful cartoon world that made good use of the beloved radio characters. Yet the idea never made it beyond lavish storyboards and drawings that can now be seen as an extra on the superb *Time for Beany* DVD, complete with the Frees-narrated, five-minute soundtrack.

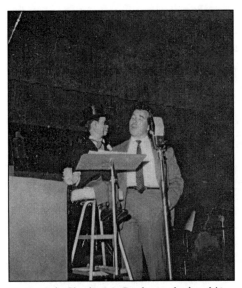

Frees with Charlie McCarthy in the late '40s.

When Walt Disney took his weekly television show from ABC to NBC, he called it *Walt Disney's Wonderful World of Color*, as it would begin broadcasting in color. For the introductory, hour-long special, a new character was created to explain the magic that was color television. Naturally, a teaching personality suited the times. Ludwig Von Drake, related to Donald Duck, was an older and wiser duck who had slightly buggy eyes, pince-nez glasses sitting on his beak, an energetic, professorial personality, a madcap, almost non-linear sense of humor, and a voice like a higher Victor Borge. Paul Frees recorded Drake's utterances in his normal pitch, which was then sped up to achieve a warm, zany, rambling effect. The first episode of the new color Disney hit was simply, "An Adventure in Color," and was pared with the ever-popular *Donald in Mathmagic Land*.

"Walt Disney gave me a lot of liberty in portraying the Professor, and I've made him more personal than any of my other characters," Paul said in the early 1960's. "The Professor is bright, good-natured, has a sense of humor, and is marvelously absent-minded at times. But, he has character. He is always driving at something and he is not beyond scolding you for lack of attention. When we have a story conference, the writers toss questions and situations at me. I ad-lib on tape and it's incorporated into the script.

"Originally, Ludwig was a supercilious character but we've given him point and shade as we've brought him along. His complete knowledge in every avenue helps bring a little culture to TV."

Fred Frees recalled, "I don't specifically remember *anything* before the age of three or four, let alone what Dad was doing. I suppose the first thing that sticks in my mind was Ludwig Von Drake. Dad recorded an album for Disney featuring the wily professor, and I remember listening to it a *lot*."

On July 24, 1961 Disneyland Records released that *tour de force*: a

Paul Frees and Ludwig Von Drake. (© *Disney Enterprises, Inc.*)

one-man album simply called *Professor Ludwig Von Drake*. It was a wonderfully madcap musical spin to push the new TV series which made Drake a household star. "I'm Professor Ludwig Von Drake" was the catchy opening song, followed by "The Spectrum Song" which showcased his wet rolling R's, especially in the word "red." The entire recording was meant to help listeners understand colors; an ambitious attack in a world of sound alone. "The Green with Envy Blues" had some great improv scat and passionate up-tempo blues singing, followed by "It Gets You," a song

Paul and the Drake. (© Disney Enterprises, Inc.)

Discussing a Ludwig Von Drake session with Ham Luske.
(© *Disney Enterprises, Inc.*)

about Mardi Gras.

On Side Two, the professor introduced all the wrong instruments which, though far away from color, was pretty funny. Frees demonstrated a mastery of timing on the LP. He illustrated different sounds/rhythms working on the same tune, "The Blue Danube." From the cha-cha-cha to rock 'n' roll. He then introduced the engineer "who thinks he's the most important thing about the recording." This bit allowed Paul to chew some scenery with vocal effects, especially running the tape backwards, all accomplished without technical tricks. Next, he introduced the echo chamber and had some amusing dialogue with the echo.

Before the last number, Ludwig had some problems with his musicians, and so made one leave the room. When he finally got the band to heed the baton he got from the local Chinese restaurant, a slow surfer's version of "Bibbidy Bobbidy Boo" began for a few bars before he called a halt to the gibberish. Once he realized that he had not been singing it upside down (a gag reminiscent, again, of Victor Borge), Ludwig continued singing the whole song, finally lapsing into a sort of baby talk. He then started interpreting it, being one of the most famous opera stars in the world (says he), in opera talk. The song, and album, finally ended on a last low tuba note. "Thought I wouldn't make it, didn't you?"

At least two songs were released as singles: "I'm Ludwig Von Drake" with a B-side of "Green with Envy Blues," and "It Gets You."

That same year Paul also voiced Ludwig for a beguiling RCA promotional release called *The Voice of Professor Ludwig Von Drake Offers Songs and Stories for Children* with the following tracks:

> Introduction
> Little Wet Riding Hood
> Jack and the Cornstalk
> Ludwig in the Circus
> Aladdin and the Eenie Weenie Genie
> Sleeping Beauty

It was a very funny 44-minute cartridge, bigger than modern-day cassettes, that could only be played in the special RCA player. It came with a two-foot tall Gund stuffed doll of Ludwig with a speaker embedded in his ear. The tracks ran continuously, though the production wasn't nearly as lavish as the Disney record. "Testing? One, two, three, testing," began the duck. "This is the part of the tape where we waste a little time so you can make sure that the sound is on, and that it is on just right." Except for a few seconds with a runaway piano sound, the introduction is done with few effects and no musical accompaniment. Over the slightly warped "Blue Danube Waltz" the Professor tells the story of "Little Wet Riding Hood" who lived in a rain forest "where it was always raining cats wit' dogs." Walking through the forest of puddles she almost drowns, calls out and is saved by the badge-toting, monocle-wearing

Stan Freberg and Paul Frees.

junior lifeguard. But it is a fake badge—a wolf in disguise. The story continues pretty much as normal, except for reviving grandma with pickle juice after the wolf's terrible drag act. Before the next story, he briefly tells of his hunting expedition which winds up taking place in the local zoo, at which he could not move due to some "joker" putting chewing gum on his chair.

In "Jack and the Cornstalk" young Jack trades the family cow in for a bushel of corn, choosing it over a bag of beans or a watermelon. He and his mother eat some and Jack puts the rest of the corn in the backyard. The next morning a giant cornstalk has grown clear up to the sky. Jack climbs it and, in the castle, comes upon an echoing voice which recites, "Jack be nimble, Jack be quick, Jack leave my castle before I take you apart and see what makes you tick." Jack grabs the golden hen and, to escape, swings through the air like the daring young man on the flying trapeze. Thus begins his career in the circus, and Ludwig's own tale of himself in his circus years, leading quickly to a recitation of "Little Jack Horner" who put in his thumb and pulled out 24 blackbirds. After jumbling other nursery rhymes together, Von Drake gives the recorded & warped music a solo spot before beginning Side Two with a whistling lesson, then performs a few magic tricks before starting the 15-minute "Aladdin and the Eenie Weenie Genie" story, followed by a bit more rambling about his many inventions. The traditional story of "Sleeping Beauty" ends the tape. "Alas, alack and Alaska, one day she disobeyed her parents and she strayed fah, fah out into de woods!" The princess had journeyed to escape an evil fairy, and came upon good ones who raised her as their own.

The Austrian-accented duck never achieved stardom on the scale of Mickey, Donald or Goofy, but the early to mid-1960s were filled with Von Drake cartoon credits for Frees, such as "Fly with Von Drake" (1963), "Inside Outer Space" (1963), "A Square Peg in a Round Hole" (1963), "Three Tall Tales" (1963), "The Truth About Mother Goose" (1963), "In Shape with Von Drake" (1964), and many more. The genius duck also lectures in the Oscar-nominated theatrical cartoon, *A Symposium on Popular Songs*, directed by Bill Justice and released in 1962.

"There was one time that my father actually had considered it possible for me to follow in his footsteps," says Fred Frees. "I remember going with him to Disney when he had a session doing Ludwig von Drake. After the session was over, he and the director asked me to imitate Ludwig. So, Dad said a line, and I repeated it just like Ludwig. They were thinking of creating the character of Ludwig von Drake, Junior. Unfortunately, they never did. But it did give me a chance to show that I could imitate my dad.

"My dad indirectly acknowledged my voice abilities when I would call him and pretend to be someone else. Of course, whenever we did speak on the phone, he expected that it would always be me who initiated the call. He rarely ever called me, and if he did, it was always a surprise. But, occasionally, I would call him and he'd answer his usual 'Yes.' And I'd do an older voice and say something like, 'Paul? Is that you?' And he'd respond, 'Who is this?' And I'd say, 'It's your son.' And he'd say, 'Fred? Frederic William?' It was always funny to fool him. And I did fool him every time I did it."

1961 was also the year Paul contributed to possibly the most popular and talked about album of his career. *Stan Freberg Presents The United States of America Vol. 1* was an amazing musical satire of America's history, from Columbus discovering America through the Battle of Yorktown. It contained enough top voice talent to keep a radio series satisfied: Freberg, June Foray, Peter Leeds, Walter Tetley, Jesse White, and of course Paul Frees as the rather self-important, slightly wobbly narrator. The hilarious, often over-the-top, 56-minute musical showed off Billy Mays' exquisite musical direction and Freberg's lifelong love-hate relationship with advertising.

Paul Frees: "I was the one who put in 'modestly.' When I narrate at the beginning, I say, 'Stan Freberg *modestly* presents The United States of America!' And Stan says, 'We can't say modestly in there. We're not going to do that.' And I said, 'Stan, we're *going* to do it.' And he said, 'No, I don't think it should be in there.' I said, 'Stan. I'm the narrator. I'm going to do it so there's no way you can cut it out. I'm not going to give you the scissors space to cut it out.' And he had to use it, and it was one of the big successes of the opening. Everybody loved it. It was a cute idea."

After the commercial success of *USA Vol. 1*, Broadway producer David Merrick wanted to stage a lavish Broadway production with more material and songs. The often-difficult Merrick held up the other proposed *USA* albums because he wanted to release a cast album along with the show. But time went by. Merrick offered to put the show up in Washington D.C., but eventually the idea was a wash out, infuriating Freberg to no end. Not only did Paul Frees not care, he never would have agreed to leave his precious California for such extended work, even if a Broadway producer *could* match the thousands of dollars a week he would lose from stepping away from the vast cartoon and commercial voice work that kept coming in. Frees estimated that he was doing about thirty-five different jobs a week at that point; and Merrick wanted him narrating on stage, microphone in hand.

For the long-awaited sequel record, *Vol. 2*, released in 1996, Corey Burton ably imitated Frees' pompous narrative style. Burton, a master impressionist and voice man, has been keeping Ludwig Von Drake, Captain Hook, and many other characters alive since the passing of the great voice men. "I never actually worked with Paul, however I did meet and talk with him. The Haunted Mansion was mind-blowing to me. It was like everything I loved in the whole world was right there. The illusions, the silly chills of it, and the perfect narration."

By 1961, Frees and Freberg had already worked together in various radio shows and cartoons. Years later, he also did at least one brief bit on a Stan Freberg radio commercial - for the National Association of Broadcasters, satirically heralding the epic abilities of the radio medium (by audibly draining Lake Michigan, casting 25,000 extras for one shout at the end, and other gags that were far too expensive for other mediums).

The weekly half-hour *Calvin and the Colonel* animated TV series was

Frees as Meowrice in *Gay Purr-ee,*
© 1962 Warner Brothers.

first broadcast in 1961 on ABC opposite *Dobie Gillis* and *Alfred Hitchcock Presents*, later dying as it went against *Bonanza* and *Perry Mason*. It was the creation of Freeman Gosden and Charles Correll who wanted to keep working even after their famed *Amos 'n' Andy* series had been knocked off television due to the racial controversy of white men performing as black. *Calvin and the Colonel* was not much different from *Amos 'n' Andy,* except that those characters, voiced more as southern than African-American, were now played as animals. The Kingfish character of radio years was now seen as con artist Montgomery J. Klaxton, while Andrew H. Brown had turned into a cigar-smoking bear by the name of Calvin J. Burnside. Paul Frees was heard as Oliver Wendell Clutch, vocally reminiscent of John Brown's deadpan Digger O'Dell character on radio's *The Life of Riley.*

Paul appeared on another classic adaptation that year. *Dick Tracy,* a popular cartoon strip for years, bowed its syndicated head via UPA (United Productions of America). Created 30 years earlier by Chester Gould, the plainclothes policeman with the strong jaw had starred in popular B-movies and on radio where he fought deformed and oddly-named villains. The cartoon series was no different, with Paul Frees, Benny Rubin, June Foray and a few others lending their voices to the enormously popular 130 five-minute cartoons.

Then in 1962, The Beary Family cartoon series began. An homage to TV's *Life of Riley* starring William Bendix, it was created by Walter Lantz, and lasted ten years. Charlie Beary did not believe in employing professionals to fix or install anything. He'd much rather die trying or blow up the house than accept help. Paul J. Smith directed most of the Technicolor series. Grace Stafford (wife of Lantz and voice of Woody Woodpecker) voiced Bessie Beary and Suzy, while Paul doubled up as the voice of Junior.

He had previously worked for Walter Lantz in a few *Woody Wood-*

The cats from *Gay Purr-ee*: Paul Frees and Red Buttons.

pecker cartoons, and introduced the character of Doc in the 1959 cartoon *Mouse Trapped*, involving the immaculate cat Doc (always dressed in bow tie, top hat and cane) who goes up against the two troublesome mice, Hickory and Dickory (both voiced by Dal McKennon).

In 1962 Frees found himself again connected with a Frank Sinatra picture, *The Manchurian Candidate*. This time he narrated a portion of the Oscar-nominated post-Korean war movie about a brainwashed soldier sent by communists, under cover of being a Congressional Medal of Honor holder, to assassinate a Presidential candidate. "This nation jealously guards its highest award for valor, the Congressional Medal of Honor," Paul intoned, reading the exposition of the soldier's history with the same confidential tone (matter-of-factly, but with importance) that he reserved for other film narrations and honorable Disneyland projects like *The Hall of Presidents*. In order to get the film moving and cover a large backlog of information, Paul had quite a few lines in the first 15 minutes of the film.

It was a year for working with the big boys. Paul stole the show with his villainous Meowrice character in *Gay Purr-ee*, a cartoon feature film. He had the most lines in the movie, though it was essentially a vehicle for Judy Garland to sing some luscious Harold Arlen (composer of *The Wizard of Oz*, among others) songs. There were no hit songs, but the film did boast a remarkable cast of voice talent. Aside from Judy as Mewsette, Robert Goulet provided the singing and speaking voice of boyfriend Juane-Tom, and Red Buttons voiced his best friend Robespierre.

Directed and designed by legendary animator Chuck Jones, the simple plot involved a country cat (Mewsette) who dreams about seeing the wonders of Paris. When a relative of her owner goes back to Paris, she jumps in her carriage and finds herself singing in the city of lights. On the train, she meets that cad of a cat Meowrice, done by Frees as a deep, French George Sanders. His oily ways convince Mewsette to let her be handled by Meowrice's sister (though she isn't his sister), Mme. Rubens-Chatte, voiced by *Gigi* star Hermione Gingold, to acquaint her with the ways of Parisian society. However, Meowrice is really making a lady cat out of her in order to sell her to a rich American cat, a Mr. Henry Phtt. The heartbroken Jean-Tom and friend Robespierre follow Mewsette to Paris, but it is futile. Meowrice, having seen an example of Jean-Tom's amazing ability to hunt out mice literally like lightning, shanghaies the boyfriend onto a ship (that needs just such a cat) on its way to the Alaskan gold rush. There, Jean-Tom makes his fortune and rushes back to pluck Mewsette away from the bad cat, and all is musically well at the end.

The film was a co-production between UPA and Warner Brothers, and enlisted some very able voice talent in small roles, such as Mel Blanc as the bulldog in the alley who takes on the bad cats and puts Meowrice's tail in a splint. Paul Frees was given two songs to sing. "Money Cat" was a comic ditty that had Meowrice's alley cat helpers, who were always shown in shadows, in harmonies done by the Haunted Mansion singers, The Mellomen. His second song was with Mewsette in a buggy ride around

Paris, explaining to her why all the couples kiss in carriages: because the horses won't talk.

The film could have used more gags, but it did give Paul every opportunity to show off, especially in one overdone scene which he narrates, while writing another letter to Mr. Phtt that Mewsette is being painted by all the known and unknown artists in Paris, everyone from Monet to Russo to Van Gogh and others. It was an odd piece of business that didn't go anywhere, but it was a rich narration, and Paul's single longest scene in the film.

Reviews were mixed. *The New York Times* called it "a nice, soft drink for the whole family" though the first half of the film was

Sabrina Frees.

"studied and even familiar." *Variety* wrote: "The artwork in *Gay Purr-ee* ranks with the finest ever manufactured in the specialized realm of the animated cartoon" and thought its weak storyline was saved by slick production values. They were enamored of the songs, especially "Paris is a Lonely Town" saying it "has the earmarks of a hit. Miss Garland's singing is characterized by her patented verve, oomph and feeling, and Goulet sings clearly and robustly."

After Paul and Joy Terry had divorced in 1962, he married a Las Vegas showgirl named Patrice, whom he took with him to Chicago for the opening of *Gay Pur-ee*, and to show her his old neighborhood. After the Friday premiere at the B&K State-Lake Theatre, the couple picked up Paul's sister Rose Ginsberg, visited with his niece Janice Fishbein and took a short tour of his old Von Steuben High School, which had been a junior high school in his day. The escapade was written up in the local paper, which pushed the two things most of the media would forever highlight in Frees' life: his anonymity, and his bank account.

"I learned early to submerge my ego for the financial success and the

Sabrina Frees.

privacy I hold dear," he told *Lerner Newspapers*. He turned that Hollywood money and privacy into time to write, paint and relax. At the time, he was reportedly in the midst of writing a novel, two screenplays and a dozen TV scripts. He had already composed music for Donald O'Connor, Sammy Davis, Teresa Brewer and others, and had stopped gambling in Las Vegas, putting his vast cash into the stock market where he would lose more in a month than in a year of gambling.

Frees was feeling good, having just celebrated his 3000th commercial account. He took a mile-long walk around the Chicago lakefront at 5 a.m., commenting that it was one of the most beautiful sights he'd seen since he was a child. But back in the limo, Paul toured the North Side, then the corner of Lawrence and Kedzie where he exclaimed, "Where's the S&L cigar store?" He showed Patrice where he had played in the street and one of the buildings where he had lived at 4940 N. Kedzie.

Paul's marriage to Patrice lasted a mere two and a half years. Their daughter Sabrina was born on June 10, 1963.

"My mom was born in Selma, California on January 25, 1936 and was the oldest of seven brothers. She came from dirt-fed Oakies, but she was gorgeous. She was a showgirl in Vegas by the name of Terry Stone, and my dad swept her off her feet. He said, 'Let me take you away from all this.' And she was like, 'Uh...okay!'

"She was about 26, 27 when they met. Dad tended to gravitate toward small blondes. My mom was 5' 9". They were living in the house on Doheny, in the hills, in West Hollywood when I was born. He was making a fortune at this time. They had twin T-Birds, twin Rolls-Royces, the whole number. But Mom was a nightmare. Drugs and alcohol. She could not stay sober to save her life. From people I talked to who knew her, she started drinking when she was thirteen. My grandmother was the same way. Runs in the family.

"When I was real little I'd see Dad every other weekend, flying from northern California to southern California. My mom moved me to Hawaii when I was about six. Illegally. She took me away from my dad. I didn't see or hear from him until I was fourteen.

"I know he felt sorry for her. She was always calling and asking for money. Every time she got into scrapes she'd call crying and asking for money, and he would bail her out. They tried to get back together a couple times. I think he married her twice, the second time in Mexico City. They got back together when I was about five, and lived in the house over in

Paul Frees and Patrice Frees. (*Keith Scott*)

Discussing a Krazy Kat cartoon.

Tiburon.

"We had first gone to Hawaii on a vacation, then she met some guy, got offered a job, and decided to stay. She was a waitress. She was painfully shy. Long legs and incredible body, and she used it. But she was really, really shy, probably one of the reasons she drank so much.

"All the time I was in Hawaii she told me that my dad didn't want to have anything to do with me. That he couldn't be bothered. Which was typical of my mom—'poor, poor, pitiful drunk, me.' When I was about fourteen Dad out of the blue got hold of my mother to tell her that her mother had died. They'd found Dad and told him. After my parents talked, I talked with him a couple more times, building up a relationship with him over the phone. I told him how miserable I was—I was stuck in a class of 3000 kids in junior high and there were 30 white kids—I was hating life. And mom was drunk all the time, and she was real nasty. I just wanted the hell out of there. So he came up with an idea to get me out to California. Not necessarily with him. Which was fine. This guy doesn't know me, he's got his own life, and the last thing he needs is a teenager. So we decided to send me to boarding school, in Ottowa, California. So Mom and I came back to California. Then

Toasting at the Bullwinkle statue unveiling party on Sunset Boulevard and Havenhurst Ave., September 1961. (*Keith Scott*)

I started visiting him around 1978. The first couple of years, when I was a teenager, I would visit with him for a week every couple months.

"I spent more time with his last wife Beverly than I ever did with my dad. Just coming from Hawaii, I didn't speak proper English, which I could see grating on him. I could see him cringing whenever I talked. We all spoke pidgin English, it was terrible.

"I didn't see him as a voice. That's what he did for a living. He didn't do voices to entertain me or anything. When it came to work, he was a well-oiled machine. He had a photographic memory. He'd read a script once, maybe twice, and bam, he did it. Nobody did it better.

"Whenever he would talk about his first wife, he would get tears in his eyes. There was love there, absolutely.

"We used to talk about being short. He used to say, if the king of the jungle was meant to be tall, it would've been the giraffe. He was always making references to being the king of his castle. He was the ruler. On a piece of paper which was taped to his desk was, 'Life is not a dress rehearsal.' And I got that piece of paper after he died.

"I remember being two or three years old, sitting on his lap, steering the Rolls down the hill. Money gives you power, and he wielded it! He had a Napoleon complex. As much as he could build somebody up, he could make them feel two inches tall. But he would talk to anyone. I would see him carry on conversations with gas station attendants. If he decided to be engaging, he would do so. And he would make everyone feel great. He loved to talk, but his number one love was food. He loved to eat. I inherited that from him too. Fortunately, it hasn't gone to my stomach."

Fred Frees also vividly remembered the Rolls. "Ah yes, the Rolls. For a while, the rare times I stayed with him into the following Monday, I would be driven to junior high school in it. It was fun at the time. I'd have the driver open the door for me, right in front of the other kids. They never knew I didn't really live that lifestyle, but it was fun pretending I did."

Sabrina: "I was a good kid. I didn't need to be disciplined. But the rewards! He gave me my first car, when I was fifteen-and-a-half. $1900 for a '69 Mustang, which eventually got stolen. Beverly was the instigator of clothes buying. That woman knew how to spend money! I still have one of those $300 sweaters, so I guess they're made well…It got to the point where I wonder if he even knew the value of a dollar anymore. Extravagant! Ridiculous! One time we had six ten-pound lobsters for three people, flown in from Maine! And then we had to warm them up in the oven—they were stuffed with creamed spinach. It was absolutely wonderful. We stood there in the kitchen and picked them apart with our fingers, we couldn't even get them to the table."

The World's Greatest Sinner, written, starring and directed by Timothy Carey, has a cult following if only for the fact that its score was composed by Frank Zappa. The political comedy, released in 1962, dealt with bored insurance salesman Clarence Hilliard who forms his own political party, "The Eternal Man," as he believes that man will live forever. Paul Frees (pretty close to his real and Ghost Host voices) voiced the snake (i.e. Satan): "Oh, yes. This is the place where a simple, average American family lives. There's Clarence, my boy. Just like any other male - the only difference is, he wants to be God. *(Horse neighs)* And that's coming right out of the horse's mouth."

When Jim Backus came back to voice the nearly-blind Mr. Magoo character for *Mr. Magoo's Christmas Carol* in 1962, Frees came along to plug in just about any vocal hole left. This delightful musical version of Charles Dickens' often-produced morality piece aired on December 18. Magoo arrives on Broadway to star in a show, singing all the way to the theatre where he's met by the frantic director (Frees). Though late, Magoo makes

Jay Ward, Paul Frees and unknown man, late 1960s. (*Keith Scott*)

no other mistakes until the final curtain and plays Ebenezer Scrooge with the relish that only a rich cartoon man could bring to the character. Frees appears again as the voice of one of the men seeking a charitable contribution from Scrooge, and later, during the trip via the Ghost of Christmas Past, as Scrooge's old jovial boss, Fezziwig. Then, seeing what life will be like after his death, Paul is heard as the tall man with the top hat trying to sell Scrooge's possessions. Here Frees excels briefly during the thieves' song, giving a partial Boris Karloff impression. The Broadway-type score was beautifully written by Jule Stein and Bob Merrill, of *Funny Girl* fame.

Frees would later be heard, along with every other top voice name

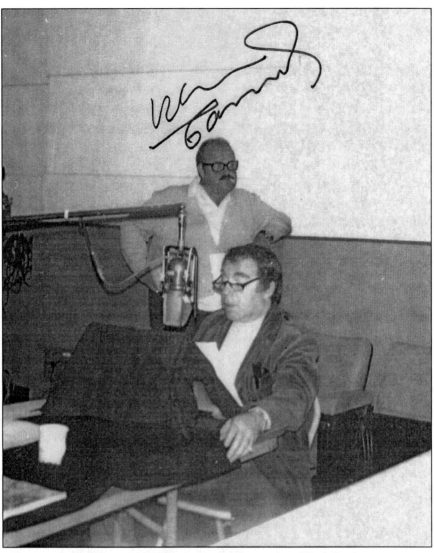

Paul Frees and William Conrad, late 1960s. (*Keith Scott*)

in the business, on another *Mister Magoo* TV series from 1964-65. He did "other voices" for *Mr. Magoo's Treasure Island* (also known as *The Famous Adventures of Mr. Magoo*), narrated by young Jim Hawkins (Dennis King). It followed the story of the classic book fairly well, except for the unbelievable casting of Magoo as Long John Silver.

More film work followed. He did the opening narration for the US version of *Burn, Witch, Burn* (sometimes known as *Night of the Eagle*) in 1962, and was heard as several voices in John Huston's *The List of Adrian*

Blood and Black Lace, 1964, Allied Artists.

Messenger, starring Kirk Douglas. He was the voice of a German knight in *The Magic Sword,* and dubbed for a few people in another John Huston film, *Freud,* starring Montgomery Clift as the famous doctor. He also took up his Peter Lorre disguise again for a promotional record for radio done for Vincent Price's movie, *The Raven.* Boris Karloff, also in the film, appeared on the record with Price and Frees.

In 1963 Paul was part of the syndicated *King Features Trilogy,* which featured the cartoons *Beetle Bailey, Snuffy Smith* and *Krazy Kat.* Since *Popeye* was proving so popular on television, other comic strips were animated for the insatiable TV programmer's diet. Created by Barney DeBeck, the hillbilly comedy of Snuffy Smith placed Frees in the vocal lead of Snuffy and Barney Google, the latter once the star of the comic strip. The cartoons were ground out at Hanna-Barbera speed, relying on several different animation studios to produce it all.

Back at Jay Ward Productions, Paul, Bill Scott and squirrel-girl June Foray lent their voices to the syndicated (1963-64) television series, *Fractured Flickers,* hosted by that other flamboyant voice, Hans Conried. Conried appeared on camera, however, introducing old silent films with new humorously-altered soundtracks. Chris Hayward dreamed up the idea which debuted in October of 1963 and ran for a scant total of 26 half-hour episodes. The imaginative shows were classic Jay Ward. Rudolph Valentino's character in *Blood and Sand* was changed from a matador into an insurance salesman. John Barrymore in *Dr. Jekyll and Mr. Hyde* became a chemist eager to create the ultimate chocolate seltzer drink. The series was a gas, though reviews ran hot and cold. *The New York Times* called it "a new program that dubs silent films with disrespectful dialogue." However, it was certainly one of the greatest Jay Ward outlets for Paul's unabashedly silly voices.

The next year Paul narrated Jay Ward's *The Adventures of Hoppity Hooper* in a slower storyteller-type voice. The show ran from 1964 to 1967 on ABC. Hans Conried returned as the conniving fox Professor Waldo Wigglesworth who traveled the country in his patent-medicine van with Fillmore the Bear (Bill Scott) and the frog hero with the little kid voice, Hoppity Hooper (Chris Allen).

It was also around this time that Paul Frees took over the narration of the Cap'n Crunch commercials from Bill Conrad. Those lasted until 1980, after which Paul would phone his lines in from his home studio.

Commercials were taking up more and more of his time, often paying more per second than narration and cartoon jobs, as he could do many in one sitting and received royalties every time the little gold mines played. "The only voice I have been unable to imitate is my own," Frees told the press in 1963. "I did a commercial once when I had a sore throat. They liked the sound I made and wanted me to add a few more lines a couple of days later. But my throat had healed and I couldn't recapture the first sounds I made."

When Pillsbury was touting its Funny Face Drink Mix in 1964, Frees was called in to give the fruity flavored characters voices on a promotional record, singing as Goofy Grape, Freckle Face Strawberry, Loud Mouth Lime, Rootin' Tootin' Raspberry, Chinese Cherry, and Injun Orange (the latter two later renamed to Choo-Choo Cherry and Jolly Olly Orange, for obvious reasons). Kids could buy matching plastic mugs (featuring the faces of the flavors/characters) that are highly collectible now. Unfortunately, the popular drink was soon taken off the market due to a controversy concerning its ingredient "cyclamate," later proven to be safe.

Frees obviously was not forsaking *any* direction of work for the sake of sponsors. By 1964 he and Tony Romano had signed up with ASCAP and had written at least six songs together: "I Ain't Gonna Take It With Me," "The Gallows Dance," "The Dream of Man," "All But One," "Wetback," and "The Old Man With a Drum."

Next, he lent his carefree narrative style to *The Carpetbaggers*, directed by Edward Dmytryk, starring George Peppard as the ambitious, dynasty-building tycoon. "Every nation has its modern carpetbaggers," he began in a quick, insouciant but streetwise style, "its adventurers who gamble everything to stand head and shoulders above other men." He narrated almost throughout the film, which was based on Harold Robbins' best-selling novel.

That same year, Jerry Lewis scored one of his silliest, biggest hits with *The Disorderly Orderly*. Paul's opening narration came somewhere between comic and dead serious. "Throughout history there have been men who have dreamed of being brave and heroic." Over this Jerry mugged several differing heroics: being a scared soldier in the Napoleonic era, having scaled one of the highest mountains in the world, and as a medical student. As the posed "heroes" of the piece stood together, Paul called, "Will the real hero of this movie please fall down." Down went Dr. Lewis. "We have a winner!" Frees was not heard again in the film.

Also in 1964 he lent his various voices to a rather dull cinematic vision of the Air Rescue Service. *Flight from Ashiya* starred Richard Widmark, George Chakiris, and Yul Brynner and dealt mostly with rescuing people from the sea, with flashbacks of each of the three rescuers during crucial moments in their lives. Paul narrates the opening and closing like an Army recruitment voice, but with a soft, tight delivery that gives the necessary honor to an otherwise bland picture. He also crops up frequently in the film, as producers knew that as long as Frees was in the studio, they might as well give him as much work as they needed done; Frees was paid $500 an hour anyway.

He also dubbed nearly every male voice on the American soundtrack to Mario Bava's *Blood and Black Lace*. Even for stars Cameron Mitchell, and Thomas Reiner, himself a famous looper and cartoon voice in Germany. Thought by many to be Italian director Bava's masterpiece, the dark, intense thriller was high on suspense, beautiful women and still compares favorably to shocker series like *Scream* and *Friday the 13th*.

Joy Terry Frees recalled the film: "Paul and I dubbed a movie together where we did all the characters, about 400 loops in one day. Made in Italy. He played all the men, I played all the women, and it was about models. And this one woman was killing all the models, so I was killing myself."

It was indeed a busy year for his theatrically released films. *The*

Paul with Cliff Gill and Vincent Price's second wife, Mary Grant Price.

Socializing in the '60s.

Incredible Mr. Limpet, which premiered on January 18, 1964, involved nerd Don Knotts a) loving fish more than people, and b) passionately wanting to do something for his country, during World War II. Alas, the armed forces just didn't want poor Mr. Limpet. The first 'thing' Mr. Limpet meets upon wishing himself into becoming a fish (with glasses) is Crusty, the hermit crab, voiced like an old timer by Frees. They part for a while near the beginning of his undersea adventures. Once Limpet gets commissioned as a Sergeant by the Navy as their "secret weapon," his main task is to see the US convoy of ships safely through the nasty Nazi U-boat-infested waters. Limpet loses his glasses and Crusty returns, wearing special armor that he's found in that vast junkyard that is the sea, and functions as the fish's extra eyes. Together, they use the Axis subs' own torpedoes against them.

The film, based on Theodore Pratt's novel, was not a hit when it was first released in 1964, but the re-release sparked interest that has continued to this day. Paul received last billing in the credits and had a fair amount of Gabby Hayes-style delivery.

This was also around the time that Paul began his 20+ year stint as the voice of the Pillsbury Doughboy, a high-pitched, squeaky little white fella with a baker's hat who loved to giggle when poked in the tummy. The Leo Burnett Advertising Agency in Chicago and BBD&O in New York were so enamored of the adorable vocal character, they literally gave Paul a run of the play contract. In 1980, the Doughboy was valued at $25 million by Pillsbury, and an item in a 1991 *Woman's Day* article revealed that "the Pillsbury Doughboy, whose voice was originally provided by the late Paul Frees, receives as many fan letters per week as Vice President Dan Quayle (200)." The character is still in use today (voiced by JoBe Cerny), with fans and merchandising around the globe. Paul probably would have giggled himself to learn that the master impersonator is even now being impersonated.

In 1964, he put voice to the introduction of *The Night Walker*. Over a spooky montage, Paul asks, "What are dreams? What do they mean?" He gives an eerie, almost masochistic breathy narration that isn't quite as low as the Haunted Mansion's Ghost Host, yet just as horrific. It is reminiscent of his lead-ins to *Escape*, with its myriad of questions chosen to invoke nightmares. He speaks of the death and blood of dreams… and ends on the title of the film, just before a woman screams. Directed by William Castle and written by *Psycho* author Robert Bloch, this gothic horror film starred Barbara Stanwyck as a wealthy woman being gaslighted by an evil attorney, played by Robert Taylor. The film was released on January 20th.

And then came *The War Lord*. The epic feudal film had a $3.5 million budget and was released in November of 1965. A tale of knights and magic and the downfall of a warlord, it teamed the *Planet of the Apes* crew up 3 years before that epic simian saga: director Franklin J. Schaffner, and actors Maurice Evans and Charlton Heston. While it would never achieve the same fame as *Apes*, it was an engaging action/love story with plenty of mud and sword clanging. Some of it was filmed in Malibu and Marysville, California.

Before the credits, over a picturesque scene of swampland, Paul narrates, "In the 11th century Europe was a patchwork of feudal states, extending from the Mediterranean to the North Sea." The straight-ahead narrative style was not as low as some of his other works, much like an informative Disney short. But he is also heard in *Pirates of the Caribbean* voice exclaiming "Peasant pigs!" and a diabolical laugh during the film's first battle, as well as "Move along!" and other overdubs. Paul overdubs for the dwarf who shows up throughout the picture, though the character is killed a half-hour before the film ends.

In August of that year Frees sang on yet another album, *Tinpanorama*, on Disney's Buena Vista label. It showcased the hot trots of Tin Pan Alley through the years, featuring songs written by the Sherman Brothers, most famous for their *Mary Poppins* score. Two of the twelve songs were sung by Frees: "Rutabaga Rag," sung in Al Jolson character to the accompaniment of Dixieland jazz, and "Although I Dropped $100,000 in the Market, Baby, I Found A Million Dollars in Your Smile," belted in a similar, happy Harry Richman impression.

Keeping busy with a fair amount of dubbing of Japanese science fiction films for Titra Sound Corporation, it was reported Paul also somehow found time to sign on to voice a Sid and Marty Krofft puppet show, with Jane Kean providing the female sounds. In 1965 he gave at least one rare TV interview, on *The Joe Pyne Show*, and met socially with Los Angeles Mayor Sam Yorty. He attended few parties, but preferred to spend his off time with his family, his creative pursuits, Federal government work, and, of course, watching television.

Fred Frees: "His favorite shows were *Barney Miller, Get Smart*, and *Mission: Impossible*. (They have something in common, don't they?) He did do a voice-over in a *Get Smart* episode, though. [It was a satire of *Casablanca*, with Don Adams playing Max as Bogart, and Frees dubbing two actors in the voices of, who else?, Sydney Greenstreet and Peter Lorre.]

He liked scary movies and he was an Oakland A's fan.

"His voice career was full-steam now and he was in the studio full time. The cartoon character actors were great, but they could never go from Bugs Bunny or Quick Draw McGraw and do the Ghost Host. Dad's range speaks for itself. But in his humble way, Dad always referred to Mel Blanc as the 'Dean' of character voices.

"He didn't practice—that's how good he was. He may have done vocal exercises and such when he was younger and had to learn lines in movies, but later on, he didn't have to practice. However, if someone sent him a script for an upcoming commercial or special, he would read it over, and perhaps 'practice' how he would do it, but he didn't do special exercises or anything else. In fact, he would usually 'save' his voice by speaking softly or not at all. Often, at the end of the day or week, his voice was 'shot' and he would say, 'YOU talk to ME. I can't talk because my throat hurts.' On the phone he would say this, and then talk my ear off for hours. But he would sometimes lay in bed, with one hand around his throat, and the other hand holding a popsicle."

Variety knew he deserved a popsicle, reporting that Frees was bringing in a princely $250,000 a year from his TV and commercial work alone, not counting the theatrical dubbing, for which he received no residuals. He could perform an average of 1,000 commercials in a year, and six different accounts in a single day. Over the course of several years, he'd received $20,000 from Pepsi alone. This was one of the main reasons he relished in his secretive government work—it was a challenge. The money from voice work was just too easy.

The Atom Ant/Secret Squirrel Show debuted with episode "Up and Atom" on October 2, 1965. The hour-long Hanna-Barbera Sunday night television series featured the continuing adventures of "Atom Ant," "Secret Squirrel," "The Hillbilly Bears," "Precious Pupp," "Squiddly Diddly," and "Winsome Witch." The cartoons ran from three to seven minutes each, with Mel Blanc voicing Secret Squirrel, and Paul Frees as the secret agent's sidekick, Morocco Mole, voiced in breathy Peter Lorre mode. The little mole wore an Egyptian hat, suit (or at least, a jacket with a tucked-in scarf) and thick glasses. They worked undercover for their boss, Double Q, living the life of James Bond in the animal world. Frees also did his Sydney Greenstreet impression for the voice of villain Yellow Pinky.

When *I Dream of Jeanie* arrived on the scene that year, much of

The Haunted Mansion (© *Disney Enterprises, Inc.*)

television was still broadcast in black and white. The first episode of the series was narrated by Paul, telling what the more famous cartoon introduction would do later with no words at all: he related that the astronaut Captain Nelson, having crashed his rocket on a deserted beach, found a genie in a bottle. She followed him back to Coco Beach, "a mythical town in a mythical state called Florida. And there, in this house, the girl in the bottle plays spin the astronaut."

The Outlaws Is Coming, which turned out to be The Three Stooges' last feature-length film, was released in 1965. It took place in Casper, Wyoming Territory in 1871, and had some clever moments, such as the shooting up of the opening credits which were painted on lights, windows, bottles, glasses, etc. "A fiery villain with the speed of light," begins Paul's narration *a la* Dudley Do-Right. The plot began with a "syndicate" of good and bad guys who had teamed up to form the first western mafia, controlling gambling, protection, liquor and every other profit-making evil. Frees also voices a brief magic mirror for Jesse James, answering the question, "Who's the fastest gun of all?" and is shot for giving the wrong answer.

Switching into album mode, Paul provided voices for the Hanna-

The 1,000th Ghost remains at Disneyland. (© *Disney Enterprises, Inc.*) (*Steve Jaspar*)

Barbera LP *Monster Shindig* in 1965. It began with a catchy title song: "Dance watusi or dance the jig, at the Monster—the Monster—Shindig…" For contractual reasons, Daws Butler, already signed to Colpix Records, couldn't play the character he created, the driving force of the album: Super Snooper. Instead Frees assumed Snooper's role while June Foray tackled his trusty sidekick, Blabber Mouse (another Butler creation), with both professionals taking on all other characters that came their way. The plot began with PI Snooper called in by an old woman to investigate her weird neighbors. Naturally, the first oddity to open the door of the dark, dreary mansion was a Peter "Frees" Lorre voice greeting, "Bad evening, gentlemen." It was Weirdly Gruesome, one-time neighbor to the Flintstones, who slowly introduced them to his creepy family and friends.

Compared to his other albums, and even most Hanna-Barbera shows at that time, the script, pace and production were rather stifled. Jokes were obvious and drawn out well beyond their creepy or gag potential, such as the "blood bank" joke from Count Dracula that could be seen coming a mile away. Still, it was good to hear Granny Witch giggle her greeting to "Drac, baby," and that perfect Lorre voice chuckle through the gathering party. The Mummy arrived in mink bandages just in time to jig to another chorus of the title song and "The Monster Jerk" before Dr. Frankenstein revealed his latest creation…

In 1965 Paul Frees recorded his first work for Disneyland. *The Pirates of the Caribbean* was reportedly Walt Disney's favorite ride, though he never got to see it completed, as it opened the year after his death. Originally conceived as a walk-through attraction in New Orleans Square, the 15-minute boat ride consisted of more than sixty Audio-Animatronics figures of fun and frolic as the good-natured pirates drank, chased women, blasted at each other from huge ships and counted their mounting treasure. Frees is heard in every scene as the boisterous pirates, often fashioned after the Robert Newton (Long John Silver) manner of speech: he first ominously warns riders that "Dead men tell no tales!" from a pirate skull and crossbones as their boats push into the darkness and down a small waterfall. Next, he is the buccaneer auctioneer who tells one flirting maiden to "Shift your cargo, dearie, show 'em your larboard side…I'm not spongin' for rum! It be *gold* I'm after! Strike your colors, ya brazen wench. No need to expose your superstructure." Paul Frees' voice is *everywhere*. In the biggest set in the ride, he can be heard above the cannon fire, which sprays delighted passengers, between the two massive ships. He is also at least one pirate voice in the biggest laugh of the ride: as the jail is burning down, three imprisoned pirates try to entice a mangy dog, who has the ring of keys in his mouth, closer to their rope. The accompaniment of the tuneful "Yo Ho, Yo Ho, A Pirate's Life for Me," written by George Bruns and X. Atencio, throughout the attraction makes it a *very* memorable and festive experience. The ride did not undergo much change during the years, with Frees' many voices still floating through the favorite attraction to this day. (Atencio, *Pirates* script writer, also recalled that Paul was a master of ad-libs, echoing the fact that he would do his parts in just one take.)

A fantastic, but limited-edition 33rd Anniversary CD of the complete attraction, including a few of Paul Frees' voice sessions and a wonderful collection of other rarities, was released by Disney in 2000. Fred Frees: "I was the pirate voice on the interactive kiosk that instructed customers on which buttons to push in order to make their own personalized CD. I also did the same thing for the Haunted Mansion's 30th anniversary CDs, which were in Disneyland and Disney World. I actually did a third one just for the park itself. But the Mansion one was the best one. I remember going to Disneyland and hearing my voice coming from the machines over and over. There was one machine in Tomorrowland and one in a store on Main Street."

Though the *Haunted Mansion* (once merely called "the ghost house") began as a sinister gleam in Walt Disney's eye as far back as the mid-1950s, Paul Frees did not come into the studio to test out voices as its narrating Ghost Host until 1966. Clutching an early script, which referred to the attraction as a "Haunted House" with a black cat that was supposed to be a recurring character throughout the ride, Paul tried several versions of the Host (self-labeled "your ghost guide"), improvising with dead-on impersonations of Bela Lugosi and, of course, the mad Peter Lorre.

The imposing, decaying house situated in the New Orleans square section of Disneyland (and later Disney World) contains a cemetery in the backyard filled with headstones etched with humorous epitaphs. Your Ghost Host begins his scare tactics on you as soon as the grim pallbearers open the door to the brief chamber that leads you to the elevator. "When hinges creak in doorless chambers…" is Frees' classic opening to the spook show. "Welcome, foolish mortals… to the Haunted Mansion." He introduces visitors to the grotesque paintings on the walls of "guests as they appeared in their corruptible mortal state." As the room stretches, the portraits (which are oddly similar to what friends would call Frees' own "academic-surrealist" style of painting) reveal a variety of gags depicting these poor souls and how they met their ultimate demise. "This chamber has no windows and no doors." His laughs are echoed while the rest of his speech has a crypt-like chill to the recording. Obviously, the Host delights in his spook strategy. "999 happy haunts are here, but there's room for a thousand. Any volunteers? (Sinister laugh.)" Though for a sinister spirit obviously intent on causing some harm, our Host still tells us to "kindly watch your step" and, almost angrily, not to take any flash pictures!

Climbing into your two-seater Doom Buggy from a moving sidewalk, your dark tour begins. "Do not pull down on the safety bar," shouts your Host through a speaker at your ear. "I will lower it for you." As the ride progresses, the Ghost Host gleefully points out the "wall to wall creeps, and hot and cold running chills." After a heartfelt plea from a decapitated medium who calls out the spirits from inside her crystal ball, the Ghost Host returns to say that the "happy haunts have received your sympathetic vibrations and are beginning to materialize." He goes away for a brief bit as the real ghost show begins: you are witness to a wonderful wraith show in the ballroom, then in the graveyard where the full song of "Grim Grinning Ghosts" sung by Thurl Ravenscroft and The Mellomen is at last fully heard. When the Ghost Host returns, he tells us all to beware of hitchhiking ghosts, followed by a menacing laugh. As a ghost joins the center of every Buggy, via the special mirrors guests face, the Ghost Host admits, "They have selected *you* to fulfill our quota. And they'll haunt you until you return." Finally, he raises the safety bar so that "a ghost will follow you home!" The laughter that dissipates is the last you hear of the Ghost Host. A softer, new chorus of the harmony song from the ghosts leaves you ready to get in line for another ride through. Sadly, there's a rule against sitting in the car and taking the ride over and over again.

Paul recorded a series of radio promos in 1969 to advertise the attraction. In one, he was old Granny Ghoul, "former Peoria socialite and silent movie vamp," being interviewed by a reporter creaking through the old house. In another, the excited reporter interviewed old Phineas Pock (Frees) who had died in 1720. "Yeah, I'm tired of resting in peace. I wanna get in there and *spook* everybody!" In yet another, he was the hide-and-seek champion Willy the Wisp.

Aside from Boris Badenov, the Ghost Host may be Paul Frees' greatest-loved vocal performance. It, and the Disney attraction, has a cult following akin to *Star Trek* and *The Rocky Horror Picture Show*, especially considering that (like *Pirates of the Caribbean*) a big-budget film starring Eddie Murphy was released in 2003.

By the time Disneyland's *Haunted Mansion* unveiled itself to the public on August 9, 1969, Frees had already voiced two other major attractions there: *Adventure Thru Inner Space*, and *Great Moments with Mr. Lincoln*.

In 1966 he narrated Monsanto's *Adventure Thru Inner Space*, which opened the next year. "As you shrink beyond the size of a molecule on this adventure through inner space," said Frees, in his most natural voice, "you will notice that there is a remarkable similarity between the microcosm of inner space, and the macrocosm of outer space." Guests rode vehicles through a new Omnimover ride system that had been developed by WED, a system used in a greater way later in *The Haunted Mansion* and other attractions. Before riding their "atomobiles" through the tiny speck of a snowflake crystal, scientists discussed the heady jargon needed to get the shrinking job done. Once all was ready, Paul's voice was the only thing guiding passengers through this strange excursion. "I am the first person to make this fabulous journey. Suspended in the timelessness of inner space are the thought waves of my first impressions. They will be our only source of contact once you have passed beyond the limits of normal MAGNIFICATION... MAGNIFICA-TION...MAGNIFICATION." A scientist himself, the unnamed character imparts an eager excitement of what he is seeing. "These fuzzy spheres must be the atoms that make up the molecule. Two hydrogen atoms bonded to a single oxygen atom, and I see it's the orbiting electrons that give the atom its fuzzy appearance. And still I continue to shrink. Is it possible that I can enter the atom itself?!? Electrons are dashing about me—like so many fiery comets! Can I possibly survive?" The ride crescendos to the moment when the snowflake finally melts. "But there is no cause for alarm. You are back on visual, and returning to your normal size."

The ride, sponsored by The Monsanto Company (makers of Roundup weed killer), was finally removed from Disneyland in 1985 to make room for the new *Star Tours* attraction, a simulation "ride" based on *Star Wars*.

Great Moments with Mr. Lincoln opened at the 1964 World's Fair along with stalwarts *It's a Small World* and *The Carousel of Progress*. It moved to Disneyland as a permanent attraction in 1966, with several changes in format through the years. It was one of Disney's crowning achievements to the theme park, built on a solid foundation of Audio-Animatronics work that showed a full-sized, robotic Abraham Lincoln talking and gesturing realistically.

The show began with lush music enveloping Paul Frees' speech. "It was from Illinois and his prairie beginnings that Lincoln went on to become the 16th President." Frees also vocally appeared in the short film made up of illustrations from the time; he's heard as several of the hecklers ("That's what *you* think, ya long drink o' water!") as Lincoln gives his speech, and as Mr. Douglas speaking against him in the famous debate. This rousing, patriotic attraction featured Paul's voice at its most natural, and has long been a crowd pleaser at the various Disney parks.

In 1968 Paul repeated his respectful performance for the expanded

Ringo, Ed Vane (Vice President of ABC), Paul McCartney and Paul Frees.

Great Moments with Mr. Lincoln Disneyland record. It gave more information on the most beloved President: his origin and slow climb to the White House. The album may or may not have been boring for kids, but it still had the same great production that the attraction claimed, ending with the resplendent "Battle Hymn of the Republic."

It was Paul's versatility that kept him in high demand for Disneyland work. Don Pitts, in charge of voice actors at the Charles Stern Agency, explained: "He was the greatest voice-over performer of all time, and I'll tell you why. He was the master of every category. Orson Welles narration. He was a great impressionist. Then he was a cartoon voice. And he also could sing! It was probably because of this that he did not tolerate fools, because when he became successful there was no *reason* for him to tolerate fools.

"I remember once, I booked him at Disney for half a day for twelve or fifteen hundred dollars. He called me up and said he was getting ready to go to a movie because there was a new man at the gate who didn't know who he was, and as his name wasn't down on the list, he wouldn't let Paul in. Disney Studios called up, irate, asking, 'Where's your client, he's late!' I told him Paul couldn't get on the lot, and this guy went on and on about how Paul should've had the guy pick up the phone and call the soundstage. Well, a week later the same guy called up for the same job for Paul. I told Paul and he said, 'Oh sure, that's fine. By the way, I want to be paid for the other day.' I called up Disney—and this guy went through the ceiling! I never talked to anyone so upset in my whole life."

Frees later recalled his Disney years to studio engineer Bob Lindner: "Paul said that Disney was a very tough business guy, and nobody got the better of Walt Disney. Nobody, except Paul felt that he had. The way it worked was that they had wanted to use him for some of these voices, and Disney asked how much it would take. He asked his people who recorded those things, how much time he thought it would take based on what other people were doing. And they gave him a figure, so Disney based his fee on this figure, but cut it quite a bit. Frees was getting a day rate to do these things. He would go down there and say, 'Oh, this will take all day.' Well, Frees would go down there and get paid a day rate and knock the thing out in half an hour or an hour, and walk out of there just smiling, knowing that he had upped Walt Disney one. It just made him feel really good."

Disney and Frees enjoyed each other's company, though, and continued a strong relationship until Disney's death in 1966. In the early 1960s Walt gave Paul a beautiful gold Mickey Mouse watch which the actor cherished for the rest of his life.

Oddly, Paul was not enamored of Disneyland, or theme parks in general, though he always received free passes. He *hated* waiting in lines, especially with "ordinary people," and had to be dragged by his son to the place. Fred: "He didn't seem to care for Disneyland, even though he was involved with it. Going on rides was all I wanted to do, and what he cared for least.

"As for Walt Disney, he was the 'boss,' and not a performer, at least, not when Dad was working for him. Dad was always gracious to the 'higher ups,' even though he knew they needed him more than the other way around.

"He had a phone in the limo. And in the 1960s, that was a big deal. I used it to call a friend when we were actually parked in front of his house. It was a big surprise then. Now, anybody can do it.

"He always came to pick me up, or had the driver (when he had one) come and get me. But my mother never dropped me off for those occasions. I'm guessing he never 'visited' me because he didn't want to see my mother or (most definitely) my stepfather. There was a lot of tension between them and my dad, and it may have colored the way Dad treated me. His parenting skills were nothing like his artistic abilities. I wanted him to be proud of me, but I never felt I ever did anything to be particularly proud of.

"Dad did his best, and I always loved him. He did express his pride in me on occasion and always told me he loved me. Basically, though, I have no complaints about the way I was raised. I had a lot of freedom for a kid and I was fortunate to have some very good friends growing up, who are still my friends, after 50 years!"

Amazingly, Paul didn't care for popular music, least of all rock 'n' roll and The Beatles. But that didn't stop him from working for creator Al Brodax (TVC) and King Features to voice John Lennon and George Harrison for the ABC cartoon series, *The Beatles*. At the height of Beatlemania TVC latched onto the animation rights, including rights to use most of the songs in the shows. One of the reasons Brodax was able to do the series at a time when everyone and their grandmother was clamoring to reach The Beatles and their constantly-phoned manager Brian Epstein was because of the lack of work The Beatles thought the series would take on their part. They would not have to record new songs, nor voice the manic dialogue. Two veteran voices were called in: Lance Percival, a hot UK TV property from *That Was the Week That Was* who had made a few records with that 4th Beatle, producer George Martin (though that connection had nothing to do with being cast in the cartoon), and Paul Frees, with whom Brodax had already worked on his *King Features Trilogy*. Frees took John Lennon and George Harrison, and any other characters that cropped up, and Percival voiced Paul McCartney and Ringo Starr.

In May or June of 1965 Frees, Percival and Brodax met in London with ABC, who had approval of the final scripts and voices, to run through various vocals. No impressions of The Fab Four were attempted; voices were auditioned to fit the personalities of the already-agreed-upon cartoon characters. Any female voices needed were done by Jackie Newman.

One controversy that arose from the choices of the final voices was that everyone was concerned that the Beatles should not sound too English for American audiences. Their Liverpool accents, which delighted so many teens in the 60s, were Americanized to represent how the US *thought* the UK sounded. Naturally, it made the cartoon voices exceedingly unpopular with the British, and The Beatles. Epstein himself decreed that the cartoons shouldn't be shown in England, because of the voices, though Brodax believed that the voices helped the show's high ratings in America.

The recordings took place in a London studio at 18 Rodmarton Street, with as many episodes as possible being recorded in one 9 to 6 session. As there was no overtime in the budget, nothing ever went beyond 6 p.m., after which Frees would often go into a nearby pub for a drink. Though Ringo was initially the only Beatle interested in the cartoon series, soon the other band members came around to see how they were being portrayed. After one such visit by the group, they and Frees went into a pub, where photos were taken. Only one picture survives from that night.

With too many other commitments pressing, Frees had to fly back and forth to London for recording part of the second season. The travel was getting to be too much of a chore, so he finished the second season, as well as the third, from a New York studio, with Percival still recording in London. Paul Frees did attend the screening of the series at TVC Cartoons animation studio when The Beatles arrived in a big black limousine to see the final product for the first time. Everyone was happy.

To facilitate the huge interest in the series, the animation was spread out for production in Australia, England and Canada. 78 five-and-a-half minute episodes were made using most of The Beatles' catalog up through their then current *Revolver* album, plus hit singles. These were the classic Beatles, before *Sgt. Pepper*, and before growing beards and their hair even longer. The plots pushed the clean-cut youths into extraordinary troubles, such as the last episode, "I'm Only Sleeping," in which John Lennon falls asleep telling a story to children and dreams he must, with electric guitar in hand, help Merlin the Magician and a Prince slay a ferocious dragon. Every mini-musical was named after the song it contained. "A Hard Day's Night" christened the series, airing on September 25, 1965. Again, they were put in a wacky situation, this time rehearsing at The Transylvania Hotel, but to escape the throng of fans, they find an empty castle that's actually full up with spooks.

"Before and during his work on *The Beatles* cartoon, he met with them," said Fred Frees. "I don't think they did any specific work together, except perhaps to discuss what he would be doing. However, I know they socialized on at least one occasion because my father had a series of photographs of them drinking together. He was rather greedy about those photos, and I was only able to squeeze one away from him. It was only of him and Ringo, each with a drink in their hand. I *really* wanted those other photos, but he wouldn't give them to me. After he died, I tried to find those pictures, but they had been taken."

Later, around 1968, father and son tried writing songs together. They'd wanted to make an album out of the material. Fred: "It was a collection of original songs he wrote, one of which I co-wrote with him. They were not exactly pop tunes, they were just his own songs (some were better than others). Nothing came of it, however.

"I liked rock and roll, but Dad hated it. I used to play piano and bass guitar. For our collaborative song, I had come up with a basic melody and he hired an arranger to expand it into a song. Then he told me to come up with a title and I came up with three, and he used one of them. The song was 'just okay.'"

Rock music continued to infiltrate the cartoon world. *Frankenstein Jr. and the Impossibles* was yet another idea that ignored the fact that Frankenstein was the creator not the monster, but this Hanna-Barbera series put Frees in the voices of narrator and Fluid Man, the mop-topped leader of The Impossibles, a group of superheroes that "disguised" themselves as a rock group in order to thwart baddies. Each hero had at least one superpower, Fluid Man's being the ability to liquefy himself at will. They drove the Impossicar, and communicated with Big D, their superior, through the two-way radio embedded in the guitar. The wacky series ran from 1966 to 1968, later repackaged with *Space Ghost* in 1976, with each show containing two seven-minute adventures.

On the *Justice League of America* segment of *The Superman/Aquaman Hour of Adventure*'s second season, Frees provided the voices for Kyro and Guardian of the Universe in this Filmation Studios epic production of nearly all the DC Comics superheroes. Only three cartoons of the *JLA* spot were made, since variety was the key to the series. *The Atom, Green Lantern, Hawkman* and a few others were also given six minutes each to save the world in 1967.

Paul went back to Jay Ward Productions that year for another series. *George of the Jungle* was to be Ward's final hit series, and is revered as the swinging cartoon spoof of Tarzan. George still spoke in broken English, but, to avoid a lawsuit if "Jane" were used, his bombshell girlfriend was renamed Ursula. The muscle-headed dope flew through the air on vines in Africa's Mbwebwe Valley, never failing to slam into a tree, though he was obviously smart enough to decipher animal noises and a strange telephone/bird which only said "Tooki, tooki!" The articulate and haughty Ape (an ape, naturally) was beautifully voiced by Frees in his best Ronald Colman, and would often be seen reading significant matter such as *The Origin of Species* by Charles Darwin. A pilot had been made two years previously, with Hans Conried as narrator, but Frees narrated the series, which was divided up into three portions: *George*; *Tom Slick*, a race car version of Dudley Do-Right; and the illustrious *Super Chicken*, a crazy Batman-type idea with a rooster in the lead.

Frees and company had returned to Jay Ward studios in late 1964 (as if he ever left) to record a second pilot for *Super Chicken*, with William Conrad as the narrator and Frees as Eggs Benedict, Fred and the Cop. In the *George*-supporting series, Frees provided narration and the voice to the hero's valet, the lion Fred—another Ed Wynn impersonation. The cluck (Bill Scott) in mask and Musketeer garb, had been a concept since 1960, and lasted for seventeen six-minute episodes.

"Tom Slick, Tom Slick. Let me tell you why. He's the best of all good guys..." began the theme song to the third *George* component, *Tom Slick*, voiced by Bill Scott in Dudley Do-Right style. Paul nasally narrated the shows in Race Commentator fashion, doubling as evil Baron Otto Matic in many of the episodes.

George and friends originally ran from 1967 to 1970, then went into constant reruns. Many of the people working on the series thought it was the best work they'd ever done for Jay Ward, with its quick, tight scripts and clean and classy limited animation. And voices.

"We're not voices, we're saxophones," Frees said at the time. "If E-Flat is wanted, we play E-Flat. I speak in three octaves. The one I'm using now is one I cultivated for conversational use and is free. The other two are too valuable to use up." He laughed. "I'm really kidding, but I do save my low and high registers for work."

He also saved his jokes for the session work. But Paul never advertised where all the gags were coming from.

Ex-vaudevillian Billy Glason of New York City had begun "servicing the stars" (Ed Sullivan, Bob Hope, Tommy Cooper, etc.) with a joke file of stories, songs and gags called "The Comedian" (AKA "Fun Master Monthly") in 1940. When Paul Frees began subscribing to it is uncertain, but he amassed a literal ton of the issues beginning sometime in the 1950s. As of 1962 at least he was still subscribed (at $45 a year plus postage), but as most of the issues are undated, it is difficult to tell when he stopped getting it. He kept the issues in good condition to the end of his life, and used the jokes and stories to keep his fellow voice actors entertained, miffed or delayed. Glason "collected" the material from various sources and gave lots of instructions on the telling of jokes and stories, even admitting that a performer could reword the stuff to make it his own. He also published (typed up and copied anyway) a huge "Blue Book" full of dirty material which he called "gags for stags." Paul, depending on the comedy, loved to recite his own versions of some of these, sometimes in the most unlikely places.

Few of his gag scripts were marked, as Frees had an incredible memory for events and comedy. Like a primed time bomb he could explode on a specific topic with just the slightest straight line. (You'll find examples of these in the next chapter.)

Voice actor Doug Young recalled, "I did a couple of commercials with that guy. He had what we used to call the Mickey Rooney syndrome. He was always on! He would distract the director and everybody and he would never quit! We would say, 'Come on, Paul, let's get this done!' But hey, that was Paul. He was okay, he just liked to ham it up. Very, very talented guy, obviously. I think he did some Flintstones characters with me, too, but not too often."

In 1966 Frees, along with Don Messick, supplied miscellaneous voices to support Larry Harmon and Jim MacGeorge as *Laurel and Hardy*. It debuted in syndication a year after Stan Laurel's death, though it had been in the works since 1960. Unfortunately, the joint production of Harmon, Hanna-Barbera and David L. Wolper was less like the classic comedy team and more like most of the other kiddie shows at the time, including the previous *Bozo* show. Apart from the assembly-line production of gags and limited animation, the series was up against opposition from a legion of Laurel and Hardy fans who would already marvel at its sacrilege. "To criticize these cartoons is pointless," stated one reviewer. "Any imitation, even a good one, simply cannot be Laurel and Hardy."

It was in 1967 that Paul's long-term association with Rankin/Bass began. Arthur Rankin, Jr. was originally owner of a New York advertising studio and Jules Bass, who worked in television, had a regular account there. The two decided to team up and began producing 130 five-minute segments of a TV series called *The New Adventures of Pinocchio*, first broadcast in 1960. That series began their popular trek into stop-motion animation, usually done for them in Japan, though they would often veer into regular animation as well. The Animagic figures usually took over a year to animate within the room-sized sets and cost around $5000 each to construct. They were made of material that wasn't meant to last more than a couple years: wood, plastic, wire, etc.

Their specialty was Christmas; even Hanna-Barbera admitted that they owned *that* season. Perhaps their biggest hit came in 1964 with the ever-popular *Rudolph the Red-Nosed Reindeer*, which spawned at least one original Christmas hit song sung by Burl Ives: "Holly Jolly Christmas."

It wasn't until R&B's fifth television special, *Cricket on the Hearth*, which premiered on December 18, 1967, that Paul Frees joined the ranks. The sixty-minute special, sponsored by Burger Chef, was another fun musical with music by Maury Laws and lyrics by Jules Bass. Writers Romeo Muller and Arthur Rankin, Jr. adapted Charles Dickens' 1845 Christmas fantasy about a poor toy maker named Caleb Plummer (voiced by Danny Thomas), and his daughter (Marlo Thomas) who turns blind after she finds that her Royal Navy fiancé has been lost at sea. They are helped by tiny Cricket Crockett (Roddy McDowall), while Hans Conried dives into the villainous role of Gruff Tackleton. Frees doubled up as Uriah and the Sea Captain. An RCA soundtrack recording was issued, produced by Laws, with Frees and the original cast credited on the cover.

In a later interview Paul told of how he would often have to voice-direct the children who had parts in these specials. Even though the project had a different director, Paul would read the kids' lines the way each child was supposed to do it (most significantly on *Santa Claus is Comin' to Town*, which had several young cast members). He would also do it for big stars who had never done animation, "because they were dealing with a medium that they had never worked in before, and it requires a special technique." Occasionally he would be credited as "dubbing director" on a film, especially for work on some of his many Japanese movies, such as *King Kong Escapes* (1967 US version).

One of the oddest cartoon series Paul fell into was *Super President and Spy Shadow*. Only in 1967 could executive producers David H. DePatie and Friz Freleng dare to broadcast an animated plot in which President of the United States James Norcross (voiced by Frees, as was the introductory narration) is transformed into a superhero when his molecular structure is altered during a cosmic storm. In his red, white and no blue suit the Chief Executive would fly through the air without Air Force One (a belt of rockets did it), changing his mass into steel, granite, or whatever element it took to fight the villain of the week. He even once changed into ozone! It must have cost the taxpayers a pretty billion to have that underground cave lair built beneath the White House, not to mention his Omnicar which could fly, become a submarine and had a weapons system that James Bond would die for.

Many adventures had SP rescuing his "adviser," the only one who knew Norcross' secret, from all manner of non-political dangers. Not only did this Pres not spend any time battling the deficit, but the timing for the series was all wrong, debuting a mere four years after JFK's assassination. Some critics called it in bad taste, and many viewers thought it just plain compost. Not even merchandising agents wanted to touch it.

The Saturday morning half-hour series contained two *Super Presidents*, separated by *Spy Shadow*, a private eye named Richard Vance (voiced by Daws Butler) who, through the "powers of inner self," can (sometimes) control his shadow (voiced by Lurch of *The Addams Family* himself, Ted Cassidy) to fight evil. In light—as it needed that alone in order to live—Vance's shadow was invincible to bullets, could easily slip under doors, and had great strength.

DePatie called the series the worst project they ever made, and thankfully the turkey gobbled for only a single season on NBC, croaking after Christmas. Funnily, during Norcross' tenure, Nixon became President.

In 1967 Paul provided the narration for a high-profile gangster movie, *The St. Valentine's Day Massacre*. February 14, 1929. Paul began with a statement of what was going on at the time (the birth of Mickey Mouse, the year of the Black Bottom, and so on). He gives the colorful and then-current history of the Chicago mobsters in an informative, impersonal tone that neither made light nor horror of the film that followed. The movie told the story of "Scarface" Al Capone, and Paul had a hell of a lot to say about the characters involved.

Also that year he did the opening narration to the CBS television series, *Mr. Terrific.*

> "A scientist both wise and bold
> set out to cure the common cold.
> Instead he found this power pill
> which he said most certainly will
> turn a lamb into a lion
> like an eagle, he'll be flyin'."

The situation comedy only lasted a season, but no wonder Frees found himself drawn to it: the Bureau of Secret Projects had invented a top-secret power pill that only worked on one man, young gas station attendant Stanley Beamish (Stephen Strimpell). Unfortunately for the government, Beamish was too gullible and compassionate an idiot and though he did his country a lot of good, the pill, which gave him super abilities for just one hour at a time, had a habit of wearing off at the worst possible moment.

Paul had meantime divorced Patrice. "One of the most memorable times my father appeared on TV was on *The Dating Game*," says Fred Frees. "I think it must have been after he divorced Sabrina's mother, Patrice, and before he married Jeri. After the bachelorette was introduced (I think her name was June), the Host said, 'And let's meet the three bachelors.' The stage opened up, revealing not three bachelors, but just Dad sitting all by himself on the center stool. He did the voices of all three bachelors. As memory serves (which is dubious), one was just a straight sounding guy, the second was a man with a southern accent, and the third was a man with a British accent (the one she picked, I think). It was a sight to see. Of course, he never used his regular speaking voice. It turned out that my dad and the woman had met once before. It was hilarious."

After this, Paul married a young woman named Jeri Jene Cole. The union did not last long. According to Fred, "I really liked Jeri. She was my favorite. My dad's relationship with her was mostly a mystery to me, but she treated me well and I thought she was very pretty. They weren't together very long and I always wondered what happened to her. Fortunately, I was able to see her again around 2007, once Ben Ohmart got in contact with her.

"When I was 14, I had one of the most memorable times with my dad ever. I flew with him and Jeri to New York. June Foray, my uncle Dave and his wife were with us. Then the three of us continued on to Montreal, Canada. It's the only time I can remember ever traveling with Dad anywhere in an airplane. We stayed at this magnificent hotel and took horse-carriage rides at midnight. When we had to cross a busy street, Dad went into the middle of the street and pretended to be a traffic-control officer. Sure enough, the traffic stopped and we crossed over.

"Later, we went to the Exposition (Expo '67). Dad had a special coin that allowed us to go to the head of all the lines. We went into what we thought was a 'science' exhibit, but it turned out to be a 'creationist' exhibit, and Dad and I walked out in a hurry. I took my 8mm camera with me, and shot scenes of him and Jeri for a sci-fi movie that I was making. I still have a video of that movie."

"I was born Jeri Jene Cole in Duluth, Minnesota in 1943," states Jeri Capella. "I worked at Radio Recorders and loved my job. Paul would come into Radio Recorders quite often. Sometimes he drove; sometimes L.C., his black chauffer, drove. L.C. made quite an impression. He was about 6'5", skinny, black and in uniform. Paul's gold and black Rolls-Royce Silver Cloud sat at the curb. I can't say I was attracted to Paul at any time. He was imposing, I guess arrogant, and paid little attention to me. Occasionally, some of us at RR would go for pizza after work across the street. Paul joined us this one time and we were all surprised and honored. He was at the top of his career then. The talent didn't go for pizza with the crew. I was always more comfortable with a group and before we went our separate ways, Paul asked me out. I was then a bit stunned. I didn't actually know much of what he had done. Just the RR stuff and I had a sense of how good he was. And of course, the idea of being picked up in a chauffeur-driven Rolls Royce to go to a movie was heady stuff.

"He called the afternoon of the date to alert me that we wouldn't be going to a movie. He said it was his preference but some people from out of town wanted him to show them around, and that I should dress to go dancing. That was not a problem; my mother taught me well. So Hubert Humphrey, his son, and a couple of secret service guys joined us on our first date. I wasn't intimidated, I wasn't too aware of any of them, because Paul was not shy; he kissed me right after I got in the back seat. The combination of over the top luxury and his incredible kiss was like

Cinderella's shoe fitting and I wore it well from that moment. We kissed at every opportunity all evening. I was in love like never before.

"I went with him on most jobs. Our joke was that I had him on a pedestal and carried it with me. He became 6'6 tall. I loved being his cheering section. His later avocation in narcotics law enforcement, which left me alone way too much, especially at night, took its toll. He became paranoid, I think, with a gun under the bed and he was almost always wearing one. When I didn't go to work with him, he would give me a couple hundred dollar bills for me to go shopping. Enjoyable to a point. I was bored a lot. He repeated stories when in a group, always needing all the attention. Actually he was probably more entertaining to himself than anyone else in the group. When we would go to the Caesars for brunch, he was with equally talented or more talented guys so then it was fabulous.

"For a time Paul and I renamed me Kristina. That was the name on the mini-slip I was wearing when my instructor cut a piece off after I flew solo at Novato airport. Paul liked to pass me off as Danish royalty somewhat as a gag. I took to wearing my long blond hair in circle braids at the sides of my head. Later a friend of his told me he didn't commit my name to memory as 'what is the point, you wouldn't be around long.' I actually was, or so it seemed. I think Paul and I were both romantics. I was his fifth wife, as you know and John, my present husband is my fifth. So much for judging others.

"Paul and I married in 1967. We lived together for about a year and a half first. We were divorced in 1969, with some reunions for another year. We were married in a hotel room in Las Vegas. Lots of red velvet and mirrors on the ceiling above the bed. What was I thinking? Kurt Berger was our witness. He was pivotal in my story. Why we divorced is a lot of the story. I have so many memories of how it wasn't working for me. And I don't think Paul had a clue, I didn't give him any. I just moved out. I very quickly met my next lover, young, handsome, artist Iain Dougherty. His mother lived on the island; she set it up. Love at first kiss was my pattern.

"A big problem arose with his daughter Sabrina; I wanted her to be our little girl and her overdosing mother Patrice was in the way. That became the major reason for my leaving. I couldn't respect Paul for not wanting to get custody and I really had no power in the situation. Paul had had a vasectomy when he was compelled to marry Patrice. He wanted no strings and then she told him she was already pregnant. So the story was told to me. Sabrina was of course a big financial string and looking back, he simply did not want a family. He wanted to be the center of attention. And Sabrina filled a big place in my heart. He talked about reversing the vasectomy and by this time I didn't see him as a husband and father period.

"Also his involvement with the Marin County Sheriff's Dept. and the narcs was difficult for me. He was carrying a gun all the time and out every night, often all night. He wanted to live full time in Tiburon and there went whatever glamour I experienced in L.A. Well, just the fun of going to the studios together and feeling that I was contributing. Even though he was just 48, he had started in the business so young and he was now retreating/retiring. He had done the big European tour with Patrice and wasn't interested in travel. I had wanted to travel all my life. My parents went around the world a couple of times.

I couldn't ask for what I wanted. He was devastated when I left. Lots of drama. I was in love with the young artist and I loved Paul very much for many years. I went back and forth for a while. Quite mentally ill at the time. I pushed onward; with a touch of therapy.

"Another disturbing thing about Paul was his hypochondria and reliance on certain drugs. He developed a close bond with a Dr. Russell in Gulfport, Mississippi who he had met through a pretty famous singer, Brother Dave someone who sounded very black but wasn't. We visited Dr. Russell and his family a couple of times. They lived humbly in a rambler on the bayou. One Christmas visit Paul went to a local furniture store and bought an entire houseful and had it delivered. Big gestures. Dr. John used to give him shots of Ritalin and lots of pills for sleeping, etc. I don't really know what all. One of those trips included New Orleans and that was wonderful for me. We bought antiques and went to see the puppet show that predated the Muppets. Another trip was with Paul's brother Dave and his wife Helen and Freddy (he reminded me of this when we met in L.A. a couple years ago) to Toronto and Montreal for an animated film festival. We stayed in a beautiful room in Montreal at the Chateau Frontenac and rode in one of the horse-drawn carriages around. Very romantic. I remember also hours spent in the rental car from Montreal to Toronto, I guess they wanted to see the countryside.

"When Paul and I were living on Hollywood Blvd; he had purchased a fabulous property with 4 or 5 Spanish-style townhouses around a pool, with lots of immense sycamore trees. Quite perfect. Courtney was the

Left to right: Sheriff Louis P. Montanous, Bill Johansen (SO Captain), Paul Frees, Al Scoma, and Captain Harvey Teague.

street. Charlie Brill and Mitzi McCall rented one of them; you may have seen them on *Hollywood Squares*. They were a popular comedy act and brought oodles of fun. This was a good period in our relationship. The painful part was flying to Fresno to pick up Sabrina handed over by Patrice and then flying her back, she would be crying so hard and clutching me, saying she didn't want to go to her mother. We were both broken hearted. She was I think 4 years old.

"Another tenant at Courtney was Sid Caesar's manager, H.F. Green. (He and my sister had an affair. They were both married.) Lots of parties. Whereas when Paul sold Courtney Place, our friends in Tiburon were Sheriff Louis Montanos and his wife Beverly who were just struggling along raising two boys in San Rafael. I was so turned off when Paul and Louie would go to Tahoe, with or without Bev and I, to gamble. Louie was from a Greek family of several brothers who were heavy gamblers. He had been the youngest Police Chief for Sausalito, then he was elected as the youngest Sheriff of Marin County. He was a wonderful, sweet, handsome man. Paul was a very heavy roller and gave Lou $ to gamble with.

Lou even had me sworn in as a deputy as a perk for Paul. How his Sheriff's Dept. connection was involved with Paul's security rating, which was very high, and with his having been given some acknowledgment from Nixon from the oval office, I don't know.

"I showed my badge to get out of a couple tickets while driving to L.A. a couple of times, speeding at 130 MPH in my Porsche. In hot pursuit of drug dealers, don't you know. We had an older Porsche 912 for a while, then bought a new green Targa. We joked that we had a front and back Porsche as one was in L.A. and one was in Tiburon for a while. Oh, by the way, that house on Corinthian Island hanging out over the yacht club cost $50,000. And was supposed to be my wedding present. I didn't claim it though.

"I remember one time we were in D.C. Paul was being given a high security clearance (G12 or something) and some kind of acknowledgement in a ceremony at the White House from President Nixon. And on one lovely night Paul, when the moon was full and there wasn't another soul around at the beautifully lighted Lincoln Memorial, he read the, I guess, Gettysburg Address to me in that full booming voice. That was a fabulous memory. Probably my best memory of our time together. He had done the narrator's voice at Disneyland for the Lincoln Exhibit, which is probably still going on. Afterwards he talked the guard into letting me into the bathroom of the empty Senate. The good old days, before 'Homeland Security.' Since Kurt Berger was a CIA agent and very close to Paul, I wonder what else Paul was up to.

"Kurt was a wonderful man who was a sobering influence on Paul. He was a psychologist, and manned the phones for the Suicide Prevention Center. And was a go-between for me with Paul. He encouraged me to leave Paul. He said I was clearly 'in over my head.' He was tall, well built, in his 50's. Always in a suit. Distinguished. He had a tragic situation with his daughter who was given LSD at a party and she was institutionalized and didn't recover when I knew him. I think he had something to do with Paul's top security clearance and meeting with Nixon."

While it's unclear just when or why Paul first got involved with his prodigious police work, Alfred W. "Tex" Teixeira was one early witness: "I don't remember the exact date I met Paul, but it was probably back when I started with the Marin County Drug Abuse Bureau in 1967. Schwedhelm, who was in charge of the Drug Abuse Bureau and my boss under Sheriff Montanos, and I had an apartment, an undercover condo there next to A. Sabella's restaurant in Corte Madera. I met Paul when he came to the apartment. He was a friend of the sheriff's and he came to meet all the undercover guys that the county had just hired for the Bureau. My first impression was 'What a big phony!' He just appeared to me to be a typical groupie. I wasn't really impressed with him for the first couple of weeks that I knew him, but after a while he started to kind of grow on you. I guess the first time I realized he wasn't a phony was when…well, you know, he was always spouting off about how he knew this famous guy or was friends with this other actor. Naming names like a lot of people do. So we were sitting there talking about Jack Webb and he said that he was good friends with Jack. I think he said he helped him get started in his career. I might be wrong about that, but I think so. Then he said, 'I have to give Jack a call,' and he got on his phone and dialed and said, 'Hey, is Jack there? Well, tell him Paul Frees called.' And I'm thinking, 'Ya right.' A couple of hours later the phone rings and I pick it up and I hear this voice say, 'Is Paul Frees there?' and talk about freezing! I almost froze 'cause I recognized the voice right away. So I told Paul, 'Hey, Jack Webb on the phone,' and he takes the phone and starts to talk to him. That was when I realized that this guy was for real, he wasn't a phony. He could talk the talk, but he could also walk the talk.

"We became close friends. The sheriff always would call me and say 'pick up Paul at the airport, take Paul to the airport, do this for Paul, do that.' A lot of it was escorting him around. To and from the Sheriff's Office; then I was taking him to work in San Francisco. I'd watch him do the voices in San Francisco; we'd have lunch, come home. We were always in the city. In the evening when we were done we'd meet the Federal and State agents and hit all the hot spots. Cop bars. It was a lot of fun.

"He always wore these capes and a fedora. One time we went into this place, I think it was called the Silver Cloud. They had Irish Coffees for a buck. We saw the sign, so we went in there one time to have an Irish Coffee. They were Taiwanese people. Nice people. One time we decided to eat there. They had a Lobster Bisque soup. Paul fell in love with that soup. All the food was wonderful. Paul fell in love with the food so it became one of our favorite restaurants. One time we parked in the alley behind the place. There were four-story apartment buildings with fire escapes and in the evenings people would sit out there. This big long alley with all these people on their fire escapes. So we were walking by this alley and he looked down there and saw all these people. He had on his fedora and cape and he started walking down the alley singing like Mario Lanza. Paul had a beautiful voice, and he's waving his arms. People were clapping. It was like out of a movie.

"Another time we were in a bar and he had on that cape and hat. The bar was pretty full and there was this older guy and he was with a pretty young blonde. We were at the bar and the guy came over to order a drink and he started talking to Paul. He said, 'Oh, if my wife only knew! That's my girlfriend over there' and he went on about his infidelity. Paul just goes 'hmm umm.' Later the guy comes over again and orders another drink and starts talking again. He asks Paul, 'So what do you do for a living?' Paul says, 'You really want to know? I'm a private investigator hired by your wife to watch you.' The guy turned white, turned around and got his girl and split.

"One time the sheriff asked me to pick Paul up at San Francisco Airport and I was waiting for him at the gate. He came off the plane and he was dressed like a hippy. He had all this makeup on, a big red bandana tied around his head, and he had just dyed his hair carrot top. He was singing and he had a bag full of pennies. He was dipping his hand in the bag as he was walking and throwing pennies up in the air. I just turned around and walked away. I don't know this guy!

"One time we were at Macy's and he's looking for a sales person. He walks up to a manikin and starts this 10 minute saga: 'why aren't you talking to me? I'm going to call the manager.' By the time he was done, there must have been 30 people there laughing like crazy. He could continue this comedy scene forever. He loved to have an audience.

"We were in the store another time and he started sing-

Paul at home. *Photo courtesy of Gail Teixeira.*

ing and tap dancing with another manikin on a platform. You never knew what he was going to do. It was a laugh a minute.

"I don't know that Paul contributed anything to the Bureau. He was just there. Well, he did makeup for undercover work. He could take somebody who was already known to people and fix them up so they could go right back in and buy from the same dealers again. He never gave anything financial or anything like that. Except that he was always treating us to dinner. We went across the street from the old courthouse to San Rafael Joe's. That was the local watering hole every night after work. Nobody could put their hand in their pocket, you know? He would always pick up the tab. He contributed a lot in that way. He was a real good friend of law enforcement. A real good friend of the sheriff's.

"If he wasn't in LA doing his thing there and the sheriff wasn't available, he was with us. Sometimes just riding around with us or hanging out in the office. It was funny, because whenever he was around he was always laughing or kidding or joking and doing one of his characters. He could do music, like sounding like trumpets with his voice. He took me one time to a session and he was talking to some old ball player, I think it was, and Paul was saying that he had a hard time doing his own voice. He was kidding the guy. Paul could do 10-12 characters at the same time. Just change his voice to a new character without skipping a beat. He could be twelve people in one shot. It was incredible.

"He was real good friends with Al Scoma from the restaurant in San Francisco, and so was the sheriff, so maybe that was how they met. I really don't know. It could have been at a narcotics conference. We all belonged to the California State Narcotics Officers Association and there was also a Federal one that we all belonged to. Paul was involved in this stuff long before he was involved with us. The old Federal Bureau of Narcotics Enforcement—he had one of their badges. He was the first one to be given one of their badges as an honorary representative of Hollywood. And he used to kid Elvis Presley, because Elvis Presley also had a badge, a Federal badge. And he would kid him and say he (Paul) got his first.

"Paul also had a few guns, but his favorite was a Walther PPK. That was the one he liked the best. He was a good shot. We went to the shooting range together. He handled a gun well.

"He went with us on a lot of raids. But he had to stay in the car until everything was secure. Then he could come in. Even though he was a special deputy—being a special deputy meant he could be there—we had orders

Paul, around 1970. *Photo courtesy of Gail Teixeira.*

from the sheriff that he was not to be put in any danger whatsoever or in any compromising position. Once we had everyone handcuffed and there was no threat or danger, then Paul could get out of the car and come in. Unless we knew it was something that was going to be easy and we knew no one would get hurt. But if we were going with a search warrant into a house where narcotics were being sold, then no. He stayed in the car. Paul never tried to push his way around or influence anyone or anything like that.

"We went on hundreds of stakeouts together. But there was no quietness to it! It was always a laugh a minute. He was an endless source of fun. The guy was ... well, I guess I saw him in down moods, but never when anyone else was around. We were pretty close friends. I think his biggest problem was women. He just wanted to be with a lot of young girls and for the most part it never worked out. It seemed they got bored with him too soon and then someone else comes along and the next thing you know, they were gone. Maybe he suffered from depression. He wanted his wives to be young but to be almost like a caregiver. He would start off strong—take them to Europe or something, but after six months it changed. That fast and free Hollywood life was only good for the first six months and then it was gone. Bring me a sandwich."

Tex and his Best Man. *Photo courtesy of Gail Teixeira.*

"I first met Paul through Al Teixeira," says Gail Teixeira. "I had gotten involved with the Marin Drug Task Force when my roommate turned me into the Juvenile Division of the Marin County Sheriff's Office. I was a very young 18 years old. Officers Chuck Prandi and Jeannette (soon to be Prandi also) interviewed me and threatened me with jail. They promised me that they would get me and my friends help in the form of counseling or whatever we needed to get clean if I helped them arrest the big dealers. Foolishly, I agreed. I started working undercover for one of the agents of the new Drug Task Force, not Tex.

"Paul enjoyed being involved with the drug officers and often did the makeup for some of the undercover work. The first time I remember meeting him was in the Sheriff's Office. He made an immediate impression, of course. Loud, funny, confident, clever. Always the center of attention. Surprisingly, I don't remember him being on actual raids or stake outs. But he may have been there.

"Eventually, my undercover work was complete and Al Teixeira (Tex) saved me from a difficult situation that resulted from my work. We

Gail and Tex's wedding.
Photos courtesy of Gail Teixeira.

began dating and eventually were married. Paul was our Best Man. He was single when Tex and I got married and he told me that if Tex didn't show up, he (Paul) would marry me. He was probably kidding, but I was still surprised that he would even think of it. He was 30 years older than me and we were friends and cared for each other, but certainly not like a husband and wife should. I think he was just lonely and liked having a young girl to show off. I was only 21 and still believed that you married someone because you were deeply in love. But I think Paul had gotten to the point where he took a more casual view of marriage. Luckily, Tex showed up.

"I remember that we were not able to put our wedding in the newspaper as an announcement before the ceremony because there were so many police and VIP's there. They were especially concerned about the narcotics officers. We spent part of our honeymoon at Paul's home in LA, visiting the set of Bonanza where his good friend,

Lorne Greene, was working. I remember Lorne telling Paul that he envied him for doing voice work for which Paul made more money for an hour's worth of work than Lorne made for days on set. That trip may have been when we went to a recording session with Paul. He did three or four different voices as if these people were having a conversation. It was so weird to see such different voices coming out of the same mouth.

Paul visits Lorene Greene on the Bonanza set.
Photo courtesy of Gail Teixeira.

"Paul lived in a different world than I did. His life was full of going out to restaurants, 'commuting' to LA, celebrities and lots of money. I was a working career woman, wife and step mother. I was happy with work, cooking, cleaning and spending time with Tex and his sons fishing, water skiing and playing. It was always a special occasion to be with

Paul. It was always fun and entertaining and you could count on unexpected and delightful things happening. One time we were in a department store and found him having a long conversation with a manikin. He was very upset that the manikin was so rude as to not answer him! But his reality was not something I was comfortable living in all the time. I went shopping with his last wife, Bev, one time. When we were ready to leave to go shopping, she asked him for some cash. He handed her about $500 and she said that wasn't enough. He handed her more—I think another $500. He

A toast! *Photo courtesy of Gail Teixeira.*

didn't seem happy about the amount of money, but she wasn't bothered. Remember, this was the early '70s. That was probably more than I made in a month and Bev was going to spend this on bed linens. We went to a store and she picked out some beautiful lacy linens and then saw some gold-rimmed wine glasses. She told the clerk to pack up a set and told me I should get some. I told her that she didn't understand that one of those glasses cost more than my entire monthly budget for food. She looked stunned that anyone lived like that. She had told me that her mother raised her to marry a rich man and she had been successful. But I do believe she really cared for Paul. Being married to Paul would have been difficult and exhausting and she did a good job of taking care of him for many years. I didn't envy her.

"I didn't see them much after Tex and I got divorced, but Tex would keep me informed about them. I worried about Paul. He seemed so unhappy and I just didn't understand why. My opinion was that he really

Paul at the wedding. *Photo courtesy of Gail Teixeira.*

wanted and needed to be loved. For himself. Not for his celebrity and certainly not for his money. Most people around him were attracted by that and loved to brag about being his friend. But few of these people would have been around if he wasn't rich and famous. And he didn't know how to recognize the people who really cared and those who didn't. So he put up road blocks to really getting to know him. If you were talking to him, he might suddenly be Peter Lorre or Ludwig Von Drake. It was hard to know when it was him and when it was a show. I remember one time he told me that he had been everywhere and done everything that he wanted to do. He was still in his 50's when he said this! I thought it was one of saddest things I had ever heard and couldn't understand why he couldn't see how much was still out there for him. It was a tragedy for such a good man to be so unhappy."

Every time Paul found himself alone and between relationships, he would call up the one woman he continued to count as a friend.

Joy Terry Frees: "He would call me in between the wives and come over and cry. And I kept asking him, 'Why do you keep getting married?' He gave me the Welles voice and said, 'Well, you know I can't be alone.'

"During that period in time he started changing, as all of us do. He became a narcotics agent. He used to go out on stakeouts; the man was walking around with two guns. It was kind of silly. I think he enjoyed the chase and the drama of it. He made a tremendous amount of money, and the work of making money was very easy for him, so he had a lot of time on his hands."

Carl Hixon, for whom Frees would do many commercials, vividly remembered those times. "I still have the card he gave me when he asked me to join the raids: International Narcotics Enforcement Officers Association, 1969. One story Paul told me about was that the narcotics squad had set up a sort of trap for various buyers of drugs and it was supposed to be taking place in a house someplace in the country. Paul was to sit outside in the porch of this place and if a car pulled up, Paul had a little mike of some kind and he would say, 'Here they come' or whatever. One time, a car drove almost up to the porch and these guys jumped out, and they saw Paul muttering into this thing in his lapel, and the man said, 'Who the hell you talking to?' He said, 'I'm talking to God,' and they all went in. They thought that was all very funny, until they were busted.

"He had an ego so big he couldn't get it through the door. He dressed so well it was almost foppish, like a late 19th century English gentleman. He had a Silver Ghost Rolls-Royce for a long time, impeccably restored, period about 1932. And a black chauffeur. He used to pick me up in this thing. He had a snub nose revolver, probably a .38, in a holster, and then he had a back-up gun, a barrette, stuffed down the back of his pants. I saw them on the raids.

"I gave him a lot of work. But you could never get Frees off the phone. If I would call him, I'd try to say goodbye about seven or eight times and he would just talk right through it. Finally I'd have to say, 'Paul, I'm hanging up!' and bang the phone down. He was exhausting. If you spent a day with him, you were tired, because he never stopped talking. He was at *all* times trying to make you laugh, from minute to minute.

"Jeri was quite young, in her 20s, a smallish blonde, cute, but not beautiful. When she threw Paul over and went to live with some other guy, he was desolated by it for a long time. Under all of his charm and his humor he wasn't happy."

"He confided everything to me," says Joy Terry Frees. "Through a series of adventures and misadventures, we did get a divorce, after we were married about eleven years. But it didn't affect Fred. The door was always open to him, he could come and go as he wanted."

As Fred grew, however, tension had grown between the two that widened as the years went on.

"It was bad enough that I had to bounce between my mother and my father, only getting to see him two weekends a month. But when I was fifteen (when I was spending a semester away at a Michi-

gan boarding school), my mother coerced me to return to Los Angeles and appear in a court battle between my mom and Dad. I didn't want to do it, and I specifically asked if this would hurt my dad. But my mother and her attorney insisted that it wouldn't. They lied.

"When Dad came walking down the courtroom hall, he was ready for battle. But, when he saw me sitting there, his entire expression changed. In the courtroom itself, I was only asked who paid for this, who paid for that. I wasn't asked to give any opinions about my mom or Dad either way. But, apparently, my appearance worked in favor of my mother's case and against my dad's. I was never told what the court dispute was actually about, but I'm sure it was mostly about money.

"Regardless, my father held it against me for the rest of his life. We didn't speak at all for three years after that. When I moved to the San Francisco area at age 19, we reconciled. The two years I spent up there was very good for the two of us. But, Dad would every so often mention what happened in the court, always reminding me that it hurt him. Just as he never really forgave me, so I never really forgave my mother.

"I hate to disenchant your image of a 'rich' father, but I grew up under the conditions resulting from the divorce settlement. Although Dad did occasionally buy me things, he felt that I was receiving enough money from child support and that it was up to my mother to provide for me. Money was a major contention in our family. It only caused resentment. Either way, I was never at the receiving end of my father's 'riches.' Nor did I want to be.

"Money was obviously important to Dad. But he did not *work* for the money. He worked because he loved what he did. He said that frequently. When he was offered huge dollar amounts for his services, he naturally agreed (if not, his agent would find that unacceptable), but he would say, 'They don't understand that I'd do it for free.' Of course, you can't survive if you actually worked for free, but those were his sentiments.

"As far as money and his family and people who surrounded him was concerned, he felt that his money was more important to them than he was. That's the downside to success. To follow up, he didn't invest his money wisely. He took bad advice. That's why he did not leave behind the amount of money people thought he had. He did not live or enjoy seeming cheap. I once looked in a telephone booth for a dime (when I was younger) and he got upset with me. I never told him I like clipping coupons!

"He was an immaculate dresser. He had dozens of tailor-made, double-breasted suits with matching ties and ascots. He never wore shoes. He had dozens and dozens of Italian-style boots (ankle high). I don't know why or when he started wearing them, but I think as he became more successful, regular shoes just didn't fit his image. He did wear shoes at first, of course, but the boots made him look taller. He also had a 'boot-buffer' machine. It had soft feathery things at either end (one red and one black) and it would spin around really fast. Those boots had to be polished! He had many colors, but I remember the brown ones the most—actually they were kind of reddish-brown.

"He had a hat collection (I don't know how that got started), but they were mostly for show; he didn't actually wear them, except for an occasional

With friends in the Department of Justice.

bowler. And yes, the hats were only shown to select visitors, especially the part when he would put on the hat and do a 'character.' He also had his fingernails professionally manicured. He was always a showcase when he went out. He would also sport a gold watch and chain.

"But at home, he usually wore one of his silk robes and not much underneath, with house slippers. I am the exact opposite. I've never manicured my nails. I don't like boots. I wear sneakers, jeans, and t-shirts. Suits and ties make me feel uncomfortable. Dad never liked the way I dressed, but I just couldn't dress the way he wanted me to. And it wasn't just looks. He wanted to see that the money he was sending my mother was being spent on my clothes. Sometimes I'd try to dress up, but I just didn't like it.

"He did have regular wristwatches, but you can bet they were expensive! He needed to know what time it was in order to get to his appointments on time. But he sported that pocket-watch only in his later years as I recall. He was stylish. I am not. I can't match anything. There was a time when he was between wives, and he seemed to fashion himself just fine."

Joy Terry Frees: "After we were divorced, he got himself a big Napoleon desk from France, and this thing was huge, with the red and the gold and the gilt, please! He used to sit behind there holding court."

His lifestyle merely reflected the amount of work he was receiving. When going along to jobs, Paul would always carry a chocolate bar around, to keep his energy up. He admitted that in television in the early '60s, "everything is so fast there isn't time to audition new voices, especially in commercial work. Thousands and thousands of dollars are spent on commercials that are often more expensive and fastidiously done than the shows they sponsor. So the work is usually given to the 'insurance policies,' the same four or five voice people each time. The secret is flexibility."

In 1968, Paul met another woman who would soon become important in his life. "I didn't even know who he was," says Joyce Post. "And actually I didn't know who he was for a long time or what seemed like a long time. I was working at the Marin County Sheriff's Department, working under Sheriff Louis Montanos. I had just gotten the job there. It was quite interesting. And I was 23, just a kid.

"I'd only been there two weeks, and I didn't know anybody. On this one particular day, Al Teixeira comes walking in with a prisoner, and my desk was about fifteen feet away from the booking desk. Now, this prisoner looked rather odd—he was a little short fat guy dressed very, very funny, in striped trousers with suspenders and red hair. I didn't know it was a wig. It was just odd. And this man is screaming and ranting and raving. So I just presumed he was a 5150, which in our code is a wacko. Tex is dragging this guy in front of my desk, and I don't know anything. They throw him in the padded cell which is right around the corner from me. I hear this man screaming and throwing himself up against the walls in the padded cell, and I'm thinking, 'Oh my God, he's a lunatic.'

"About ten minutes later, this odd person comes running past my desk; he's escaping. So I'm going nuts! I'm going, 'My God!' And the boys are after him. Well, then about ten minutes later, they come back in, and they're talking with this guy. Well, as a joke they'd thrown him in the padded cell, but they hadn't locked the door. They said, 'We were just playing a trick on Paul Frees, he's a friend of the sheriff, don't worry about it, no big deal. He helps us with undercover cases.' So that was sort of the end of that.

"I didn't think much of it until a few weeks later when Paul came in, dressed as he always did in his white suit, looking rather refined. I was getting ready to leave the office that day and was walking out, and he was talking with Tex and the boys, and Tex says, 'Oh I'd like to formally introduce you to the gangster that escaped from the padded cell.' I thought it was rather funny, so I was very cordial to him.

"Paul always liked to have a gorgeous woman on his arm; that was sort of his trademark, and at the time he was dating a girl, I can't remember her name, but the boys used to call her Paul's wind-up toy. I knew also that he had a home in Tiburon, and that he lived in LA, that he came up here and would play around with the boys. So he then asked who I was, blah, blah, blah. And he asked me if I'd like to come over to his house. So I kind of looked at the boys like, 'What *is* this guy? Who is he?' They said, 'Ah, he's harmless. Go on over.' I guess they were sort of trying to promote him having another young chickie. So that's how the relationship developed, and it developed into an incredible relationship. It started out rather crazy, and I did go over to dinner, still not really knowing if you're supposed to know who he was. To me he was just this man that I met.

"We had a lovely, lovely dinner. It was like being around a twelve-year-old. He served pink champagne with the salads, regular champagne with the dinner, and was actually a fabulous gourmet cook. He conjured up some fabulous little goodies you would find in a French restaurant. I mean, I was really impressed. And, of course, he was obviously trying to impress me. But at twenty-three, I was pretty impressionable.

"The house in Tiburon was kind of a shack hanging on the hill. Now Tiburon's a very, very lovely area in Marin. The property values just absolutely soared. If you're going to live in California, you want to live in Marin. But this was kind of a dumpy little two-bedroom house with a fabulous view of the city. He went on to remodel the house, and when he passed away it was simply gorgeous: five stories, beautiful, with an elevator. At the time, it was rather modest.

"After we met he had apparently decided to give up his wind-up toy. I can't remember her name, it was something silly like Trixie, and he started exclusively, or what appeared to be exclusively, seeing me when he'd come up from L.A., which was generally on the weekends. I never did see where he lived in L.A. He used to come up every weekend or every other weekend, and would spend the weekend with me. We became very close. I gradually learned from him and the stories that he told that he was, of course, the voice of the Pillsbury Doughboy. And that never really meant much to me until I really got to know him, then I would ask. He's constantly on television, on all the commercials.

"He was very, very special to me. I've had a couple of really great loves in my life. But Paul was the love of my life. I mean, I absolutely idolized the man. I just idolized him. Oh, he was a character. When he played Boris Badenov, I mean that is just *him*, except of course, without all the meanness. He demanded a lot of attention in every respect, in his personal life, too. I think he was just trying to make up for the fact that he wasn't exactly Rock Hudson.

"Our relationship was hot and heavy, and I really know that he loved me. I was certainly smart, rather than being a wind-up toy. He told me that he really would have loved to have married me, but he didn't want to get involved with anyone who had a small child. In '68, I had a four-year-old, but he said that it would be okay to keep doing things the way we were on the weekends when he came up. So I settled for that. I really wasn't interested in getting married. Why would I want to be married? I'm self-supporting, I come from a very good family in the county.

"He was very, very demanding. I was staying with him at his place on the weekends. I came home one weekend and he and I had a tiff. I told him, 'You know, this is ridiculous.' And he screamed at me, 'You walk out that door, and I'll get married next week.' Of course, I took that as just another twelve-year-old stunt. But he went down to L.A. as he did when he left Tiburon, and he met Beverly, and he married her. That quickly. And he kind of threw it in my face, in that he took her to Rome or somewhere over there, I don't know, and he called the Department from Rome to tell the sheriff to line up a Justice of the Peace because he wanted to come back to the sheriff's department and be married by one of our judge friends. Of course, I was devastated.

"The part that he played in the police department, which is interesting, is that Sheriff Lou kind of liked to have Paul around because that made *him* important because he knew somebody that was important. And actually the impression I got was that everybody thought Paul was important. It was important to know Paul Frees because then you could tell everybody that you knew Paul Frees. I loved him because I loved him. Well, it would have bothered me if he had been a garbage man. They would let him tag along on these crazy capers. We used to call them capers. When they were trying to catch criminals, Paul would play the idiot clown-type person. They never gave him a gun, but he would actually go out on some really serious cases when the seriousness of the case warranted having someone around who really wasn't a law enforcement officer. But he added a lot of zest and a lot of life to the department. I mean he *really* did, and he thought he was a sheriff guy. I mean, as far as he was concerned, he was one of the boys.

"I think he was doing it for the adventure. I think his life was really, really boring in a lot of respects. I can only presume you've got that problem when everyone knows who you are, but no one knows who you are. We would go into restaurants, and I can recall that a waiter would come up and say, 'I think I know you. Do I not? That…*voice.*' So everyone knew, but no one knew. And he really liked the anonymity. But he was quite the showman whenever he met anyone new, it didn't take them long to know who he was. He wanted to make everyone know who he was. And I think that it was difficult trying to keep that anonymity of 'Who is that strange voice?' and on the other hand letting people know that he's accomplished something. He considered himself, and so do I, up there with Orson Welles. I mean, he was just the greatest.

"One caper I was told about was one of the times they actually shut down the Golden Gate bridge. The Department asked that the bridge be shut because they were after a suspect who they suspected was going to try to escape to San Francisco. It was a rather high-profile national case. I believe it was the William Penn Patrick case. And they brought Paul along on this thing. They finally determined this fellow was in San Francisco, upstairs in a high-rise apartment. They told Paul to stay down in the car, because when it came to the serious stuff, he really shouldn't be busting through doors. They parked in the garage, and left him with an unloaded revolver, which of course is worthless, and headed up in this elevator. When they get up to the apartment, they realize the suspect is not up there, so they're headed back to the elevator. Meanwhile, Frees is sitting in the car in the garage, and sees the suspect walk out of the elevator and head towards a vehicle. Not running. He's acting very cool and calm and is just walking over to a vehicle. Paul gets out of the car, and as the boys are getting out of the elevator, he starts singing the song, 'In My Merry Oldsmobile.' I wasn't there, of course, but I could just see him skipping like he would, 'In My Merry Oldsmobile.' The suspect was getting into an Oldsmobile, and of course was apprehended.

"Later on, the San Francisco police got involved and when Paul heard that the media was coming, he said, 'Where's the makeup? I've gotta look good.' Just like he had been responsible for the apprehension of this perpetrator. The boys would tell crazy stories like that, which I know got embellished immensely. I can see him, of course, down there with no revolver, getting out of his car, just plain as can be, just dancing and singing 'In My Merry Oldsmobile.' It was that type of thing that was just nuts about him. We'd go shopping and he'd sort of be doing a two-step or tap dancing or doing pirouettes in the aisle. I mean he was wacky, wacky, wonderful. I just adored him for it."

Fred Frees: "I'm afraid I can't tell you much about his police work, since his operations were always confidential, and I was never privy to any of it (and he hardly talked about it). But I chanced upon his disguise kit (a wooden box) one day and found various beards and mustaches. He did confess about the purpose of the disguises (undercover work—he mentioned 'international conspiracy' occasionally), but that was about it. Knowing his abilities, one can only imagine what 'personas' he adopted. He did mention pretending to be a German soldier when he was in Normandy in World War II when he was rescuing his buddies there, so 'disguising' himself was not something I found unbelievable."

"It wasn't really serious undercover work," says Joyce Post, "but it was. They did have him go out because he could disguise himself. As I said, he wasn't being paid. He was more like a charm for the sheriff's bracelet. He was fun to be around. He made anything hysterical, and he was fearless, completely fearless. I mean, he was never given the capacity to where he would ever be able to go out and actually arrest someone."

Dave Frees: "Paul carried his gun in a belt holster. When he was working for the sheriff's office of Tiburon, I forget what rank he was, one time they were on a drug raid. He pulled out his pistol and held it on this one guy, but he had also pulled the holster off so he was pointing the gun in the holster at the guy."

But not even Joyce knows anything of Paul's work for the Department of Justice. She had seen the badge and ID card, but it was an area of his life that Frees would not talk about. He did have identifying business cards made up, however, which stated: "US Department of Justice, Washington DC. Paul H. Frees. Special Assistant to the Director. Bureau of Narcotics and Dangerous Drugs. Los Angeles, Calif. 213-688-2650." Found among his papers after his death was a bound copy of "A Primary Course in Narcotic Investigation, Presented by Marin County Drug Abuse Bureau," which gave the history, effects and hiding techniques of drugs. The introductory statement to the heavy reading easily explains why he kept mum about it for more than twenty years.

"The information contained in this text is exclusive to members of law enforcement. Officers' friends, families and teenage children are not privy to its contents. We must protect our knowledge and investigation techniques from delusion so that they will remain effective."

In 1967 Paul began a four-year stint on Hanna-Barbera's *The Fantastic Four* as the voice of Ben Grimm/The Thing and others.

Fred Frees: "Without actually thinking about it, he would do voices or imitations when we were together, usually while watching TV. On the weekends I visited him, we usually went to the movies; he loved to see what other actors were doing. One time we walked into a crowded theatre, the movie [*King of Kings*] already in progress, and from the screen was the voice of Orson Welles. At the top of his lungs, my father exclaimed, 'Looks like Orson got a job!' I was somewhat embarrassed and slunk into my seat. He did things of that sort quite often, however, and I should have gotten used to it.

"He was also able to get whatever he wanted, whenever he wanted, or at least he seemed to be able to. One time, we were driving around late at night, and he wanted a box of popsicles, to soothe his throat. We drove by a Thrifty Drug Store, which was closed, but he pulled in front of it anyway. I said, 'They're closed, Dad. You can't get in.' Without saying anything, he got out of the car...went to the front door...a few minutes later, some lights came on...and he returned... with the popsicles.

"Dad was also a daredevil. When I was about ten (that would be 1963), he owned a dark-blue Corvette. He was living in the Hollywood Hills at that time, and he scared me to death...driving around those curves as fast as he could. Maybe that's why I tend to drive conservatively. Patrice once crashed the Corvette and had to have her mouth wired shut because she was so badly injured.

"When I was nineteen, I moved to the Bay area and was able to visit him several times a week for the (almost) two years I was there. I stayed in a guest room, at whichever house he was living in at the time.

"He loved Italian food, and was fond of calamari. He always had a big breakfast, usually bialies, eggs, and I suppose coffee, though I don't remember him drinking a lot of it. I remember he made a great bouillabaisse, and recall him cooking things when I was around ten years old. But I don't remember him making anything in the 70's and 80's. Usually the wives did the cooking.

"We would go to 'hot spots' for breakfast or usually 'brunch,' such as Canter's, or Nate & Al's, or Art's Deli. We would go to places other actors tended to go to like Schwab's and Musso Frank's. I was fond of Diamond Jim's restaurant. He would often have humorous encounters with people he knew.

"One time, we were eating at Ah Fong's and Ross Martin and his family came in, and Dad called him over to our table. Dad immediately insisted that Ross 'Try this,' and he, holding chopsticks, would shove it in Ross's mouth. Then Dad said, 'You have to try this,' and stuffed another piece of food into Ross's mouth. It was pretty funny.

"I remember whenever Dad saw someone he recognized, which was often, he wouldn't remember their name...so he would quickly recite the alphabet, hoping to chance upon the name. For example, he would say, 'A—Alfred, Arnold...B—Bob, Bill, Burt...C—Chad, Curtis...,' etc. By that time, the person would come up to Dad and say 'Paul, good to see you,' or something like that, but Dad would not have finished his alphabet yet, and still wouldn't remember the name.

"He also liked to follow fire engines to the scene. I remember one time he approached a fire captain who initially tried to tell him he was not allowed; then Dad showed him some kind of identification and the captain saluted him and walked away.

"There was one thing I regretted not doing with Dad. During the time Dad was recording the Beatles cartoons, he brought back from England a special gift for me: two front-center-box tickets to see The Beatles at the Hollywood Bowl in 1965. Instead of inviting Dad, I invited my best friend to see them. In hindsight, my dad could probably have arranged for me to meet them, but at the time, I didn't think he'd want to actually sit through the screaming at a concert, especially since he already worked with them. Besides, I couldn't have lived my whole life having seen them without my friend being there, also (and he and I are still best friends). I know it's a selfish reason for something I regret my father and I didn't do together, but as I said, I don't feel that I 'missed out' on doing anything with my father. Being with him was all that mattered.

"In later years, we would just stay home and watch TV. Of course, in Tiburon he would play with his pet birds.

"He wasn't really into visiting relatives, but when he was still living in Los Angeles, we would occasionally visit Uncle Dave. Usually, the other family members would be visiting there also, and that's when I'd see my other uncle (Manny) and my Aunt Rose and various cousins.

"Of course, during voice sessions, Dad was always 'the life of the party.' One incident about his voices got me in trouble at school once. They used to have 'what do your parents do?' day at school. So I naturally said that my father is the voice of so and so, and so and so, and that he was on Saturday mornings on channels 2, 4, and 7 simultaneously. No one believed me and I was even called 'a liar.' I remember Dad coming down to the school to prove I wasn't lying (talk about reluctantly doing voices!). But I was never called a liar again after that.

"He never went out of his way to hear himself performing. However, I always got a kick out of his Disney attractions, when I went there on other occasions, especially the Haunted Mansion and the now-closed Monsanto ride. To him, acting was his profession. He never showed much interest in any job, once the job was over. He may have secretly enjoyed hearing himself, but he never publicly showed it, and I never knew him to go out of his way to hear something that he had done. He definitely lived to work. He loved his profession. He loved doing the best job he could do, which always turned out better than planned.

"I don't recall him turning down a job, but he may have felt certain jobs didn't pay enough or were beneath him. I know he was supposed to be the voice of H.A.L. in *2001: A Space Odyssey*, but he was already doing the voice of the computer in *Colossus: The Forbin Project*."

His main meat and potatoes continued to be the ever-rich field of commercial voice-over work. Ron Boltz, a fellow "voice," remembered Paul vividly: "Paul was an extremely big talent. Really amazing. But he was short, and he had a complex about this. One time, he was giving his readings, but it wasn't the way the producer wanted it. It was the way Paul felt it should be read. And he knew Paul had a Napoleonic complex, and knew that if he said anything, the session would be over. But he took a chance and said, 'Now, Paul, what I need—is a tall reading.' And that ended the session! With that, Paul closed up his copy and walked out.

"I was going into a recording session at Coast Recorders in San Francisco and he was working at Coast that same day in another studio. Both our sessions had been delayed for whatever reason, so I had a chance to talk to him. To me, this was a thrill, because I always had Paul on a pedestal. We talked. I remarked that he was known nationally. 'Nationally, Ron? Ron, I'm known… *inter*nationally!' He went on to say what he'd done for other countries. Then toward the end of the conversation, I wanted his card because I wanted to send him something, thanking him for his time, so I asked him for his business card. 'Card? Ron! Why do I need a card? The world knows what I do.' Well, there I put my foot in it again."

In the press, Frees' fees for commercial recording sessions fluctuated, depending on who was reporting it. In 1967 one paper claimed his scale for a two-hour recording session for ads was $123, which is incredibly low compared to other reports. That same notice suggested that he would have two vocal roles in the new *Wonder Woman: Who's Afraid of Diana Prince* TV pilot, as FDR and Westbrook Van Voorhis.

Possibly the weirdest film Paul was ever involved with was narrating bits throughout *Wild in the Streets*, a cheaply-made, yet epic fantasy-satire from 1968. Nominated for a single Oscar (for Best Film Editing), this very 1960s-conscious movie contained not only good pop songs of the era, but an uncanny ability to laugh at itself *and* try for a large dose of *very* political comedy at the same time. The plot involved pop star Max Frost (Christopher Jones) who rises from being an abused child (basically terrorized by mother Shelley Winters) to, ultimately, President of the United States. He uses his love of youth to forge a new world, one in which youth (meaning those under thirty years old) is applauded and credited for being 'real' and being the only important definition of character. All 'old' people are eventually rounded up into camps and force-fed LSD. The young people of the world start the motions going to abolish war and hunger—by getting rid of the Army, the FBI, CIA, etc.—but in doing so, the groundwork is laid for hatred by the even younger set: those under ten years old.

The film cost a million dollars to make, though the look of it was rather inexpensive and relied heavily on stock shots of masses of teenagers. Released on May 29th, it grossed a whopping $10 million at the box office. Paul didn't have much to do, but there were more than just a few lines of his scattered throughout this incredible and incredulous movie.

Back to cartoondom, Frees became "Evil Vangore" in "The Arabian Knights" cartoon portion of the manic Hanna-Barbera animation/live-action TV series, *The Banana Splits Adventure Hour.* Sponsored by Kellogg's Cereals, the series ran for two years (1968-70), alternating cartoons with a lot of men in furry suits running around the live-action sequences.

Frees, along with Jim MacGeorge, Irv Shoemaker and others, also supplied voices for the cartoon version of Bob Clampett's classic puppet series, *Beany and Cecil.* Also known as *Matty's Funnies with Beany and Cecil,* the series ran from 1962 to 1968, telling of the adventurous smiling little Beany and his pet sea serpent, Cecil. The scripts were clever, but even today many view it as a pale imitation to Daws Butler & Stan Freberg's original puppet show of the 1950s.

The Mouse on the Mayflower was another enchanting one-hour cartoon from Rankin/Bass, narrated by William Mouse (Tennessee Ernie Ford), the first rodent to set foot on Plymouth Rock after that horrendous (yet, fun and musical!) 1620 voyage. Eddie Albert spoke as Miles Standish, John Gary as John Alden, Joanie Sommers as Priscilla Mullens, and June Foray as Mistress Blake. The Thanksgiving special, which debuted on November 23, 1968, told of the hardships and hurrahs of settling the colony and making friends with Indians (mouse Indians, too). Frees was a ship's captain again, greedy Captain Jones, as well as his own dire seamen, Quizzler and Scurv who plan to steal from the Captain the gold that has financed the Pilgrims' voyage. Once they land at Plymouth Rock and begin exploring, Paul is also heard as Smiling Buzzard, the only bad Indian in the bunch.

His last credit for 1968 was the popular TV special, *The Little Drummer Boy,* again made by Rankin/Bass. Sponsored by the U.S. Natural Gas Association, the half-hour Animagic production premiered on NBC on December 19th. It was the touching story of the orphan Aaron (voiced by Teddy Eccles) who is kidnapped by Haramed (Jose Ferrer) and made a slave member of a band of musicians. All Aaron had in the world was his camel, which was sold by Haramed. After escaping with the aid of two animal friends, Aaron journeys to Bethlehem to save his friend. He arrives at Jesus' manger and gives the gift of a song. It was a touching half-hour story narrated by the soothing voice of Greer Garson. The Vienna Boys' Choir joined in the music, while Frees voiced Haramed's henchman Ali, one of the Kings there to see the baby Jesus, and several other characters. So successful was this special, that it prompted a sequel in 1976, also narrated by Ms. Garson.

When Hanna-Barbera launched their ambitious NBC series, *The New Adventures of Huck Finn*, combining live-action and animation, top voices like Don Messick, Janet Waldo, Hal Smith, Paul Frees and others were called in for the cartoon segments. Mark Twain's classic book had been turned into a dramatic version of *Peabody's Improbable History*, with protagonists Huck Finn (Michael Shea) and Tom Sawyer (Kevin Schultz) chased through time by evil Injun Joe (Ted Cassidy, who also provided his voice in the animated portions) in revenge for their testifying at his murder trial. The prime-time series collected bad blood from reviewers who thought its wholesale tinkering with Twain's original story was sacrilege and that it might keep many kids from reading the thick book. The *Adventures* lasted a mere twenty weeks, opposite ABC's *Land of the Giants*, broadcast from September 15, 1968 through September 7, 1969.

Also that year, Frees, June Foray, Bill Scott and Daws Butler climbed aboard the *Hawkear: Frontier Scout* pilot, made for Jay Ward. In the 19th century North Woods, scout Hawkear, possessing super-hearing, is assigned to track down a long-lost baby, and ends up causing the first Indian uprising in thirty years. Daws Butler put on a brilliant Gary Cooper impression as the scout, with able assistance from Frees as narrator, Commander and an Indian Chief. Unfortunately the cartoon series did not sell.

Next, he breathed life into the opening narration to the TV series *The Immortal*. "This man has a singular advantage over other men." Ben Richards, The Immortal, was immune to every known disease and old age. A transfusion of his blood could give others another chance at life—and a longer life. Because of this, he is valuable, very valuable, and so "he runs from the human hounds who would cage him," says Frees over the credits. The pilot was broadcast on September 30, 1969, but the series itself didn't begin until September 24, 1970. The hour-long series lasted only a single season (16 episodes total) on ABC and starred Christopher George. This clone of *The Fugitive* was probably too fanciful for the average viewer. As *Variety*'s review stated, *The Immortal* may have antibodies immune to disease and dying, "but it is very doubtful they can save him from dying of incredibility before another TV season."

He put his newsreel voice back on for a brief stint in the dream sequence of the Hollywood ego satire, *The Comic*, starring Dick Van Dyke. His slightly nasally, pompous vocal was an interesting if over-the-top performance in an over-the-top sequence as he related how tough the world was taking the death of Billy Bright. "Speaking for myself, I know it will be difficult to ever smile—again."

On December 19, 1969 Paul had one of his biggest Rankin/Bass hits broadcast on CBS. The half-hour Frosty the Snowman was narrated by big-nosed Jimmy Durante and was one of the most often repeated Christmas cartoons ever made. With a little embellishing from regular writer Romeo Muller, the story followed the famous song by Jack Rollins and Steve Nelson, sung here by Durante. What brought the snowman to life was a magic hat owned by an unsuccessful magician, Professor Hinkle, voiced by Billy De Wolfe. Jackie Vernon gave voice to the lovable song-and-dance snow guy. Little Karen (originally voiced by June Foray, but later replaced) helped Frosty get to the North Pole, so he would never melt, in spite of the treachery laid upon them by Hinkle to reclaim his working hat. The villain ultimately locks Frosty and Karen in a greenhouse (yes, at the North Pole), turning the jolly snowman into a puddle of water. Luckily, Santa Claus (Paul Frees, of course) arrives and, because he was made with Christmas snow, is able to bring Frosty back to life. Santa promises Hinkle a new hat if he mends his evil ways, and everyone sings a cheery "Happy Birthday" before Karen is flown back home on Santa's sleigh. The show was a delight and is still counted among the five most successful Christmas specials ever made for television.

Burgermeister Meisterburger
The 1970s

THE 1970S BEGAN MUSICALLY. *Paul Frees and the Poster People* (MGM Records), a novelty album of modern pop songs 'sung' in impersonated voices, was released in the fall of 1970. One of the funniest of the bunch had Frees talking through an extended version of Three Dog Night's classic "Mama Told Me Not to Come" (in the persona of W.C. Fields), with unaltered lyrics that sounded as if they'd been written for the comic himself. It was released as a single, and was the first track on the record:

Side 1:
Mama Told Me Not To Come – The voice of W.C. Fields
Raindrops Keep Fallin' On My Head – The voice of Humphrey
    Bogart
Let It Be – The voice of Warner Oland in the character of Charlie
    Chan
The Look of Love – The voice of Boris Karloff
Sugar Sugar – The voice of Sydney Greenstreet

Side 2:
Hey Jude – The voice of Peter Lorre
By The Time I Get To Phoenix – The voice of Clark Gable
Games People Play – The voice of Bela Lugosi
Up Up and Away – The voice of Ed Wynn
Everything Is Beautiful – All of the voices

The lavish production was a brilliant arrangement of then-popular songs, with Frees invariably staying pretty close to the original lyrics, but with more than occasional asides in character. As Peter Lorre spooking

"Hey, Jude," he holds it together pretty well until the chorus comes in, though he does admit early on, "I'm knitting a straight jacket for my sweetheart." Once the chorus begins the "na na na na" part, Lorre goes *crazy*, shouting oddities over the music for the remaining minute. "Why do I call you Jude when your name is Seymour?"

Without advance warning to reviewers, *Poster People* arrived unheralded in the mail. *The LA Times*, which ran an article on the weird little record on November 28, 1970, was at once enamored. "Sheathed in a jacket so nondescript it was almost given away unplayed to a friend, the album turns out to be a serendipter's delight, an unsung sugarplum you'd almost swear Santa dropped off in advance."

It also praised the spontaneity of the session, calling it "an unforgettable piece of listening," as well as musical director Artie Butler's arrangements that "would do justice to any pop singer on today's charts." But the best part seemed to be Frees' large talent "that makes you forget, for a moment or two, that all those great ones have gone."

"They really didn't give me much time," Paul said after its release. "The music tracks were already on tape when I got to the studio. So I had

to wing each of the cuts right then and there. It was lucky that I'd been doing all those people for years. It was all my agent, Charlie Stern's idea. He called Mike Curb of MGM and sold him the notion in two sentences. The next thing I knew, I was cutting the album."

Artie Butler remembered one other character on the album: Paul Frees. "I first met Paul between 1967 and '68 through Charlie Stern's office. Through the years Paul would call me sometimes in the voice of a character and ask for somebody else. It would break me up because I truly never knew who it was. There was one time he called and said, 'This is the Pillsbury Doughboy,' and I remember just cracking up. As a joke, he would leave Clark Gable on my answering machine, things like that. The thing that is so sad is - whoever thought to keep those messages, you know? Through him I had Ed Wynn calling me, Boris Karloff telling me jokes. He was really a wonderful, kind guy because he did it all. When I went through Disneyland I realized how much of it was Paul Frees!"

There was more to Frees' input on the album, however, than just winging it. Butler: "When we did *Poster People*, he came to my house for a couple of creative meetings before I started writing, to get his keys and whatnot. We'd be rehearsing and he would switch from one character to another in the middle of a sentence. He truly, continually knocked me out. And he would have arguments between the characters. It was really too much. I'd say his Clark Gable was the best. His Ed Wynn was exceptional. Everyone does Boris Karloff or Louis Armstrong, but he'd do people that just aren't done that often.

"Charlie Stern and I picked what songs to do, but Paul decided which characters felt comfortable. Our meetings lasted a couple of hours. Since he knew his characters so well, there wasn't need for a lot of adjustment time. I'd give him the basic format of the song on piano, and made him a temp tape that he could take with him and practice with. When he got to the studio, it was practically second nature to him.

"I remember when we did the sessions, we just laid down the music tracks. He came in to overdub them later, and I remember the people in the control room just freaking out, cracking up.

"One time Paul, Charlie Stern and I went out to lunch, and as Paul ordered, he'd change into several characters. I don't know if the waiter knew who all these voices were, but he was in shock that it was happening. And the people at the next table were hysterical."

The album was a hit with fans and is still fondly remembered. Paul enjoyed doing the impersonations, his favorite being Clark Gable reciting "By the Time I Get To Phoenix." Paul: "I really try to recreate rather than impersonate. You know, sometimes when I'm talking to someone about this album, I'll catch myself saying something like, 'Listen to that. Gable sings it just as if Jimmy Webb wrote it for him.'"

To promote the album, Paul appeared on several radio shows, including an October, 1970 *Gary Owens Show* on KMPC in Los Angeles.

Around 1963 while Owens was working on *The Nut House*, a zany pre-*Laugh-In*-type show for Jay Ward, he met Paul. "He was very nice to me. A lot of people didn't understand that a lot of his talk was a put-on. He'd say, 'Well, I was a famous opera singer at the time' and people would believe it. He just kind of put people off by these grand claims.

"When not working, Paul would drive his Rolls-Royce to the unemployment office to pick up his check. After all, when you're freelancing, you may make a hundred thousand dollars one week, but the next week nothing. That's why he was such a character. He was like something out of *The Great Gatsby*, or the Algonquin Hotel in New York. He was very bright. I'd see him once a week when we were doing commercials."

Paul told Gary the secret to his mounting commercial credits. "For the Pillsbury Doughboy, sometimes I'll go in and throw tags on maybe fifteen, twenty of them, so you're really doing twenty of them in one half hour session. I'll do between 1200 and 1500 commercials a year at that rate."

On Owens' show, the two did a hilarious brief bit together where Owens interviews Frees as the underwater man—the last remaining U-Boat commander—in gargly German accent. They made a great comedy team, trading unpronounceable names and snickering all the way. When Gary interrupted Paul before taking a commercial, he said, "Here's something you can sink your teeth into - a glass of water." It gave Paul the giggles. Paul later did a welcome to the show in his Queen

DOUGHBOY Logo ™ & ©
The Pillsbury Company.
Used with permission.

Mary voice (low, foghorn-like enunciation), and when Gary speaks to Dr. Ludwig (Frees), the Danish guest admits there is no Paul Frees. "Dere's just detached voices in the effluvium!" Owens' own absurd humor is perfect when he requests listeners to return after the news when Paul Frees will imitate the entire city of Santa Monica.

It was a year of impressions. On April 7, 1970, Rankin/Bass' *The Mad, Mad, Mad Comedians* debuted on ABC. It was a half-hour cartoon, with animated caricatures conceived by Bruce Stark, and assembled an incredible wealth of classic comedy talent. Voicing their own animated caricatures were Jack Benny, George Burns, Groucho Marx, the Smothers Brothers (who sang two songs), George Jessel, Flip Wilson (as a campy Christopher Columbus), Phyllis Diller, Jack E. Leonard, and Henny Youngman. The only ones who did not appear as themselves were Chico and Harpo Marx, and W.C. Fields. These came from the Frees machine. Reminiscent of the *Laugh-In* formula, this fanciful comedy was a collection of sketches, expertly realized. In one scene, Groucho is Napoleon, putting up with Chico and Harpo running around with his girl, Josephine. Groucho was quite amazed at Frees' imitations of his brothers. Paul also worked as the cop in the skit in which Jack Benny and George Burns have to drive under the toll bridge after Jack resists the inflamed toll which had just been raised from 25 cents to 50 cents. Last and best comes Frees' W.C. Fields bit: stuck on a ski slope with his future mother-in-law (also Frees), ultimately the red-nosed humorist takes the liquor from underneath the St. Bernard's neck and replaces it with the poor woman herself.

Interestingly, according to Rankin, *Comedians* held the highest ratings they'd ever had for a special, even beating out their top child *Rudolph*, though coming on just before the 1970 Academy Awards didn't hurt. Yet, this amalgamation of comic talent has yet to see release in video or DVD format.

Joyce Post: "Paul was the only one who was authorized by the W.C. Fields estate to do the dubbing of any of the movies that W.C. did, if the voice needed to be inserted or corrected because it had deteriorated."

It was also around 1970 that Paul got to meet Elvis Presley at La Scala Restaurant on Santa Monica Boulevard, via The King's chief of security (and their mutual friend), John O'Grady. O'Grady claimed that Frees had been involved with around 200 drug raids in Marin County, and sometimes he would throw detainees in the back of Paul's Rolls-Royce to cart them off to the station (though Fred Frees does not remember Paul having the Rolls in Tiburon). It was Frees' work for the Bureau of Narcotics and Dangerous Drugs that claimed Elvis' attention, not the voice credits. The two were soulmates in their dislike of the Beatles and "other drug users" in the rock world. After performing an array of voices, at Presley's request, Frees showed the hit-maker his flat leather wallet out of which flipped his official ID card for the Department of Justice, with its official seal and insignia of the Bureau of Narcotics and Dangerous Drugs. Along with photo, fingerprints and vital statistics, it displayed "Agent At Large" to the *very* impressed singer. Elvis, passionate about police work, had collected badges from various police stations, but this was the pinnacle.

For a guy who reportedly did *not* like pop/rock music, Paul Frees found his name linked to many top acts in the field. In 1971 he gave his voice to *The Jackson Five Show*, starring, of course, The Jackson Five, another Rankin/Bass vehicle. This time, a TV series. The Jack Davis (of *Mad Magazine* fame) art of the series graced the covers of *Ebony* and *Creem* magazines and was even used in The Jackson Five's tour programs for 1971. The series ran from September 11, 1971 to September 1, 1973 over one season's worth of 23 episodes, then was rigorously syndicated after Michael Jackson's *Thriller* album became such a huge seller. Paul Frees, Edmund

Silvers, Joel Cooper and others supported the Five who sang two songs per week within their slight plots. The series used a laugh track and grooved its opening credits over the band's biggest hit, "ABC."

Just one season later, on September 9, 1972, *The Osmonds* began its two-year run for Rankin/Bass, with Frees in the role of talking dog Fugi, a Japanese Akita, who accompanied the white version of The Jackson Five as they toured the country as goodwill ambassadors for the United States Music Community. The bellbottoms, flared shirts and psychedelic plane dated the series enough to stop a true resurgence of reruns, but it was quite popular on first broadcast, though only seventeen half-hour shows were made by the Halas & Batchelor Animation team in London. Like *The Jackson Five Show*, songs were sung in each episode, canned laughter was used, and the Osmond brothers (Alan, Wayne, Merrill, Jay, Donny and Jimmy) provided their own voices, supported often by Iris Rainer and Paul Frees.

Independent-International Pictures' *amazing* 1970 film *Horror of the Blood Monsters* starred John Carradine and Robert Dix, and was produced and directed by Al Adamson. Using much footage from the Filipino film *Tagani* (1965), its over-the-top credits, music and breathy vampire narration make one wonder if this terrible film is all a put-on. The plot involves a group of explorers, led by a doctor (Carradine), who has located another solar system beyond their own. But when they reach a planet there, they find it inhabited by prehistoric animals and people, and strange cave-dwelling vampires. Frees is first heard growling for most of the cavemen and vampires - must've been a fun gig. At the film's midway point, Paul's voice is heard almost constantly as the cavemen fight the dreaded blood-suckers. At times he sounds like a miniature Inspector Fenwick; for other characters, he speaks like a slow-thinking Hobbit.

This was also the year that Frees could officially claim his "Voice of God" nickname, having monotoned the bad guy computer voice in *Colussus: The Forbin Project*. Why Paul was chosen for something so ordinary and filtered is hard to say: he sounded much like any Cylon from *Battlestar Galactica*. Yet even within the heavy electronic distortion, the Frees intonation is clearly discernible. Paul's unseen but frightening role as the computer was unquestionably the lead character in this thriller. His use of stresses was the only variation he had on the monotone; quite a different piece of work than he would have accomplished as the voice of Hal in *2001*.

"Stan Kubrick," said Frees, "who was a friend of mine, and Jim Harris, wanted me to do Hal for *2001*. Unfortunately, I would've had to go to England and I couldn't get out of my contracts to leave for that long a time. I had to turn it down."

Colossus did not have a voice until the second hour of the film, but the dominating aspect of the super computer built by Dr. Charles Forbin (played by Eric Braeden, who later found steady fame in TV soaps) remained throughout the film as Colossus took the world hostage. It was built to prevent war, but suddenly the USSR was found to have created a similar being by the name of Guardian. Once Colossus and Guardian found each other, they slowly began to dictate to the world by threatening destruction whenever their demands were not met. Colossus requested Forbin to build him a voice, and Paul first introduced his electronic self with the words, "This is the voice of Colossus. This is the voice of Guardian." To the lazy ear, that last phrase can quite easily sound like "This is the voice of God."

Based upon the classic sci-fi novel by D.F. Jones, the movie was nominated for the prestigious Hugo award for Best Dramatic Presentation in 1971.

Frees had also been a part of the big award-winner of 1970. When *Patton* won Best Picture, Best Actor, and other Oscars, few knew that the uncredited Frees had been doing his bit in post-production, dubbing in about as many voices as he had in *Spartacus*. He could be heard as the Moroccan leader, as the voice reporting that Rommel has an earache, as a reporter while Patton trots in on a white horse, etc., etc.

Then came a Christmas classic.

One of Paul's most endearing and enduring Rankin/Bass specials originally aired for ABC on December 14, 1970. *Santa Claus Is Comin' to Town*, narrated by Fred Astaire, remains one of the most beloved of all Christmas shows. It told the origin of Kris Kringle, AKA Santa Claus (voiced by Mickey Rooney), how the legend became a reality, why presents were put in stockings, why the reindeer flew, and everything else. Frees literally played the heavy as the grouchy Burgermeister Meisterburger who had outlawed toys since he was always tripping over them. Not since Bullwinkle had Frees walked into such a villain-you-love-to-hate role, his booming German accent even singing the delightfully wicked "No More Toy Makers to the King."

With a brilliant script by Romeo Muller and memorable songs by J. Fred Coots & Haven Gillespie (title song) and Maury Laws & Jules Bass, the stop-motion Animagic puppet special delighted television audiences for

The Burgermeister and Santa: Paul Frees and Mickey Rooney.

the next 20+ years in reruns. A promotional soundtrack album was released the same year on the MGM label, who had also produced *Poster People*. Maury Laws called it his favorite of all the Christmas scores he did.

It was also Frees' favorite role for Rankin/Bass and the one to which he is most associated. At first he didn't realize that these specials would last more than the year for which they were made, but when they began to be repeated constantly, on top of all the *new* Rankin/Bass work he was doing,

Paul Frees and June Foray outside TV Recorders (for Jay Ward), Summer, 1971.
(*Keith Scott*)

that company quickly became one of Paul's favorites. Also, according to Frees, it was how he first met his last wife, Beverly Teresa Marlow, whom he married two weeks later in Rome on June 15, 1971. Her friend Arthur Rankin had arranged a first meeting for the two in the Polo Lounge at the Beverly Hills Hotel.

Paul claimed Rankin and Bass as two of his closest friends. Frees and Rankin's humor especially clicked. Rankin recalled one memorable *Santa Claus* session: "I walked into the studio one morning and waiting to work for me for the first time were Fred Astaire and his manager/agent Shep Fields. Shep Fields was formerly an orchestra leader during the big band era. His specialty was holding up a brandy glass with water and with a straw, he would blow into the glass and make bubbles. His act was billed as Shep Fields and his Rippling Rhythm, and of course this was an insane idea, but Shep Fields had a certain prominence, mostly as a joke. In his retirement he had become an agent. His brother Freddy owned the largest agency in Hollywood, and had set up Shep to be Fred Astaire's personal agent. He went everywhere with Fred, who was a very quiet, unassuming, cooperative gentleman.

"Fred Astaire had arrived early and was sitting there, waiting to be told what to do. The three of us are all sitting side by side in the control room as Paul Frees walks in. I said, 'Good morning, Paul, I'd like you to meet Shep Fields and Fred Astaire.' Paul walks down the line of chairs, passing the three of us and says out loud, 'Not *the* Shep Fields?'"

Vocally, Paul Frees was a part of everyone's Christmas. But his own was a different matter. Fred Frees: "As for the holidays, even though he worked on *Mr. Magoo's Christmas Carol* and *Frosty the Snowman*, for example, he didn't really celebrate them. Like I told you before, he was a member of the Church of Religious Science (considered a cult, really), but he didn't observe the standard holidays much. He seemed to live a rather secular life, but then, he didn't say much about it one way or the other. He never impressed or influenced me with any particular point of view. So I was on my own."

The *Lassie* satire, *Fang, the Wonder (?) Dog*, was made for Jay Ward in 1971, but failed to catch on as a cartoon series. Perhaps it was the publicity hook: "'Fangie,' the heartwarming story of a family and their rabid dog." The pilot saw Fang attempting to rescue Freddy and his Grampa Appleknocker from an abandoned mine shaft. Unfortunately, the pooch causes more harm than good, marooning police cars and fire trucks in the pit, and puts poor Grampa in the hospital at the end when Fang decides to get the family up with dynamite. Paul narrated, and lent voices to Pa Appleknocker and Policeman #2.

He could also be heard briefly singing "Darktown Strutter's Ball" as Al Jolson during the death of the man in the frog party mask in *The Abominable Dr. Phibes*. The eerie, camp horror flick starring Vincent Price as the brilliant lunatic organist Dr. Phibes was popular enough to spawn a sequel (and a remake, if you count *Theater of Blood*) the following year. But it was on the soundtrack record that Frees would have *much* more to do.

> *The Abominable Dr. Phibes* LP, 1971 (American International Records)
> Darktown Strutter's Ball (Paul Frees as Al Jolson)
> All I Do Is Dream Of You (Paul Frees as Chico Marx)
> Elmer's Tune (Paul Frees as Ben Bernie)
> Over the Rainbow (Paul Frees as Ronald Colman)
> Charmaine/Dr. Phibes Medley (Dr. Phibes Clockwork Wizards)
> Vulnavia (Dr. Phibes Clockwork Wizards)
> One for My Baby (Paul Frees as Humphrey Bogart)

The Abominable Dr. Phibes & Mr. Frees.

Charmaine (Dr. Phibes Clockwork Wizards)
You Stepped Out of a Dream (Paul Frees as Skinnay Ennis)
(What Can I Say) After I Say I'm Sorry (Paul Frees as W.C. Fields)
Dr. Phibes Theme (Dr. Phibes Clockwork Wizards)

He tackled a low Chico Marx impression with "Get-a you footsy-wootsy ice-a cream bahs here! Ha, ha!" before giving a broken Italian version of "All I Do Is Dream of You." The old-timey songs especially appealed to Paul's Tin Pan Alley side. "Yowsa, yowsa, yowsa. All you guys an' gals, it's the ol' maestro," he began in another filtered, talk-through-type track, exactly cloning vintage bandleader Ben Bernie. The songs appeared on the soundtrack recording, much to the chagrin of some listeners who expected merely the music *heard in the film*. As part of the Frees repertoire, however, it's hard not to be amused by his impression of Ronald Colman reciting "Somewhere Over the Rainbow" in true *If I Were King* fashion. In some ways the album was a "classic" sequel to *Poster People*, tongue against cheek and sticking out at Hollywood songs. His gravelly Humphrey Bogart version of "One for

My Baby" and its loser jazz sound was one of the better entries; a different arrangement of the song, sung by Scott Peters, was heard in the film.

Next, Paul lent voice to the French Police Commissioner on *The Pink Panther Show* until around 1978 (the cartoons featured were re-packaged DePatie-Freleng theatrical shorts). He also began a long stint as Toucan Sam for Kelloggs' Fruit Loops cereal commercials, regally enunciating his Ronald Colman again as the voice of the colorful bird.

He and June Foray appeared on TV's *Truth or Consequences* in 1971, hosted by an energetic Bob Barker. A lady picked out people from the audience to do imitations of Zsa Zsa Gabor, Humphrey Bogart, Mae West and Peter Lorre, the second of each done by a hidden Frees and Foray. Once their cover was blown the two were introduced on stage by Barker. Paul talked a little about his *Poster People* album, but the audience really came alive after they vocally disrobed as Rocky and Boris Badenov.

Here Comes Peter Cottontail was inspired by the hit song (popularized by Gene Autry), and premiered on ABC on April 4, 1971. The stop motion animation special was made by Rankin/Bass and based on the book, *The Easter Bunny That Overslept* by Priscilla and Otto Friedrich. The musical, narrated by Danny Kaye, did indeed concern the plot of what happened when the Easter Bunny overslept one year and couldn't deliver his eggs: Peter Cottontail (voiced by Casey Kasem, best-known as Shaggy in *Scooby-Doo*) and the sinister Irontail (Vincent Price) agreed to a contest to see who could give away the most Easter eggs. The winner would become Chief Easter Bunny. When Peter overslept, he was helped out by the top-hatted Seymour S. Sassafrass (Kaye) in his Yestermorrow mobile which took him through many years' holidays until he found good people who would take his eggs on St. Patrick's Day. Paul Frees again played Santa Claus at the Christmas stop, plus a few incidental voices on this sixty-minute special. Again, only a promotional soundtrack recording was released, on ABC Records.

1971's *The Point* was a musical special made for ABC that taught the sublime moral that being different was a *good* thing. Frees, in the role of a Father, told this story of prejudice to his Son, voiced by Michael Lookinland: Little Oblio (also Lookinland) was the first round-headed boy born in the Land of Point. The pointy-headed people exiled him to the Point-less Forest with his dog, Arrow. While there, he encountered characters such as the genial Rockman (voiced by Bill Martin), giant bees, and Frees again in the guise of Leafman, a tree in the leaf-selling business. The unusual fantasy taught Oblio that life did not have to be pointed, and that conformity was not necessarily a distinguished virtue. Called the first made-for-television animated movie in the United States, *The Point* spoke to many children who still remember it fondly to this day, including Sabrina Frees. The 74-minute feature premiered on February 2, 1971 and was brought back at least twice more, with Dustin Hoffman narrating the original, Alan Barzman narrating the 1974 rebroadcast, and Ringo Starr narrating the home video version in 1986. The songs were written by hit-songwriter Harry Nilsson, who also wrote the story (teleplay by Norman Lenzer).

At some point in the 1970s Frees ceased writing scripts and concentrated on voices—even at parties.

"Dad was always 'on' when socializing," says Fred Frees. "It is impossible to think of him at a social event and not entertaining everybody all the time. This is a strange contradiction when you consider that in private—like when I would have a friend over—he would hesitate to 'do voices' on request. I would usually have to badger him into it. Although, sometimes at home, he would just automatically be entertaining.

"As for celebrities, he did either socialize with them (since they were the people he knew personally) or he would be with his law-enforcement buddies, who were definitely not celebrities—although he probably considered them to be extra-special people. My dad did not like to congregate with 'the masses.' He even had a saying which he was very fond of, and repeated often: 'The masses are asses.'"

Paul could never go to a party—even those of high society—without always being asked to do voices. "Paul, can I poke you in the tummy and then do the giggle?" they would request of the Doughboy.

"He knew everybody and everybody knew him," says Helen Frees. "He could walk into a room and say, 'I'm Paul.' Everybody would be paying attention. He had a light within him and was fun to be with and would often make himself the butt of jokes. He would never hurt anybody—intentionally.

"I remember one time when we were invited by Paul to come to a film festival in Canada—in Montreal—and he took us to the most wonderful, and expensive, restaurant. He began to put on airs with the maître d and in a very loud voice he introduced me as a Countess! He was very unpredictable."

When Pete Duel, star of *Alias Smith and Jones* (a television version of the successful *Butch Cassidy and the Sundance Kid*), committed suicide on New Year's Eve, 1971, Paul was brought in a week later to dub Duel's

voice for some key scenes. He saved the show, until a replacement actor, Roger Davis, could be cast. "I'd never seen the show," admitted Frees. "They were left with bits and pieces of exteriors for about seven or eight segments. All they had were vocal tracks that they played for me, and I had to loop his voice for about six to eight segments. They said it came out frighteningly close." He was paid $1500 for approximately 120 loops for that one episode.

Reports from the same time period showed Frees' commercial accounts were fattening up. He was heard as Pittsburgh Paint's peacock, and the Little Valley Villager who asks the Jolly Green Giant "So what's new besides ho-ho-ho?" And, for who knows what project, he could also do perfect impressions of Lyndon Johnson and Senator Everett Dirksen.

Fred: "I *always* knew my dad no matter what voice he did. I always knew it was him. So did my mother. I suppose there was a recognizable tone or characteristic or inference to his vocal patterns that allowed me to discern that it was my dad, and not someone else. It just didn't matter who he was impersonating or whether I knew ahead of time if he had done a particular voice. He certainly never told me what he was doing all the time. It still didn't matter. I know the sound of my dad's voice no matter what. It amuses me when I hear people who are amazed at his range. I always took it for granted."

Frees worked with Bill Schallert on Raid and Jolly Green Giant commercials in the 1960s and 70s. Schallert remembered Paul as "fun, way talented and funny, and an ego maniac."

"I usually take a vacation for a week after a Raid session," Frees told an interviewer, "because it rips everything I have out of my voice." Among other characters, he would have to shout the "RRRRRRRRAAAIIDDD!!" in the cartoon commercials, before the bomb goes off killing every ugly little roach in sight.

"I get paid many different ways for each commercial I do," he told an interviewer, "including residuals for things I did many years ago. One of the union rules is that you get paid for each individual character you do. In one Green Giant commercial, each little farmer held up a sign that said 'Ho!' As a result, they were considered three different characters, and I was paid separately for each 'Ho!' in addition to the other voices I did for that commercial."

One report put union scale for his commercials at $102 for the first play and $50 for each play thereafter. Most of these would play about 75 times on national TV, and 1200 times on a host of local stations. For just the recording, Frees was paid $512 per network radio commercial. He was making more than $50,000 on his Pillsbury account alone.

"Why should I do on-camera work?" Frees asked in the early 1970s. "I'm having fun. There's nothing glamorous about sitting around a sound-stage with a bunch of electricians."

Engineer Bob Lindner: "That guy had a clock in his head. He would say, 'All right, how long does this one have to be?' I'd say, '4.6 seconds.' He would read it and say, 'What was it?' I'd say, '4.8.' The next time he'd do it, it would be 4.6 on the *nose*. Incredible. I've never seen anyone else approach that. I recorded Alexander Scourby one time, and he'd have to have a stopwatch in his hand to see where he was! Frees just had it down.

"I worked with him at Coast Recorders from around 1973 or '74 until he died. The way it would work usually was they would call Paul, or his agent would call him and say, 'Paul, I've got a session for you for Kellogg's on such and such a date,' and then the agent would call the studio and make the booking. Or, the agent would tell the client, Kellogg's or whoever it was, to call the studio. Paul didn't drive a lot - he wasn't real crazy about driving around, he'd much rather be driven - but he knew how to get to Coast which was an audio facility. We did basically sound-only things. In our first location, which was the first time I ever saw Paul and Bev, we were down on Folsom Street in a building that had American Zoetrope, Francis Coppola's company, upstairs. And Robert Duvall was coming in when they were cutting *THX 1138*. We did a lot of musical jingles. We did a lot of regular music sessions. A lot of stuff on the Concert Jazz label was recorded at Coast Recorders.

"Beverly came to a lot of the sessions early on with Paul. She was constantly on his arm. Pretty. A very pretty girl. He was proud to have her on his arm. She would sit in the control room. She kept her mouth shut. She didn't try to direct which sometimes wives will try to do, which was definitely the wrong thing to do in that situation. And, you know, I liked Bev, though her personality was never really given much of a chance when Paul was around because it was all Paul. It was his show, his act, and by God, he was not going to be eclipsed or shaded by anybody. Sometimes Paul would trade banter back and forth with other voice people in the sessions, but nobody ever upstaged Paul. Impossible. You couldn't do it."

Frees was infamous for his ability to joke through most of a session then get exactly the right spot done almost in real time. Here's a typical extract from a commercial session tape that would happen throughout a recording:

"Wanna buy some extra time? I told you I want to buy a tie, didn't I? Did I tell you I want to buy a tie? I didn't? Oh, the hell with this. We'll get back to this in a minute.

"A man is in the desert, and he's crawling, and his clothes are in shreds and tattered. His lips are cracked. His face is burned and blistered and torn. His fingernails, from crawling on the sand, are completely ripped apart. This man is on his very last moment. He gets to this tiny little ridge, and he doesn't even have the strength to pull himself over, so he just turns over in absolute defeat. The sun is burning down from this desert sky, and burning into him, and he knows his last moment's come.

"At that time, a figure of some kind blearily obscures part of the sun, and he tries to focus. Dimly, he sees a man in a blur with a black moustache and a beard. The man is looking down at him, and he looks at the man, 'Water. Wa-wa-wa-water…' The man looks at him and says, 'You wanna buy a tie?' 'What?' He says, 'You wanna buy a tie?' 'I've been five weeks out in the desert in the sun. I'm dying. Wa-water.' 'You don't wanna buy a tie? You don't wanna buy, all right. You want water? Why don't you go to the restaurant and get water? It's right over the hill.' Guy disappears, and he doesn't believe it.

"He turns back over and starts crawling with a renewed determination. Gets over the tiny little hill, and sure enough, there is the most elegant, beautiful, colonnaded restaurant with zipping lights, 'Open 24 Hours,' 'Good Eats,' everything in Arabic, of course. And he goes, with the last strength that he can summon, and lifts himself on his two feet. He starts walking, staggering, half-running toward the restaurant. He finally collapses at the front door. He picks himself up on these large, huge doors to the restaurant, and he pulls one open, and as he does, the *maitre de* is standing there in a tuxedo and he says, 'May I help you, sir? And he says, 'Wa…wa…water.' And the *maitre de* says, 'Well, I'm terribly sorry. I can't let you in without a tie.

"'Wanna buy a tie?' Isn't that cute?"

And again, during the same session:

"A reporter is interviewing W.C. Fields at his estate, and Mr. Fields is luxuriating out in his back garden on his wicker chair, as is customary. The reporter says, 'Mr. Fields, the world knows of your many accomplishments. Director. Writer. Juggler. Performer. But what the world would like to know is personal things. Do you have any hobbies or anything?' Fields [in voice] says, 'Yes, I have a hobby.' He says, 'You do, sir? What is it?' Fields says, 'I collect bees.' 'You - you collect bees? Well, sir, I've been all over your estate, you showed me your entire estate. I don't see any bees or beehives.' Fields says, 'Oh, no, no, no, I keep them in a cigar box.' 'You keep *bees* in a cigar box? How many bees do you have in your collection, sir?' 'Ah, last count there were 60,000, 70,000 bees.' 'You keep 70,000 bees in this little cigar box. Won't they suffocate and die?' 'Fuck 'em. It's only a hobby.'"

"There were a lot of wonderful things, a lot of childlike things about him," says Lindner. "The kid in Paul was very much alive. He was a very complex person, and I'll tell you, he was a very lonely person. Because of who he was and because of his nature, he wasn't the most social person in the world. He had one great buddy in town here, and here's somebody you should try to get hold of: Joe Scoma. Joe was his buddy, and after every session, he and Bev showed up. Paul was always dressed to the nines. He very often wore a white suit with a big gold chain and a huge gold watch in his front pocket.

"Now, the studio was not in the grooviest part of town. There was a big welfare office a couple doors down, and there were often some pretty shady characters hanging out on the street. It never gave him pause. Paul would march up there with Bev on his arm, also dressed to the nines, with glittering diamonds and all this gold displayed. He never had the tiniest smidgen of fear. Partly because he always had this little .22 Derringer. It was really a tiny little two-shot thing, and would fit easily in the palm of your hand. He just kept it in his pocket.

"He kept it because he knew he was a target. He was not a very tall man, and anybody who saw him walking down the street knew he was made of money. They knew he had a wallet full of cash, so, quite naturally, I think he was smart enough to try to protect himself a little bit. In his situation, I would have done the exact same thing. It's not my nature to be in any direction toward ostentatious, but he was flamboyant, let's say.

"The sessions didn't take very long because he was such a master. Sometimes it was a phone hookup, so the sponsors could hear what we were doing on the other side of the country. Or, most often, they would just send a script with timings on each line. He'd come in and rip through his lines, and then he and Bev would go off to Scoma's for lunch. That was his big deal after a session."

Scoma's Restaurant, located on Pier 47 in San Francisco, was Paul's favorite eating place for years. Started in 1965 by brothers Al and Joseph Scoma, the award-winning seafood restaurant still caters to nearly half a million patrons annually.

Al Scoma: "The stations all wanted to interview Paul, but he didn't want to do them, he was busy enough. But he said, 'Well, I'll give you an interview, if you give Scoma's a plug.'

"What a man he was. All those voices. He could do *anybody's* voice. One voice guy once called him the King of Voices and I told Paul that, to which he answered, 'He's right, you know. I am the *Emperor.*'

"He would come in two or three times a week, at *least.* He didn't drink much, but he liked *every* dish here. He was razor sharp. He had a comeback for everything. *Very* intelligent guy. We were good friends for ten or fifteen years until he died."

The San Francisco Chronicle ran an article on Frees on February 5, 1980 after an interview given at Scoma's. As pan-fried calamari was served, the conversation turned almost entirely to gourmet food. The reporter described Paul as "a smallish, sixtyish man with an RAF mustache, silver hair brushed forward to conceal a pate beginning to reflect rather too much of the light, and a gold chain and watch-fob securing a plaid vest girdling the round tummy."

"Life is a succession of dining tables and good restaurants to me," he told the reporter. "My ultimate dream of success? I want to eat in every fine restaurant in the Bay area."

He would lunch at a different restaurant every day of the week, often with his lawyer Nate Cohen, restaurant owner Al Scoma and sheriff Louis Mountanos. Apparently, he would also sometimes dine at Stefanino's off the Sunset Strip, frequently arriving for dinner in cape, top hat and medals, playing the role of someone called "Baron Obelesky." In Russian dialect, of course.

Recording a Cap'n Crunch spot. *(Keith Scott)*

On February 9, 1972 Paul recorded "a voice on the phone" for *Johnny Carson's Sun City Scandals '72* at NBC's Studio 4 in Burbank. The cast list included Bette Davis, Eddie Foy, Jr., Beatrice Kay, Jack Oakie, Gene Sheldon and Ethel Waters.

TV Guide ran an article on Frees and voice actors in their May 13, 1972 issue, reporting on two Cap'n Crunch commercials that he and Daws Butler did for producers Jay Ward and Bill Scott. Again, Frees kidded around for twenty minutes before doing his three stentorian announcer lines. Five minutes later he was finished, at which point Ward gave him a candy bar.

As of August of 1972 Paul was still setting up house in Tiburon. His small recording studio had not been completed yet, but he was still able to make demos and taped letters, occasionally to the fans who sought out his hidden presence. The getaway home was quickly becoming his haven from the rigors of Los Angeles and its non-stop schmoozing community, and was a major factor in his eventual retirement. Frees had begun assembling his castle years before, stocking it with antiques and expensive trinkets which glorified the make-over the builders were giving the dwelling. Ultimately, it was a work of art, which he slowly began not to want to leave.

Joyce Post's sister, Carol-Lynn Fletcher, was a frequent visitor to the Tiburon home many times in Frees' later life.

"As I recall, it was a five-story house with one or two rooms on each floor. The house was about twenty feet wide so all in all there wasn't much space for many rooms per floor. The top floor was Beverly's bedroom.

"The main floor (where you entered the house) had two doors, one by the kitchen and the front door that entered the living room. There was enough space to park two cars but just barely. The kitchen was at the back of the house (street side) and the living room was the view side. Beautiful view of Tiburon and other parts of the bay. There was a small deck that was glorious to enjoy the weather, the boats, the tourists, the peacefulness of the house and its location and the company. There were flowers in pots and comfy chairs.

"Paul loved Napoleonic-era furnishings and had some furniture from the Emperor himself. At least that is what he told me. He had a desk from that era that was very ornate, as you might imagine (black and gold), that he used more for display than a desk. The couch was very comfy with puffy pillows.

"The dining area was in the living room as well and there was an enormous stained glass above it from a 15th century church in Europe somewhere. He had it installed on the side of the house and also installed bulletproof glass in front of it so that nothing from the outside might damage it. Yikes, it was gorgeous! The ceiling was pretty high in that room.

Tiburon, California, 2009. Photo courtesy of Mayumi Ohmart.

"The third floor was my favorite. It was the dressing room and Paul's small studio. I *loved* that floor. The dressing room was cool with built-ins for the clothes but it was the small studio/office that I visited every time I went to the house. How small? Maybe 6x6 or 6x8, but I could always feel Paul's talent in there. As I recall, the room was partially padded for rehearsal purposes. I don't know if it was used for anything other than rehearsal. It had a mike and some small recording equipment, but nothing that would be mistaken for an actual professional studio.

"The fourth floor was the master bedroom with an aviary for Bubba and the other birds he kept. The bed faced the view and was the length of the house. Paul had an armoire that housed three TVs that he told me he would watch simultaneously so that he wouldn't miss anything. He was a voracious TV watcher. He had a closet made for videotapes that was next to the elevator. I loved that closet, too. It was built for videos and at that time (1986) that was a very cool thing. He had hundreds that he had recorded. As I recall, none were purchased. He had recorded all of them. He told me that whenever he went out he would have all the VCRs going so that he wouldn't miss anything. That set up was way cool to me because once VCRs came out I was so thrilled to have the option of seeing a show over and over. Paul and I had that in common, too. We would talk a lot about TV and the current season of shows, etc.

"The aviary was tiled and was longer rather than wider. It was the first time I had seen one in a house. And it had the best view on that floor. Paul kept the drapes pulled in the bedroom because he slept late and watched TV. There was a shade in the aviary but that was always open when I was in the bedroom.

"The bathroom was behind the bed (street side) and ran almost the length of the bedroom. I think it was mostly marble with two sinks and a separate toilet area. I think it had a separate shower and tub.

"The fifth floor was at the bottom of the house and it was a wine cellar that the elevator didn't go to. It had small windows and was like the basement but not as easy to get to. I had to climb a nicely built ladder, like a boat's gangway, but I don't think that Paul could make it down there anymore because it was steep.

"There was an elevator that was installed on the outside of the house that moved between four floors. It was slow but very useful. There were a lot of stairs as you might imagine, making the house, which hung on the side of a hill, quite long."

The goodies that filled it up were equally as majestic: a framed, leaded glass panel depicting a coat of arms; sixty bottles of Italian, Californian and French wine and champagne; a gilt-decorated regency design side chair in the bath area; and a Kenmore refrigerator in the closet, along with fourteen bottles of California wine, books (mostly novels), two porcelain steins, a Girrard turntable and a cast metal figurine of Shakespeare.

On the stairway, there were seven oil and acrylic paintings by Frees plus a "cast bust of a gentleman." In his office: a pair of white and red painted three-tier cabinets, a 19th century continental pewter stein, a "gentleman's jewelry box," a lovely contemporary, polychrome-decorated fall-front secretary, two televisions, an English marble pen/desk set, a folding director's chair, two regency design leather upholstered armchairs, several mugs (contemporary and 19th century), portable radios, tapes, tape recorders, a typewriter stand, a hand grenade, and other wonders. Upstairs was a Louis XV design leather surface salon table and marble top cabinet worth over a thousand dollars. He also kept a collection of a large number of St. Gordon's twenty-dollar gold coins, many Mexican fifty-pesos gold coins, and a European gold coin collection in a presentation book.

When asked why he didn't desert his home and go to Los Angeles more often for work, Frees raised his eyebrows and replied, "Leave paradise? I wouldn't leave here to live anywhere else in the world. And I've been everywhere, and seen a lot of things. Anybody who lives in this area should get down and kiss the earth at least ten times a day in gratitude for being able to live here."

For *The ABC Saturday Superstar Movie* on October 14, 1972 Paul voiced Iguana, a talking pet, in Rankin/Bass' sixty-minute cartoon, *Willie Mays and the Say-Hey Kid*. The social fantasy involved an eccentric angel granting Willie Mays' (voiced by himself) wish to catch a fly ball, thus winning the National League Pennant. In exchange, the baseball legend has to provide a home for the troubled orphan Veronica, who had been named his godchild without his knowledge, and her pet Iguana. Complications arise when, after inheriting a fortune, her real parents show up to claim the now-rich girl.

To the sound of eerie electronic music/sound effects Paul narrated Poe's "The Telltale Heart" for a radio broadcast on Halloween of 1972 (although what went to air was actually the recorded rehearsal, much to

PRESENTING *Paul Frees*

ANNOUNCER, NARRATOR, VOICE SPECIALIST, SINGER

THE PAUL FREES STORY:

Paul Frees, one of Hollywood's most respected talents, is noted for his work as a voice specialist with most of the major animation companies. He reigns as the heralded "King of Commercials," having been a consistent award winner at all the significant commercial film festivals. Paul also excells as a commercial Announcer-Spokesman, and his highly interpretative narrations have been responsible for great sales increases on the part of many sponsor's products.

Few people know of his singing abilities, but his very distinctive singing style has appeared on many best selling record albums and also in award winning television commercials. It would be safe to say that Paul Frees is truly one of the most versatile talents in our industry.

A demonstration tape is available upon request.

For further information, contact:

CHARLES H. STERN AGENCY   TAFT BUILDING
ARTISTS' MANAGER   HOLLYWOOD & VINE
HOLLYWOOD 28, CALIFORNIA
HOLLYWOOD 6-4304

"REPRESENTING LEADING TALENT FOR RADIO AND TELEVISION COMMERCIALS"

Frees' chagrin). He relished in the character of the murderer who questions his madness as he slowly turns to killing the old man with the eye of a vulture. The voice was one of the closest to his normal speaking voice, though the semi-confident, slightly surreal, pausing character was far removed from anything he'd done since *Suspense*'s demise.

The following year he looped Spanish-born Aldo Sambrell in *Shaft in Africa*, showed up on the car radio and in its end narrative in the violent *Dillinger*, and was reportedly set to narrate Mike Nichols' sleeper hit, *Day of the Dolphin*. Also, Hall Bartlett, director of *Jonathan Livingston Seagull*, sent Paul the script to his film to see if he'd like to be "the voice of Jonathan in Part 3." But Frees didn't care for the script.

In 1974 it was announced that Paul would narrate the "March of Time"-like opening to George Pal's final project, the feature film *Doc Savage: The Man of Bronze*, co-written by George Pal, Joe Morheim (who co-authored the novel *The Time Machine II* with Pal), and Kenneth Robeson (a pseudonym used by publishers Street & Smith). Unfortunately, Pal did not direct the weak film. Strangely, though Frees *did* narrate the feature, he did not do its trailer.

One trailer he did do was *The Milpitas Monster*, a sci-fi thriller about a monster created by pollution. "I had met Paul Frees," says special effects animator Stephen C. Wathen, "while animating commercials early in my animation career. I got involved in *The Milpitas Monster* while working locally as a graphic artist. When Tennessee Ernie Ford wouldn't let his original narration be used for a more extensive release of the film I immediately thought of getting Paul, to place it firmly in the B-movie sendup category. So I put Bob in touch with him, he liked the project and did a couple of versions of it (one more comedic and one straight—we used the straight one). I didn't know Frees well but he was generous with his time and liked a good laugh."

Director/writer Robert Burrill adds, "My students and I prepared a well written letter upon our Samuel Golden Ayer letterhead and submitted a formal request to Mr. Frees via Steve Wathen's lead to Coast Recorders. Mr. Frees liked our letter and the merit of our community-made film production and accepted our request to read and record our new narration for our Samuel Ayer High School Production which at that time had been optioned by producer William Thrush of Texas.

"Paul Frees knew a good title when he saw one, and 'The Milpitas Monster Movie Makers' appreciated hearing his comments and appreciation for 'our well written script' which was truly the work of talented David Boston of San Jose, CA. David's script was written with a classic Narration-Introduction, perfectly suited for Paul Frees, if not Tennessee Ernie Ford, who truly does narrate the first 16mm film version of *The Milpitas Monster* which premiered at the Serra Twin Theatres on May 21 1976.

"Looking back, we had time to add additional narration for a trailer since the opening and closing narration was no more than one minute. So with Paul Frees in mind, David wrote the words for a 15 sec., 30 sec and 60 second trailer. So along with the original script, we added a couple pages of trailer."

He could afford to be more particular these days as to his acting jobs. Just for voicing the Pittsburgh Paint Peacock, the Undeer in 7-Up, Fruit Loops, Shell Pest Strips, the new Pan American spot, and Ogg of Cocoa Crispies, the *San Francisco Chronicle* wrote that he was making $300,000 a year.

"You can't relax," Paul said at the time. "After all, you can't walk into an account that's spending a hundred million dollars a year and say, 'Gee, I'm kind of tired, guys, so this won't be my best.' You can't do that. It has to be perfect every time. But that's why—at least by the hour—I'm the highest paid person in the business today.

"People like Rich Little and Frank Gorshin are impressionists. I'm a duplicator. All I need to do is hear the voice once, and I have it."

He admitted that there were only four others with voices to match his: Westbrook van Voorhis, Alexander Scourby, Orson Welles, and William Conrad.

Variety reported in 1975 that Charles Stern had over 400 clients, from Gregory Peck and Telly Savalas to Joe Namath. The price for a day's work was already sky high, and celebrities who were wanted for a commercial voice session, even if they were not actors, didn't take much coaxing for that kind of money, according to Stern. He also handled the jingle team of Perry Botkin Jr. and Mark Lindsay, who had just composed the music for nine Busch commercials. Frees was again singled out as a top money maker, though Gregory Peck's three-year contract with Travelers Insurance at a million dollars was the top Stern act at the time. A close second was Joe Namath's $250,000 for a mere five Faberge commercials.

Stern admitted to *The Commercial Actor* magazine in its August, 1976 issue that he owed much of his agency's success to Frees.

"I was in San Francisco doing public relations and advertising for various accounts relating to the entertainment industry. One of our accounts was Ray Conniff. I moved down here with Ray as his manager and toured the country with him. It was during this time that I began to see the potential in the commercial field. This was in 1960. There were only two other agents who were active at that time - Jack Wormser and Bob Longnecker—so I

Paul at the Broadcast Industry Conference, 1976.

thought there was room for some competition. I resigned from my position with Conniff and started a commercial talent agency here with three clients. It took off, I would say, within a two-year period.

"We really began to roll when Paul Frees signed on as our first major client. Paul actually taught me a great deal about the commercial business. He continues to be the leading voice-over performer in the industry, even though he lives in Tiburon. Paul is really a fabulous talent. Many other great performers joined up with us after Paul began his affiliation with our agency."

Though according to Frees, in a later conversation with Keith Scott, "Juney Foray was really his first client. She came to me one day and said, 'There's a new agent in town who I think would be good for you.' I was having trouble with my agent who was a very good friend. His problem was he was selling me for less than I was worth." The last straw was a deal that his agent, Jack Wormser, had made with an advertising agency for $15,000 less than the deal Frees had made with them. He had done that three or four times previously. June introduced Paul to Charles "and I fell in love with him, and he's been my big brother ever since. We never bothered with contracts or anything else. He handles my corporation, he handles my money. We own all kinds of huge real estate deals together. He feels to this day that I am the very top of the industry. But I left the center of the industry and I think of myself as semi-retired. I called the office just today because I have a couple of jobs to do all day tomorrow. I said, 'Why am I doing all this if I'm living up here?' And they said, 'Because you're our top client.' I said, 'How can I be your top client if I'm living up here?' They said, 'Well, you are. There's nobody does more work than you.'"

Stern repeated this sentiment often: "Paul Frees is the premiere voice talent in the world. We turn down more work than we take. No one can equal his range."

In April of 1976 Frees was recognized for that range, receiving the Preceptor Award for Outstanding Contributions to Broadcasting. He shared stories and advice with an audience in Studio One on San Francisco State University's campus at a luncheon given by the Broadcast Industry Conference.

"Think of yourselves as balloons," he told the crowd, "and don't be afraid to blow up that balloon to the fullest extent, or to find out what configuration that balloon is going to take. And, don't ever stop."

Red Skelton and Paul Frees after recording *Rudolph's Shiny New Year* in 1976.

He told *The San Francisco Sunday Examiner & Chronicle* the next month how he'd never stopped. "I've paid my dues. When I was working my tuchis off in Los Angeles, it was not uncommon for me to do thirteen jobs a day, with a full-time driver and two phones in the Rolls, sleeping in the backseat between studios. I won't deny it, the popularity was wonderful. But the reward for success is work and more work. At one time I had five houses, I'd fly to Paris for lunch. But until I met Bev, I was just a commodity. I wasn't living the way I wanted to live. Now I do.

"I have designed my life, with the help of my sweetheart mommy baby here, the way I want it. I have absolute freedom. I've been asked to appear in pictures. What do I need with that crap? I've been asked why I don't appear on talk shows—Mike Douglas, Merv Griffin—they ask for me at least ten times a month. Why should I? What am I supposed to do, go on the tube and say I do the Pillsbury Doughboy? Is that something to be proud of?

"If you want to know the truth, it's a very self-conscious thing for me to think that here I am, a grown man, doing this for a living while other people are being writers and philosophers and nuclear physicists."

Yet, he knew where his bread was buttered, and around the same time told *The Saturday Evening Post*, "I know my business and I love it. I don't need lots of takes and many times I do my own directing. But I'll do a hundred takes if necessary. I'm not doing this for my ego—I'm trying to turn out the best product I can. I always make sure the client gets his money's worth."

"He didn't work everyday," Bob Lindner recalled. "He came in and worked maybe once a week. Maybe twice a week on a busy week. He would come in and do a session that would earn him thousands of dollars, and it would take him a half-hour.

"He spent a lot of time in his pajamas, in his bath robe, watching old movies. He liked old movies and baseball. And, you know, he kept weird hours, too, because if you don't have to get up in the morning, why get up? And so he would sleep late. He had a very undisciplined life, in a lot of ways. But he had complete control, and was extremely disciplined when it came to his work.

"A session with him was really interesting because he would always do the same thing. He would have a new client, and they would book an hour. Frees would show up. He was never late. *Always* on time. He would show up to the session and walk in and immediately start telling stories, basically, in a lot of ways, performing. We'd be standing around the control room, and I would just be sitting over there grinning and giggling because I knew what was going on. He would be talking with these people and playing to them, but at the same time, he's watching every reaction. He goes through his act. He's watching them. He's reading them. It was his way of figuring out what it was they wanted from him.

"So finally, he's been talking for forty-five minutes, and they've got fifteen minutes left. And he notices they've been looking at their watches for the past twenty minutes, wondering oh my God, and they're afraid to interrupt him or say, 'Can we record this?' And finally, Paul will say, 'Oh, well, let's do this.' And he'll step into the studio, take the copy, and just ask maybe a question or two about it, because he already knows exactly what he's going to do. He had an uncanny ability to know what was right, so he'd go in there, and he would do three takes, four takes, maybe five max. That's it. He's out. Goodbye. I saw that time after time after time. I loved it.

"It was wonderful because usually in sessions, it's the other way around. It's the talent that squirms. I've been on the talent side of the glass before, and they can make you squirm. 'Well, could you try it again this

Jack Frost (Paul Frees) and Crystal (Shelley Winters).

way? Or could you try it that way?' When they start doing that, it makes you sweat. And nobody made Paul Frees sweat.

"There was a session with a director who I won't name who had a terrible reputation for beating up talent. This guy would just kill them. He'd go in the studio to record one line, like 'That's the end.' And the voice guy would say, 'That's the end.' The director would say, 'No, like this: that's the end.' They would give it right back to him. No. He would do seventy or eighty takes on just one line like that and make people wonder if they were in the right business. Maybe I should get a job selling shoes or something, you know? This director just would kill them. Well, the guy tried it on Frees. Frees went for it for a few minutes, and then he finally said, 'I've given you what you need. Goodbye.' And he walked right out. Of course, he *had* given him exactly the right thing, but Paul wasn't going for it. I loved it. I loved him for that."

With commercial work still steady, if not overflowing, it's difficult to imagine why Frees or Stern thought the great voice man needed a new demo tape in 1976. Possibly it was to remind the upcoming new advertising executives, continually younger than the previous management, just who this old workhorse was. Frees' manifold skills began with words of poetry and was tailored mostly to showcasing his vast backlog of commercials. It was, after all, a worktape to secure yet more voice-over jobs for commercials.

Bob Lindner: "Everybody else's demo tape, like today, they run two minutes; two-and-a-half minutes is a long one. Back then, three minutes was considered long. His was over five minutes long. He wasn't to be shortchanged or outdone by anyone. But, he had the material. We left out so much stuff and tried to trim it down, make it as tight as we could. We just put together all the things that we could think of, a lot of them were lifts from things that he had. Then a fair amount of it was stuff we recorded, and I just put sound effects and music to it."

Obviously he needed no help in securing more Rankin/Bass work. In 1976 Robert Morse, Stan Freberg and narrator/singer Burl Ives were heard in *The First Easter Rabbit*, sponsored for television by Sunshine Biscuits. The jolly holiday musical was adapted from the book, *The Velveteen Rabbit*, and included, along with the usual line-up of original Maury Laws/Jules Bass songs, Irving Berlin's famous "Easter Parade." The half-hour animated Easter special told the story of Stuffy (voiced by Robert Morse), a toy bunny given as a Christmas present to a small girl. The bunny is brought to life by a kind fairy in order to dispense Easter eggs to the children. First, he would have to trek to Easter Valley, near the North Pole, where eggs were decorated and baskets made. After meeting Santa, Stuffy has to weather several enemies, including a frozen fiend named Zero (Frees). Paul also doubled as a rabbit named Spats. *The First Easter Rabbit*, as most Rankin/Bass programs did, played for many years in repeats. A promotional album of the entire soundtrack was also released in a limited pressing.

Rudolph's Shiny New Year premiered on ABC fifteen days before Christmas of 1976, and was one of the more popular Rankin/Bass hour-long features. Billie Richards, the original voice of Rudolph, returned to the role to find Happy, the Baby New Year, who had run away from Father Time (Red Skelton). Santa Claus (Frees) sent the well-lit reindeer out into the midnight fog to hunt for the child who, if not found, would cause it to remain December 31st forever. Frees also appeared as the villainous Aeon, an evil monster-bird who *wanted* time to stop. But with the aid of a whale, a caveman and some bright songs by Johnny Marks, Rudolph searched the isles of time to find Happy who had run away because his huge ears made him feel ashamed; Rudolph commiserated with his glowing nose and all ended well. The stop-motion Animagic puppet special also enlisted the top

Talking to *The Commercial Actor*. (*Charles Fretzin*)

voice talent of Frank Gorshin, Morey Amsterdam and the Great Gilder-sleeve himself, Hal Peary, as Big Ben. Frees is also heard as General Ticker, Benjamin Franklin, and, on the island of fairytales, Humpty Dumpty.

Midway, the epic World War II strategy film, was also released that year, and contained one of Paul's most celebrated dubbings. While most of the Japanese actors working on the film had no problem with giving their lines (they were really American actors, after all), Toshiro Mifune had still done most of his films in his native land. Frees had dubbed for him back in 1966's *Grand Prix*; a decade later, Mifune's accent and English language clarity for this new American production were still proving problematic. Paul looped for him again, giving the character that deep, pensive, slightly (of course) Japanese accent. He even invited Al Scoma along to Universal to watch.

On Admiral Isoroku Yamamoto's (Fleet Commander of the Japanese Navy, played by Mifune) flagship, Yamamoto plots his war strategy with his high-ranking officers in attendance. Unfortunately, the Admiral is the only one who sounds as if he is in a studio, since everyone else's vocals are kept as filmed. "I have traveled widely in America, my friends," said Yamamoto. "Their industrial might is awesome. I'm convinced our only hope for victory is one massive strike at Midway." Most of his lines are given in the first hour of the film. But when all is lost in the battle of Midway, an honorable but long face slowly intones his final line, "I am the only one who must apologize to His Majesty."

Some of the scenes used Korean planes and ships, and some stock footage was usurped from 1942 newsreels and the Oscar-winning *Tora! Tora! Tora!* (1970). *Midway* was originally shown in Sensurround, a system which had special low-pitch woofers for sound effects.

Before filming, Walker Edmiston came into the studio and recorded all the Admiral's lines so that Mifune could learn them phonetically. But it didn't help much.

Paul Frees: "Mifune would leave these huge holes in his speech in *Grand Prix* when he was trying to come out with the English words. Your head is bobbing with his every word, hoping he can make it. The director came to me and said, 'I don't know what to do. He's making all these motions and his dramatic interpretations aren't right in this thing. Name your price, I'll lock you in a room and you'll *do* it. Goodbye!' So I'd sit there and invent words that would fit into these gaps and into the way his mouth moved, and I'd redo things that were not as dramatically correct as they would be in English."

The end of 1976 heard Paul as Jack Frost in the successful sequel to *Frosty the Snowman* called *Frosty's Winter Wonderland*. Wanting to spend the winter a little further south than the North Pole, Frosty (Jackie Vernon again) rejoins his young friends who build him a snowgirl, Crystal (voiced by Shelley Winters). The snowman has never been so happy, and plans to marry Crystal. But Jack Frost, angry at being left alone at the North Pole and jealous at always being second to Frosty, gets even by blowing the snowman's magic hat off. But true love wins when Crystal kisses him on the cheek, bringing him back to life. The kids then build a snowparson to marry the two, and Crystal invites Jack back to be best man. The half-hour cartoon enjoyed years of repeat holiday plays after its initial broadcast for ABC on December 2, 1976. The complete soundtrack to the special was released on Disneyland Records.

At some point the next year, Paul voiced a few TV commercials for the Fantastic Animation Festival which presented, among other things, sixteen award-winning animated films. He also did some very well-received promos for San Francisco's KFRC radio station; in his best, gruffest, Isaac Hayes-ish voice he sexily uttered, "The rhythm…of San Francisco…" before and after local residents praised the area.

Because of his high profile in soap selling, in April of 1977 Paul was named Commercial Actor of the Month in *The Commercial Actor* magazine. It was the 1st anniversary issue with white-suited, cool-shaded Frees pictured on the cover. The in-depth interview and photo spread inside, taken at his Tiburon home, was perhaps the most comprehensive promo piece ever done on The Voice of God.

"When I left Los Angeles and came up here, I was prepared to fly down two or three days a week if I had to. I left at the height of my career, right at the moment when I was working twenty-four hours a day. It was a scary move, but it was what I ultimately wanted to do. We had a beautiful estate in Hancock Park, and my loving wife Bev and I were coming up here to our island hideaway whenever we could. Finally she said to me, 'Why are we living in L.A. when this is where we really want to be?'

"As it turned out, I've been able to do everything from San Francisco. Producers from all over fly up here. Who doesn't want to come to San Francisco? And for those producers who can't be here in person, the industry hardware has become so sophisticated between the tape and the telephone hookups that I can work with people thousands of miles away. For example, I'm just finishing some work on the Midland CB account, and we did a great many of the spots via the patch-in. The agency producers were in Detroit on the phone in conference call, and my friend Fred Wolf and the production gang were in Los Angeles with the music. And it was all junctured into the studio in San Francisco where I was working and patched-in on earphones. They spoke to me as though they were sitting in the booth. This is how I've been doing a lot of work for the past three or four years. And so I'm really available to anybody anywhere. But I must admit that I am happy and dazzled at the same time.

"Recently, just out of curiosity, I asked one producer who had flown to San Francisco, 'Why did you go to all the trouble to fly up here to work with me? There are forty or fifty thousand actors in Los Angeles, and a lot of them could have done this particular job. Why me? Why not some other performer?' He said, 'You just answered it yourself. You're not just a performer. You're an insurance policy.' When he said that, I began to understand something that I'd like to get across to the young people that are just starting out in this business. I know that a lot of your readers are the newcomers who are trying hard to figure out what it really takes to succeed, and I'd like to direct this interview to them.

"Let's face it. I talk the same way that everybody else talks. Maybe my range is great, but there are many actors who have a great range. It's something more than just vocal ability. For the new people, I think they have to begin by envisioning themselves as professionals. What you think of yourself is what others will think of you. If you think of yourself as a lucky amateur who is sneaking in by the skin of your teeth, then that is what is projected to the people around you. It's a professional attitude, and I think that this professional attitude can actually exist without a profession. A boat without a cargo in its hold is no less a boat. The hull is there, and the superstructure is there. No matter what happens, it's going to float. And that's exactly the attitude that we have to have when we go into the studio. We have to exude a confidence that comes from a professional attitude, not from the profession.

"Professionalism means that you have the pride, dignity, and assurance of knowing what you can do. It must be an honest evaluation. It's as if you were a shoe salesman. You say, 'Yes, Ma'am, you want a 6 1/2C in black patent leather with a rhinestone buckle? I have that.' Now if you say you have, you better have it. And if you don't have it, say so. But performers sometimes overstate their abilities out of frustration or thinking that by some magical chance they might get this job even though they're not suited for it. They're afraid to say, 'No,' and so the reliability of their estimation of their capabilities becomes less. As a result they go in and do something they shouldn't have done, and they're not going to get called back. There are no second chances in this business.

"When you're out there in that hall and they hand you the script and you look at it and see, 'That's not me,' you've got to be strong enough to say so. 'No, I do not have a 6 1/2C in black patent leather with a rhinestone buckle. I cannot sell it to you because I do not have it.' If you develop a reputation for having that kind of judgement, you'll have a reputation that will work in your favor.

"Beginning is always difficult. But beginning is an adventure. Learning and developing your skills is exciting and becomes the reflective memory that stays with you the rest of your life.

"Being an artist, I used to spend a great deal of time sitting around in parks and public squares where there were people, and to this day I'll talk to everybody. And I absorb all of this. If you have this natural ability, you will absorb these things and put them in your mental library, and then you just draw on them. The person you play may be someone you heard or it may be a composite of five people you heard.

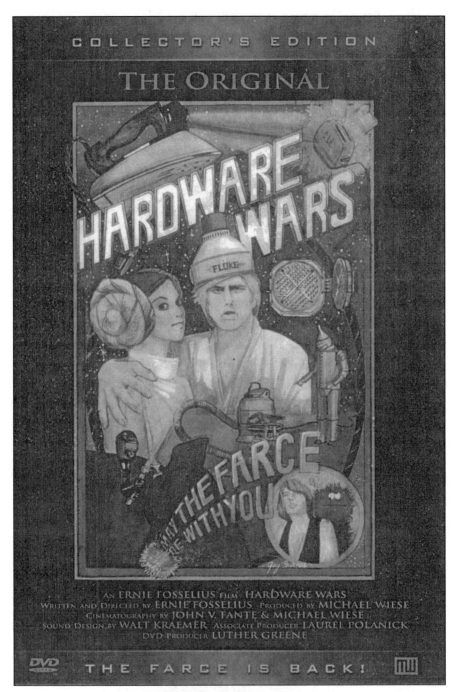

(Ernie Fosselius/Michael Wiese www.mwp.com)

"You have things within yourself you don't know exist. Sometimes you find out about these things from the auditions where you don't get the job. That's how you grow. In show business you learn what to do and what not to do, depending on the response that you get. You must learn how to edit out the things that don't work for you. If you are a director of the film—and that's what your own personal life story is, it's your story, your film—you must learn to, with all the guts in the world, edit out the chunks that don't belong in your story. Just because you've shot this piece of film doesn't mean that you have to use it. Learn to distinguish between what is usable and what is not.

"Fortunately, the majority of people who come to me want my help. If they don't know that I'm going to offer suggestions, then they've never worked with me, and they're in for a big surprise. Somebody once asked Arthur Rankin of Rankin/Bass, 'You direct Paul Frees? How do you direct Paul Frees?' Arthur smiled wisely and said, 'With a chair and a whip! How else?' Well, I've never been pugnacious about it, but I guess I have always wanted to participate. Being a creative person and a director and writer myself, it was never sufficient for me to sit and have somebody tell me, 'Do it this way.' Of course, when a producer says to me, 'We really don't quite know what we want,' that's all I have to hear. If they don't know what they want, then I'll come up with suggestions. We'll go through an entire spectrum and try to open up avenues that nobody thought of. Even if they

(*Ernie Fosselius/Michael Wiese www.mwp.com*)

think they know what they want, I'll say, 'Have you considered this other idea?' If you're working with creative people, they appreciate the fact that you're going to come up with something that they never envisioned. It's fun and exciting to explore all the ramifications of these various ideas and characters. Of course, if the producer and director say specifically, 'This is what we want and we can't change it,' for legal or whatever other reasons, then I feel you should do it their way without question.

"I've never liked the audition part of the business much. And yet it has to be done. If you're a wine salesman and somebody wants to buy your product and they've never tasted it, you have to give them a sample. Show them what you can do. It may be humiliating. It may be embarrassing, but people have the right to ask it of you if they don't know what your product is. Auditions are part of the business, and if you think of yourself as a professional, professionalism is overcoming the indignity of sitting somewhere and not getting paid for it after you've gone through all the effort of shaving and putting on your suit and tie, working yourself up into a beautiful state of self control.

"I think that Charles Stern is the one who started the practice of getting scripts and doing audition tapes with your own agent, having somebody that you're comfortable with direct you in surroundings that are familiar. When Charles became an agent, I was probably his first major client. We interrelated and grew together, and we're the closest, dearest friends in addition to working in the industry together.

"Another problem that I'd like to mention is one that occurs in this business as it does in any business. I think that if you mentioned philosophy from business people, you'd find that they tended to separate philosophy from business. They'd say, 'Philosophy is fine. We'll have to talk about that sometime, but right now I've got to go make this deal.' Now, that's the most magnificent way to cheat yourself out of life, and this is what I've seen happen to many of my contemporaries. It probably happens more to people in the business end of it than to talent because we are closer to the philosophical aspect of things. But because of the business aspect of business, people become something they were never meant to become, and they're very unhappy, and they don't know why.

"I have developed what I call the Strawberry Principle, which is a very simple philosophy. If it takes a ton of manure to grow one beautiful strawberry, it's worth it to see that strawberry come to fruition. But what happens is that a great many of our colleagues end up becoming the biggest people in

Arthur Rankin, Don Messick, John Stephenson, Paul Frees, Jack De Leon,
Orson Bean, Jules Bass, and Hans Conreid.

the manure business and have forgotten about the strawberry. How do you relate strawberries to commercials? I like to think of commercials as minute musicals. I think that some of the greatest techniques for motion pictures have come out of commercials along with some of the greatest abilities and the greatest talents and the greatest music. People might think that because it's only a minute that that's not long enough for it to be good, but I say that if you're going to tell your message in a minute, it's got to be perfect. It's a beautiful industry. It really is. But let's not forget the strawberry."

Frees was harvesting many a berry at that time. *Valley News* reported that when Dudley Murphy died in 1969 his Holiday House, a celebrated oceanside restaurant/hotel in Malibu that catered to every star imaginable, was purchased by Frees, Charles Stern and Perry Botkin, Jr., and other investors. They quickly turned the rooms into private apartments and refurbished the restaurant, hoping for another booming mecca of high-class prosperity. Barbra Streisand, Steve McQueen, Telly Savalas, Raquel Welch and others of Hollywood society dined there. The manager-host was Freddy Kernbach, once *maitre d'* at Scandia and The Sportman's Lodge. The menu's emphasis was on fish dishes, plus veal chops and an ample wine cellar of expensive Burgundies. Only the best. Under Kernbach's sage management, the restaurant upped from 40 to 200 patrons a night on average, while the average Sunday brunch increased from 75 to 350 customers.

The hotel itself offered a mix of 1930s décor and contemporary style: pedestal chairs with salmon and red upholstery and chrome basses; Boston ferns hanging before beige, white and silver wall coverings on arched walls; mirrored paneling in the bar and lounge. Movie stars could enjoy the paradise of an outside patio with brick banquettes. And the sea view was breathtaking.

Yet even with its success, it was soon back on the market at a $6 million price tag. It was probably too costly to keep up at its stately 27400 Pacific Coast Highway address.

A long, long time ago, in a kitchen far, far away, there was a brilliant parody of *Star Wars* which replaced Tie Fighters with toasters and the Death Star with a waffle iron. It dubbed Fluke Starbucker, Ham Salad, Augie Ben Doggie and everyone else who used The Farce to squash evil Darth Nader's plans like a bad Japanese monster flick. You wouldn't think that the now infamous *short*, short film *Hardware Wars*, which boasted a "$2.98 budget," would have had the wherewithal to have Paul Frees as its narrator. Writer/director Ernie Fosselius explains:

"As a kid I watched Rocky and Bullwinkle faithfully, and not just for the wonderfully cheesy animation, either. It was the voices: Paul Frees, June Foray, Edward Everett Horton. Stan Freberg used a lot of the same people, too, especially with Daws Butler.

"Paul Frees was a hero because he seemed to be behind the scenes everywhere. Few people, I think, know how many times they've heard his voice in their lifetimes. I always seemed to be aware that there were actors creating these voices and even as a kid I could identify who was doing what character. I have friends today who say that if there were a game show in which the contestants won money for identifying voices, I'd be a millionaire.

"Because of this early brainwashing, I wound up doing voices myself all my life and did voice-overs as a kind of avocation later in my film 'career.' I have screen credits on a few features, notably *Ernest Scared Stupid*, in which I did Trantor the Troll, Ernest's evil nemesis.

"Okay, *Hardware Wars*. I was making a parody of a movie trailer for a cheap *Star Wars* rip-off. Of course, I could only hear Paul Frees when I thought of the voice-over announcer. I knew he lived in the San Francisco Bay Area and I knew other people in 'The Biz' that could find him, but our

Dennis Day, Walter Matthau and Paul Frees.

budget for this short film was $2.98. How could I ever afford the legendary Maestro Frees? So I was all set to do a bad imitation of his voice myself. Then Walt Kraemer, who produced funny radio commercials then and was helping me create sound effects for *Hardware Wars*, casually mentioned one day that he went to Paul's home studio regularly to do maintenance on his recording equipment.

"We hatched a plan. Walt would show up for the regularly scheduled maintenance, explain this fun little project he was involved with, and because we loved his work so much and idolized him (no lie there), could he see his way clear to recording just six lines in exchange, say, for one equipment maintenance session? He agreed and recorded the six lines which, although it seems like more because they are spread throughout the film, are all I had to work with. Walt wanted him to read the lines again for protection, and Paul boomed: 'Why!? I just did them right!' He was correct. How can you improve on that? For me, his voice makes the film.

"Later, when *Hardware Wars* began to be shown everywhere, Mr. Frees saw it and was reportedly shocked and angry. He got my telephone number somehow and in a wonderful and scary moment I heard this thundering Voice of God coming over my phone, 'How did you get my voice!?' He

Addressing the Broadcast Museum Conference in the 1970s.

apparently didn't remember the two-and-a-half minute recording session in his home studio and our little 'deal.' Once I recovered enough to explain and refresh his memory, he was quite pleasant."

Walt Kraemer: "In retrospect and because I had great admiration for Paul's abilities, I wish now I could have created commercials and an environment where I could have taken advantage of his comedic talents. He was L.A.'s gift to the Bay Area for such a short and opportune time.

"Someone had given him a pair of high-powered World War II binoculars (which were claimed as belonging to Erwin Rommel), so he had them mounted on the railing of his Tiburon house's deck. He invited, actually encouraged, me to spy on his neighbors... something he practiced quite a bit, apparently.

"With his God-given penchant for imitation, he would loop a number of feature films including those of Humphrey Bogart. He told me once he was on a dock as Bogart was about to set sail for the afternoon when Bogart was reminded he had to loop some dialogue from one of his pictures. According to Paul, Bogart said to him, 'You do it, you sound more like me than I do.'"

"I worked with Walt Kraemer at Imagination, Inc. for almost two years in 1973-74," says Fred Frees. "I'm sure Dad forgot about the *Hardware Wars* 'session.' He often forgot what he had done since he did so many things."

Michael Wiese, author of several film books, produced the short which George Lucas later called his favorite *Star Wars* parody. "My job was cinematography," says Wiese. "I oversaw the production process and marketed the film over the last 22 years. It's won something like fifteen first place awards, and took six days, I think, to shoot. The interiors were an old laundry that we rented. It actually cost $8000 to make. The DVD production cost three times that. It's the most successful indie short film ever made."

Before the massive hit trilogy of recent years, Rankin/Bass premiered their TV version of *The Hobbit* on November 27, 1977. Frees had little to do in the ninety-minute feature, but it put him in good company among warhorses Hans Conried, Don Messick, John Stephenson, as well as Orson Bean (the Hobbit himself, Bilbo Baggins), Richard Boone, Cyril Ritchard, Theodore and Jack De Leon. The cartoon animation was a departure for Rankin/Bass' style, but fit perfectly with the Middle Earth concept so popular with author J.R.R. Tolkien's many fans. Frees was heard as some of the trolls whom Baggins meets on his lengthy journey to find the elusive rings in *The Lord of the Rings* series. Not only was *The Hobbit* Rankin/Bass' most decorated special, winning the prestigious Peabody Award and the Christopher Award, but a major soundtrack album set was released by Disney's Buena Vista Records, including three albums, a poster, a book and T-shirt iron-ons.

Frees was taking fewer roles these days, already claiming to be semi-retired. But he continued to travel to Los Angeles whenever Rankin/Bass wanted him. They wanted him for *Nestor, the Long-Eared Christmas Donkey*, which aired on December 3, 1977. Based on the title song by Gene Autry, Don Prummer and Dave Burgess, the half-hour Animagic special has the theme of *Rudolph the Red-Nosed Reindeer* about it. Nestor is the donkey that Mary rode to Bethlehem, but he has a complex. He's always being ridiculed about his oversized ears, and being friendless and an orphan (his mother had died in a snowstorm) doesn't help his sad eyes either. But after delivering Mary and Joseph through a perilous sandstorm, protecting the mother with his huge ears, Nestor arrives at the stable a contented creature, as he watches the coming shepherds and kings make their way to the new child of God. The half-hour special was again filled with songs, and starred Erik Stern as Nestor, Linda Gray as his mother, Brenda Vaccaro as Tillie, and Paul Frees as the desert merchant, Olaf, who gives Nestor to Mary and Joseph.

Two days before Christmas of 1978 *The Stingiest Man in Town* premiered on NBC. It was yet another (and Frees' second) version of the often-produced *A Christmas Carol*. Tom Bosley voiced narrator B.A.H. Humbug, a bug named after Scrooge's well-known saying, who began the story in the present after Scrooge had reformed. But, naturally, most of the musical story involved how he got that way. The title character was shouted out by Walter Matthau, with able support from the likes of Dennis Day, Theodore Bikel, Robert Morse and others. Paul Frees doubled as the two talking ghosts: of Christmas Past and Present, and sang "One Little Boy" with Matthau. He made the most of his short time on screen, but again, sadly, he was underused for this one. The score by Fred Spielman (music) and Janice Torre (book and lyrics) was a great piece of work. The special was again designed by Paul Coker, Jr., took a year to complete, and cost $1.5 million to produce.

For *Jack Frost*, another Rankin/Bass special in 1979, Paul put on his Boris Badenov voice once again to portray villain Kubla Kraus who taxes the poor people of January Junction to the point of starvation. Living alone in a towering, dreary castle atop Miserable Mountain, "King of the Kossacks" Kraus is such a nogoodnik that all the Kossacks leave him. So, he has to build mechanical acquaintances (butler, horse, even the mice in the walls) to stop from feeling so lonely. Again, he was the villain of the piece, narrated by groundhog Pardon-Me-Pete (Buddy Hackett), but also portrayed the mighty Father Winter who lets Jack Frost become a real man for one season. If Jack (voiced by Robert Morse) could acquire a wife, horse, home and pot of gold within this time, he could remain human. Unfortunately, the woman he falls for, Elisa (Debra Clinger), meets and marries a true knight in shining armor. Jack realizes all is for the best and that he enjoys being the icy spirit of winter. The sixty-minute musical premiered on December 13, 1979, and again featured Animagic puppets. It was one of Frees' largest Rankin/Bass roles that decade.

The last Animagic feature that Rankin/Bass released that year was *Rudolph and Frosty's Christmas in July,* which teamed up many original voices from other Christmas specials: Billie Richards as Rudolph, Jackie Vernon as Frosty, Shelley Winters as Crystal, and Mickey Rooney as Santa Claus. Frees voiced the heavy - baleful King Winterbolt who rules the North Pole with an icy hand. Scheming against Santa for control of the top of the world, Winterbolt deliberately tries to burn Rudolph's nose out, but must lure the reindeer away in order to make him use his red nose for evil. The 97-minute production was a recap of many of the best elements of the previous specials, including Rudolph and Frosty in a duet of "We're a Couple of Misfits." Jack Frost (Frees) returns at the end to bring Frosty back to life after Winterbolt swipes the magic hat. But some of the new elements worked best: Ethel Merman as Lilly Loraine, the singing circus owner, who also closes the show with "Rudolph, the Red-Nosed Reindeer"; and one of the best new characters, the cave-dwelling Scratcher, voiced by the ever-effervescent Alan Sues. Johnny Marks returned to compose the score, with character designs once more by Paul Coker, Jr.

Unfortunately the theatrically-released film wasn't a hit at its premiere, partly due to being released in the summer rather than the more lucrative Christmas season. One newspaper review liked the script and voice work, singling out Frees' character Winterbolt as "wonderfully drawn to tantalize youngsters of five and under."

There was a downside to the media attention. The trouble with being the recognized top "voice" was that Frees was always being sought after for free samples. He even finally had to give up his resourceful answering machine message because "I was having to put up with 25 minutes of people laughing and hanging up, and there wouldn't be any work calls."

From annoyance came creativity. An article on the subject in *The New York Times* on May 26, 1977 gave Charles Stern the idea of a series of funny celebrity messages that the agent hoped to pitch toward the

Ansaphone and Phone Mate distributors. That same day he wrote to Paul asking him to record the following on 7.5 IPS tape quickly to use as a demo to get in on the fad.

> W.C. Fields – "Hello, my little fruit flies. I'm out at the moment. However, if you'll leave your name and phone number, I'll get back to you shortly or is it monthly, whatever."

> Bogart – "Hello there, friend. It's cocktail time but if you care to leave your name and phone number, I might return the call."

> Clark Gable – "Hello, beautiful. Yours truly happens to be away from the phone. It sure would be nice if you left your name and phone number, and I will get back to you."

> Jimmy Carter – "Thank you, dear friend, for calling. Your kindness will be long remembered. If you happen to get to it, please leave your name and phone number and I will get back atcha."

> Boris Karloff – "Uhmm, you're sounding good enough to eat. Before I draw any more blood, please leave your name and phone number."

Stern wanted five or six more characters, as well as a friendly one as Frees himself. Unfortunately, nothing came of the idea.

Fred Frees: "Actually, I don't recall that he had an answering machine at all. He always answered his phone with his usual matter-of-fact 'Yes.'"

The Eternal Doughboy
The 1980s

AFTER FREES HAD BEEN SENT the script of *The Bushido Blade* in 1979 to again dub lines for Toshiro Mifune, he began 1980 with voicing promo spots for the epic TV mini-series *Shogun* (and probably more looping for Mifune who was in the series). Two years later, he would dub for Mifune again in *The Challenge*.

Paul now consolidated his L.A. trips so he could do both film dubbing and record plugs for radio stations like WXLO in New York City, plus commercials for Wang Laboratories, and work for the Hill, Holliday, Connors and Cosmopulos ad agency headquartered in Boston. According to Charles Stern, the last time Frees came to Los Angeles was to narrate *Shogun* (though his Rankin/Bass work continued through his final years). Orson Welles was credited with narrating that series, but as it is known that Paul would do overdubs for the famous actor (when retakes were needed and Welles was already on another job or out of the country), it's possible that that's what he did this time as well. Possibly in the very same session as the promo spots.

It was to be his last work in Los Angeles because that very day there was a first-stage smog alert. "That's it," he said. "I'm never coming back." He didn't need to.

Sabrina Frees: "He was a hermit. He would hold court in his bedroom, and would rarely come out. When he came out, it was an event. Most of our conversations were held over the intercom.

"It was a five-story house, and I would stay in the top bedroom, until I got completely bored. I would hope that Bev would get up, because they would sleep forever. They were night people. They would stay up till three or four in the morning, finally crash, then get up around noon. So I'd be sitting up there bored to tears. Then usually we'd have a big lox, bagel and cream cheese breakfast, which was great.

"My dad rarely went out. I remember when he had to go to work it was just a nightmare. For him, it was like pulling teeth. Looking back on it, I wouldn't be surprised if he was agoraphobic. I know he had panic attacks. If he knew he had to go to work, a couple days before he had to go, he would work himself into a tizzy. When I was real little, I remember that things weren't that big a deal. But then I was a little kid, so I didn't know.

"He would work once or twice a month, and spend most of his time in that bedroom watching TV. With the drapes drawn, in darkness, with

(*Charles Fretzin*)

the birds. I think he got the 3rd VCR ever created! And I got it, afterwards. It's like a Sony VCT400 and it's huge. He would sit up in that bedroom and not want to come out, and it was really kind of sad."

"I have no idea how he got into birds," says Fred. "Maybe Beverly started it. But he ended up building an aviary next to his bedroom. He had cockatoos, and/or cockateels, parrots and some little bird he used to let walk all over him in bed. I think I have a picture of him and the bird somewhere. In fact, one of the parrots used to imitate him. It was hilarious."

Sabrina: "Bev was more than just his wife. She was his caretaker, his Mommy, everything. She was his biggest cheerleader. She was amazing. She was like a sister to me. She was the buffer between me and Dad. We were best buddies. She would advise me all the time. 'I want to talk to Dad about this.' She would say, 'Well, here's how you do it. Don't do that, do this.' Or if I needed to ask my dad for something, she'd be the one who'd go and ask him. She was the go-between, if it was difficult for me to approach my dad. I was very intimidated, probably by the voice. I remember he yelled at me—once—and I was just destroyed. I can't remember what it was about, and it really wasn't that big of a deal, but there was just something about that man's voice that just made me fall apart."

In a phone interview with Keith Scott, Frees said, "I consider myself semi-retired, but I'm making more *money* now than I have ever made before, because we charge a *great* deal more for them to come up here or do the phone patch thing. I only have top accounts, and that's about all that I do. Charles Stern has been so wonderful."

Frees was growing weary of the business. As early as 1974 he told a fan, "It was a lot better [in radio days] than it is now, because we were always together, and it was like a club! You saw the gang everyday, and you traded different thoughts and jokes and had lunch together—it was a really wonderful thing. It's not like that now…" Coupled with a growing resistance to the changing cartoon business, and bosses now younger and dumber than he, was a growing fear of going out.

The 1974 audio letter to the fan continued, "I don't live in town, and even if I lived in town, you just don't work together all the time, unless you're on *one series*, which I won't do, because it's just too much work for me. My idea of living—and it's a very important idea—is to take a lot of time at home. We listen to good music, and we go out, and we have a nice dinner, cook a good dinner. We see our friends once in a while, when we get to L.A. We work with some of the guys or look up some of the guys, but it doesn't happen too frequently."

In his perpetual showbiz slowdown, he didn't seem to mind giving up jobs to others. "As far as voice men are concerned," said Frees, "I think Mel Blanc is *the* voice man. Of course. He's the undisputed king of the cartoon world. Nobody is better than Mel. Nobody. Including myself. If Bill Scott were not a writer/producer, if he were just a voice man, he'd be right up there with me. Sammy Davis, Jr. thinks I am the top impressionist in the world. I remember one time sitting ringside when he was in Vegas. He went to do Humphrey Bogart and a couple of impressions, and before he did them, he said, 'Excuse me. Before I do these, I would like to acknowledge the fact that a person that you probably don't even know is sitting ringside and is probably the greatest impressionist of all, and I am very embarrassed doing these in his presence.'"

Frees also continually complimented Alec Scourby, and thought Bill Schallert was "one of the finest of the light voices." He could afford to be generous.

Bob Lindner: "I said once, 'Do you mind me asking—how much are you making from all this?' He would admit to about three-quarters of a million a year just for the session work. But, he also had investments. He bought Mattel when it was brand new. That was another thing about him. This guy had an uncanny ability to pick winners. He would go to the track, and here is somebody with all the money in the world, and he would just bet and bet and bet and come away from the track every time with more money than he had when he went in. I asked him, 'What's your secret, Paul?' Well, he goes up and sits in the Turf Club and has a steak. He's sitting there, and he takes his fork and closes his eyes and waves it over the racing form and stabs it down, and wherever he hits, that's the horse he bets on. He really did that. He told me the story, and Beverly's nodding, 'Yup, yup. That's how he does it.' Incredible."

Joe Else's much-lauded documentary, *The Day After Trinity*, told the story of genius J. Robert Oppenheimer, who helped develop the Atomic Bomb. Frees narrated the 1980 film, which won a Peabody Award and was nominated for an Oscar for Best Documentary.

When the sequel to *The Hobbit* came around, Paul Frees found himself with a little more to do in *The Return of the King*, a two-hour animated feature debuting on ABC on May 11, 1980. The original cast returned in this third book in *The Lord of the Rings* trilogy, with Orson Bean as the elder Frodo Biggins, and John Huston as Gandalf and the narrator. Frees vocalized Elrond, at the opening birthday party, and one of the fighting Goblin Orcs. *King* fared just as well as the first film, securing a new generation, and different cult following, for Rankin/Bass' current productions.

In 1982 Paul had another demo constructed, this time actually recording a new intro to it, a la "Stan Freberg modestly presents..." This time it was quite short.

On June 27, 1982 he gave a lengthy interview with Morgan White, Jr. on his WITS Boston radio show, in which he told how he kept his voice fresh.

"In taking care of my voice, I abuse it so much. Since I have a range where I can go from a very deep narrator to a high kind of a voice, I arch my voice. I try to speak higher than I normally do. I would never use in normal conversation, my low register. So I'm keeping that range open and exercise it. If I spoke in my low range only for a week, it would settle into a one-octave, lower range area and may not come out of it." He would not do lower narration in the afternoon—even Charles Stern vetted such inquiries—because it disturbed his lunch (the big thing in his life those days, he quipped). He preferred to record at 11 and be through by noon, so he could go to lunch. His voice was freshest and deepest in the morning, after a good night's rest.

"You know what's difficult to take at my time of life?" he half-jokingly asked the interviewer, after his vast radio and TV credits had been discussed. "Here, instead of calling it history, the world has decided to call it trivia. While we thought we were building monuments…we were building pebbles."

The International Animated Film Society (ASIFA) sponsored a Rocky and Bullwinkle get-together with Bill Scott and June Foray in 1982, but even for that reunion Paul would not leave his precious Tiburon. He reiterated to Scott why he lived there. "If I live in Tiburon, I'm semi-retired. If I live in Los Angeles, I'm unemployed." It was a buoyant excuse to free himself from unnecessary travel commitments. Yet, in interviews, Frees continued to speak positive thoughts. "Success isn't making money. I found that out many years ago. The adventure of living: this is all we have."

Around this time Frees was awarded the Preceptor Award from San Francisco State University, given "for broadcasting excellence, and for having become a part of the American culture." Frees considered it one of the most prestigious awards of his long career, as Walter Cronkite had been its recipient just the year before. On stage with Paul was Steve Allen, being recognized as the inceptor of the talk show, along with one award for journalism going to Bill Moyer.

The Last Unicorn was Rankin/Bass' last animated feature film, released in 1982. A beautiful fantasy, with a strong score by Jimmy Webb, the movie nevertheless did nothing for Paul Frees' career. He was merely heard as the talking cat who helps the lead characters find their way to the Red Bull who had trapped all the unicorns in the sea. Alan Arkin as magician Schmendrick and Mia Farrow as the last unicorn who turns into a woman gave inspired vocal performances.

The New York Times wrote: "Children, except perhaps for very small ones, ought to be intrigued by it; adults won't be bored." They liked the unexpected and touching ending, and loved the cast, "with Paul Frees doing a particularly amusing cat imitation."

Instantly switching from cartoon character to solemn orator, Frees put narration to the 90-minute documentary, *Routes of Exile: A Moroccan Jewish Odyssey*, which screened at the San Francisco Jewish Film Festival. It followed the journey Moroccan Jews have taken from "yesterday" through the 1980s' turbulent Middle East, combining rare archival footage with contemporary interviews with Jews living in Morocco, France, Canada, and Israel. Though the narration was not mentioned in *The New York Times* review, the paper did call the film "fascinating... What the documentary lacks in slick cinematography it more than compensates for in the dramatic theme it explores."

Also in 1982 he narrated the hour-long documentary, *The Case of Dashiell Hammett* which employed movie clips, interviews and newsreel footage to tell the life story of the creator of *The Thin Man* and *The Maltese Falcon*. Lyle Talbot was heard as the voice of Hammett.

Luckily, around this time John Dunning, master radio historian and author of *On the Air—The Encyclopedia of Old-Time Radio*, instigated one of the few in-depth interviews that Paul ever gave. "I was lucky to get him that one time. He was a fairly elusive interview, as I recall. 'If you call me, I may be here,' Paul said. 'If I'm here, I may talk to you.' But once I got him on the air he was great. I still remember a couple of lines from that—at least I think I do. One was where I suggested that he and Bill Conrad had million-dollar voices, he said something like, 'Oh, you mean we took a cut?' The other was when I said, 'We'll have to endure a commercial now,' and in a very scolding voice he said, "We do not *endure* commercials in this business.' It was a good hour as I remember it, definitely one of the best ones I did."

One of Paul's best friends in the last years of his life was Peter Davis. "I met him in 1982 or '83, when I worked for the Tiburon Fire District. One morning, when I was getting off shift, our fire inspector came to me and said that someone had called down and requested someone come up and change some batteries in a smoke detector. I wasn't doing anything that day, so I drove up to Paul's house on Corinthian Island which is above downtown Tiburon.

"I knocked on the door, met Paul and his wife, and told them I was from the fire department and was here to change some batteries in his smoke detector. Paul was, you know, not very tall, and I'm very tall. I'm 6 foot 4. He said, 'Well, let me go get a ladder for you.' I said, 'I don't need a ladder.' He says, 'Ah, let me get a ladder.' I said, 'I don't need a ladder,' so I just reached up and took it off the ceiling and changed the batteries and made sure it worked. He chuckled and gave me a bad time about that. He basically said that he had been challenged all his life, not being able to reach anything tall. And as we talked, I told him I was also a contractor, and he asked me what I could do. I said I could pretty much do a lot of different things. He said, 'Well, I have

Paul Frees and Pete Davis.

a leak problem in the front stairs of my house that no one's been able to fix. Would you be willing to look at it?' I said, sure.

"A month or a couple months later he called back and said, 'Let's try and take care of this.' So I went up, and I ended up tearing up the whole front brick entryway out of his house and redoing it, because that was right above his wife's fur closet. It was a tedious job, but I got it done.

"A few more months went by and he called me back up and said he had some other things that needed to be fixed. So, as I'd go up there and fix things for him - I worked on his elevator and all kinds of different stuff - he would always tell me stories about doing his voices and his acting and stuff as I worked. He was very, I guess what you'd call, nocturnal. He was often sleeping during the day and awake at night. So, I'd have to plan to either come late in the afternoon when he was awake, or I oftentimes worked when he was asleep. I also did a lot of odds and ends for him for awhile.

"I had worked for the Tiburon police department before I went to work at the fire department, so we often talked about that; we had some mutual friends. He was trickling off on jobs, but he was still doing voices for different corporations. Mainly commercials.

"One of the cars I had was a Cadillac Seville, so he asked me if I would be willing to drive him into the city when he had a job. I said, sure, no problem. He said he didn't like to drive there, so I guess I chauffeured him into San Francisco four or five times. He had a relationship with the drug enforcement agency, so he said, 'Well, since you have a background in the police department and firearms training, I'll get you a concealed weapons permit. I want you to be my bodyguard and to carry a gun.' He was very secretive of that stuff. So, he ended up buying me a stainless steel Walther PPK. Pretty much the same kind James Bond used. And a holster. I had to have it when I took him into the city. It was kind of funny.

"I wasn't surprised at his requests because of the stories he would tell about being involved in the DEA and things. I believe that Paul felt that the dark side of his life was more intriguing than his normal every-day existence, but that was his request. And I honored it for him. I never thought at any time there would ever be a problem with stuff. It was more of a feeling for him that he was protected. There was never any indication that there was anyone out to get him in any way or anything like that. For me, it was more of a charade type of game.

"He carried several guns. One was a stub-nosed .38, and he also had a Belgium Brownie high-power 9 mm which he often carried. He bought them for the look of them, because I did fix a couple of gun holes in his place where he'd discharged them."

Though he never stopped working, in the mid-1980's he did extensively slow down. His list of credits show this. Yet, it wasn't from lack of offers.

In 1980 he had narrated Jay Ward's unsold *Rah! Rah! Woozy!* pilot about two lab animals, Morey Mouse (Bill Scott) and Hamilton Hamster (Daws Butler) at Woozy State College. Morey was a genius who had invented a radio-controlled football in order to help poor coach Weepy Mudbank win his first game in thirty years. The delightful Alex Anderson/Bill Scott script had perfect voice work from Frees as the football announcer and a footballer, with June Foray as a cheerleader. It was a superb last cartoon from Jay Ward Productions.

Paul's last outing with Jay Ward may have been when he suggested the idea for a restaurant he wanted to open that would be themed with Bullwinkle characters, as well as Underdog, Tennessee Tuxedo and other cartoons. He had pitched the notion to Jay but nothing came of it for Frees. However, in 1983 the first Bullwinkle's Family Food 'n' Fun Restaurant opened in San Jose, California, featuring a gift shop and large game room. The enterprise lasted more than a decade, but was not financially satisfying to Ward.

In May of 1984 it was announced that Paul would do narration and voice-over promos for Roger Corman's New Horizon production company. Frees' first film involvement was to narrate *World War III*, but nothing came of it.

As the decade wore on, Paul took on fewer and fewer jobs, depending mostly on his investment income and the continuous Rankin/Bass, cartoon and commercial royalties. It just wasn't worth leaving the house anymore.

Fred Frees: "Not only did he not visit me, he would hardly ever call me. Communication between us was my responsibility. He called me once—and I was surprised to hear his voice on the phone at the time—because a 'Fred Frees' was reported killed in a plane crash. Obviously, it wasn't me. But he was concerned enough at the time to actually initiate the call. I was actually glad that something motivated him to call. There may have been several weeks or longer between conversations. Our relationship was strained for a while, but it was better when I was living near him. It wasn't difficult to 'keep up' with his career. I'd either hear what he'd been doing from him, or from someone else, or the trades, or just tuning in to TV.

"In the early 1980s, I remember talking to him on the phone one day when he was having problems with his VCR. This is one of those areas where he had no expertise. He had all his equipment installed by someone else, and it took everything he had just to make the stuff work. Well, apparently, one day, a tape jammed in his VCR and he couldn't get it out. He was getting so worked up about it, that he threatened to shoot it with a gun. I wouldn't say he was maniacal about it, but he really was threatening to shoot it. He put Beverly on the phone and she also said he was going to shoot it. Fortunately, I never heard any shots fired."

Commercials were nearly the only things Frees worked on in his last years. In a May 29, 1985 letter from producer Larry Lauter of Evesiage Productions, Charles Stern was profusely thanked for Paul's doing the public service announcement publicizing the wearing of seatbelts that was produced for the American Trauma Society. "Paul's distinctive style enhanced the impact of the important message. At a recent press conference involving national and local Bay Area press, the PSA was very well received and garnered much media attention."

But there was still a little cartoon work he couldn't pass up. Rankin/Bass' *The Wind in the Willows* was a 95-minute cartoon special for television that premiered on July 5, 1985. Appearing in the 7-9 p.m. slot, it contained a loving story of friendship, based on Kenneth Grahame's famous novel. The voice talent was first rate—and often better than the acting of the drawings—including a brilliantly cast Charles Nelson Reilly in the title role of Toad of Toad Hall, Roddy McDowell as Ratty, Eddie Bracken as Mole and Jose Ferrer as Badger. Unfortunately, it was another non-lead gig for Paul Frees who was heard first as one of the men in the car who picks up Toad; a Frees-like character with a round belly and wild black mustache. Could it have been drawn with Frees in mind?

Later, he found a greater, but nearly just as short, role as the sea-farin' rat Wayfarer who boomed like a cross between the Burgermeister Meisterberger and Boris Badenov. He suddenly appeared when Ratty was feeling wistful about the changing season. When Wayfarer related his poetic spiel of a grand life of travel he'd had on the high seas, he made Ratty want to leave home for an invigorating taste of the world.

Frees' final Rankin/Bass special—and in fact the last TV special that Rankin/Bass would make—was for the two-hour cartoon, *The Flight of Dragons*. Oddly, Paul was uncredited for his work as Antinquity. Based on *The Dragon and the George* by Gordon R. Dickson and *The Flight of Dragons* by Peter Dickinson, the main voices for the cartoon were John Ritter, Harry Morgan and James Earl Jones. Whether or not Paul was tiring of starring roles or disliked the travel they required, even working for Rankin/Bass was becoming a chore.

Dave Frees: "I used to go down and watch him work in the studio occasionally, but we weren't that close. We were both very busy. I manufactured auto accessories and was on the road quite a bit, so we didn't get together as often as it could have been. The last time I visited him was a few months before he died. He was sick. He had something that caused him to bleed through his rectum. He was pretty upset about it. It kept him from going to Los Angeles or actually going out on jobs other than around San Francisco. He was more or less tied down there. He never knew when he'd start bleeding. He had to wear retainers to catch the blood. It didn't hurt. He'd been to every doctor he knew in the San Francisco area and nobody knew what it was. He had an operation but they couldn't find anything. They didn't know where the hell it was coming from. It was pretty bad and he was pretty miserable about that."

"I found out about that when I got back together with him in '86," says Joyce Post. "Dr. Watts had gotten that absolutely under control, so there was no Depends. None of that. But he was a homebody. He wouldn't go on planes. He became very reclusive. We would go outside, and we would go to the supermarket. But as far as traveling, he wasn't interested in going anywhere. Period. And I think that's why he liked being here at my house: because I liked it, number one. Particularly during the remodeling. He'd walk around in these striped pajamas outside and direct the boys. They called him the Baron. 'Good morning, Baron. Have you had your coffee, Baron?' We always called him Baron. When they were remodeling, he would walk around like he was foreman, and say, 'A little to the left on that.' Of course, he did not know what he was doing.

"He was a brilliant, brilliant man, but he was a crazy driver, in that he would drift. He had a bad eye and had doughnut vision in that you can see around the doughnut, but you can't see the hole in the doughnut. It was in his left eye, which, of course, in the driver's seat, that's the eye you need the most, so I wouldn't let him drive at all. I drove him when he had to go to the studio, which was often, but not all the time. At least once a week. I would be in the booth with him. As a matter of fact, I got a couple of speaking jobs. I do have an unusual voice.

"Once I was standing over him in the booth when he was recording, and they took a break in the session and I said something to him. And the producer goes, 'Who's that?' And Paul says, 'That's blah, blah, blah.' The producer says, 'Well, she needs to say this,' so I'd say a few lines. That kind of pissed him off a little bit. He didn't want me becoming a star. But if you have a connection like Paul Frees, do you think I would have made it or what? All you need is a foot in the door.

"I know one time we went, he did a commercial with the Jolly Green Giant for, I think it was Alpha Beta or one of the supermarkets or something, where the Doughboy was talking to the Jolly Green Giant. He did that in about forty seconds, and the Jolly Green Giant took two hours. Yeah, he was quick, and he was serious when he was doing it. But in between, the outtakes, they were incredible. It was *hysterical*.

"One time Pillsbury was giving away $25,000 towards a college scholarship. All he had to say was, 'We won.' That's all the Pillsbury Doughboy had to say. He spent thirty minutes telling Pillsbury that they were nothing but cheap mothers to not offer $100,000, and he was doing it in the voice of the Pillsbury Doughboy. It just had me rolling on the floor!"

When styles collide.

Around the second week of February, 1986 *Adweek* reported that Paul would celebrate his 25th anniversary as voice of the Pillsbury Doughboy. He briefly described how he got into character for the little soft-tummied chef. "I thought warm thoughts and began talking one-on-one with a wide-eyed wonder. When I walk into a studio I begin moving my hands like he does and I can see my face moving like his."

Paul revived his Ludwig Von Drake for the February 14, 1986 hour-long special, *Disney's DTV Valentine*, broadcast over NBC. The Professor joined Mickey Mouse (voiced by Les Perkins), Donald Duck (Tony Anselmo) and Jiminy Cricket (Eddie Carroll) to host this sweet look on love via a collection of classic Disney cartoons done to the tunes of modern and classic rock songs, sung by The Eurythmics, Whitney Houston, Elton John, Madonna, Elvis and others. DTV was Disney's answer to MTV and could be heard for years on the Disney Channel, before it became another Nickelodeon.

Paul's last two feature film credits were for writer/director Arnold Leibovit. *The Fantasy Film World of George Pal* (1985) was a lush and loving tribute to "the gentleman director" who scored enormous hits with Frees' own *The Time Machine* and *War of the Worlds*. Under "Special Thanks" Paul was given the distinguished and last credit.

"It is no accident," began Frees over modern sci-fi film scenes, "that the fantasy pictures of today have captured our imaginations." His voice sounded a bit older, a bit gruffer, a little more tired perhaps, but it still held a magical tone that fit perfectly with the content. Frees' narration credit fittingly got its own screen beneath a *War of the Worlds* spaceship blowing Los Angeles City Hall to pieces. The narration was interspersed with interviews, both on screen and audio only over stills and behind-the-scenes pictures from Pal's classic films and shorts.

"I was originally going to have an on-screen narrator," Leibovit explains, "and there were a lot of proposals that I made. I met with William Shatner, for instance, and other people that I thought would be good for the genre. But none of that really worked out. Then I just realized that there's no better person to do it than Paul, because he really *was* the voice of George Pal's movies. It was such an obvious conclusion."

Paul had such a great love for the old days, and considered George Pal one of the finest directors he had ever worked with. He asked to see Arnold's film and a copy of the script. "He wasn't paid. He did it as a favor because he loved George, as everyone did. Most of the people that worked on the project did it out of respect for George Pal, and their love for his work and for him as a person. Paul spoke quite a bit about that. There wasn't anyone who worked with George Pal who didn't love him and have great things to say about him. I had a list as long as the industry itself that I got in touch with when I did my film. It involved everybody in the business. People just opened up in amazing ways; so did Paul."

During this time (1985) Leibovit was slowly developing *The Puppetoon Movie*, which would be released theatrically in 1987, the year after Paul's death. The Puppetoons were Pal's inventive and award-winning stop-motion puppets made from rubber and/or carved wood (for the many heads and expressions, etc.).

It begins with Arnie the Dinosaur (Frees) flubbing his menacing role as a deer stalker in pre-historic times. The trouble is, ever since he was cast in a George Pal movie, he's been a vegetarian. Once Arnie takes his teeth out, he explains, "George Pal taught me everything I know. His films were so positive. He showed me even a villain can have a good side." But this annoys director Gumby who doesn't understand why Arnie can't just pretend. To illustrate his strong feelings, Arnie brings Gumby and a few others into a room away from the set to watch a collection of Puppetoon shorts which comprise most of the movie, ending with Pal's last and perhaps most memorable musical short, *Tubby the Tuba*. Once the rousing compilation has finished, Gumby fully understands Pal's genius and wants to be a part of the film they've just watched. They exit from the screening room where all kinds of characters - including the Pillsbury Doughboy (Frees again) - shout their praise to gentleman Pal. "Hi," the Doughboy says for them all, "we came by to thank George Pal, too." For this end crowd scene, Frees reportedly recorded 100 voices, together with old friend Dallas McKennon.

Arnold Leibovit: "I wrote the script for it and came up with this dinosaur that was called Arnie, named after me really. The name just kind of stuck. But it should have been Paul the dinosaur because that dinosaur was really Paul Frees. In physicality, in every way, we patterned him after Paul. I kind of created a little pot belly on the dinosaur and made him look as much like Paul as you can for a dinosaur."

Instinctively, Paul knew what to do when Arnold explained the part over the phone the night before the session. "Arnie, you don't have to worry," soothed Paul. "You're not going to get a chicken. You're going to get a dinosaur."

Frees' voice work for both Pal tributes were recorded in only a couple hours at the same session, in a San Francisco studio that Paul chose because he had worked with the people there many times before. "With hardly any preparation at all," says Leibovit, "he ran right through it almost perfectly the first time. He did the whole narration, although I did have to do pickups [single word or line retakes] with him.

The Puppetoon Movie, 1987, Arnold Leibovit Entertainment. (*Photofest*)

"He was such a pro. I mean, he was amazing. He was like one of those great musicians in the orchestra where they could sit down and do a composition. The first time it's perfect, almost perfect, and the second time it's totally perfect. You didn't have to tell him very much, and he just did it. He was that good."

At first Frees appeared "crotchety" to Leibovit, but as the discussions for the films progressed, Paul warmed to the material easily and began calling Leibovit "boychick" as they got to know each other better "because he was a Jewish fellow, as I was. And I never knew he was Jewish. So I think that helped a lot because he knew that I was, I guess, part of the family.

"Critically, *The Fantasy Film World of George Pal* did very well. Financially, it did well. The investors got their return on the investment; *Puppetoon*, not quite as well as the other one, but they did very well. I mean, they had a good response. They've sort of become cult classics in a way, at this point, because they're the only documents done of George Pal's career. And *Puppetoon* is the only one of its kind. They are now out on DVD with a plethora of extras.

"Paul was loving, full of great feelings and memories of the past. We talked on and on about George, and Paul's relationship on the movies and his love of what he was doing; and Pal's professionalism.

"Paul's astuteness in defining a part or knowing the material and delivering it in the way it was intended was really incredible. I mean, those are my memories of Paul. I'm sure that's the memory a lot of people in the business have of him. Just a real pro. Some people just called him the Voice of God, or the Voice of the Movies. But at the same time, he also was the voice of these unbelievable characters. I mean, to see him go from Arnie the Dinosaur in a narration to the Pillsbury Doughboy was amazing to me. He was so quick to switch gears and change into whatever it was that he was doing.

"He did make a big impression on me. Paul was a wonderful man. He was sweet. When you really got to know him, you know, he was really a decent guy, and when he passed away, I was really taken by that. I really got to feel quite affectionate for him, and I did a tribute to him on the *Puppetoon* movie. It's dedicated to Paul. It meant that much to me because he had done a fantastic job."

One might say Frees' film career had come full circle: from George Pal to *George Pal*. *The Puppetoon Movie* was released by Arnold Leibovit Entertainment on June 12, 1987, showing:

In Memory of
Paul Frees
1920-1986

on the last screen after the credits.

"I didn't see Paul much, maybe a few years, before he died," says Al Teixeira. "I wasn't working for the Sheriff's Office anymore and I got married and moved to San Leandro. Toward the end he was hanging out a lot with Joyce Post. He hung out at her house or she hung out at his. She was absolutely crazy about Paul. He cared about her, but I think his last wife just broke his back. He just wanted to be loved so badly. But he wouldn't be interested in anyone his own age. Just these young girls. The problem with Paul was that he would pick these young girls, but when he got home all he wanted to do was just lay in bed. He never wanted to go anywhere or do anything and he like imprisoned these women and they got bored. As soon as he got home he got out of his clothes and put on his robe and climbed into that damn bed. I used to tell him that it was like a coffin to him. But he loved it. He would sit in that bed and have a sandwich or something and have his dinner served to him in it. That's all

(*Charles Fretzin*)

he wanted to do. He told me once that Sid Caesar was like that and Paul was his friend and he used to tell him, you can't do that. Well, Sid Caesar turned it around and got back into life and started living a good life, but then Paul ended up doing the same thing. And that's where he died.

"I last saw Paul maybe about a year before he died. I was remarried and living in San Leandro, not working for the sheriff any more. I'd talk to him on the phone sometimes. Mostly his wife, Bev, would call me. I wasn't around the area and the friendship seemed to have gone stale. It just kind of died out. He would spend a lot of time over at Joyce's house. Anytime I was in the area, I would stop by and he was there. He had some fireman doing all the stuff that I used to do for him. Next thing I knew Joyce called me up and told me he was dead. He had tried suicide before, but someone had always come and saved him in time. I think it was one way for him to get attention. A cry for help. This time I think he went too far. I don't think he really wanted to die. He just went too far.

"He was hypochondriac #1. He was always complaining about all these problems. It was always something with Paul. He had this or he had that. But I read the autopsy report and there was nothing wrong with him like he had said. I think his sickness was that he didn't want to do anything. Just get back home, get into bed and watch TV. He had tapes upon tapes of shows. Hundreds of tapes. He would watch documentaries, news, anything. I used to think, what a waste. He could have done so much for people. Little kids loved him…all those voices."

In 1986, there didn't seem to be a lot left in life that interested Paul Frees. Except television.

"He loved anything that had his friends in it, like Vinny Price," says Joyce Post. "And of course everyone was his friend. He loved documentaries and anything that chronicled. He would record lots of documentaries."

He had thrived on challenges all his life, pushing himself to do more and more. But in his last year, the only challenges Paul confronted were health and family problems.

Fred Frees: "Around 1983-84, Sabrina's mother arranged for the two of us to fly up together and visit our dad. Beverly had left him, and he was all alone in the house. It was great for me, because I had a chance to be with my sister. And even though we had been at the Tiburon house at the same time years earlier, this was the first (and only) time that we went there on the same plane. Dad was very surprised and glad that we were there, although we didn't do very much after that. I remember watching him several days later when we drove away in the taxi, and he was standing outside his house, in his usual striped robe; crying. It was really sad.

"What I didn't know then was that it would be the last time I ever saw him.

"I did speak to him on the phone quite a bit the next couple of years. But the last time I ever spoke to him was three weeks before he died. He told me that he was going to get married again. So, he put Joyce Post on the phone to talk to me. We said 'Hello' and not much else. She told me how much she loved my dad and I said something like 'Yeah, it's hard not to do that.' Then I told Dad that whatever he wanted to do, I was behind him. It was the only time I can remember that my dad seemed to be asking for my approval. (It was usually the other way around).

"Three weeks later, my mother gave me the news that he had died, and my life would never be the same since."

Eddie Brandt: "I knew he was going to die when I saw him the last time because he was too fat. He was stubborn, and did nothing to keep himself in shape. He just laid in bed all day, in this great big waterbed, and watched TV. He'd do his commercials and everything right from his home in Tiburon. But he could hardly breathe, he had gained so much weight. He was too heavy."

"He hated the fact that he was growing older," says niece Janice Fishbein. "He *really* hated it. He told me that."

He also hated being alone.

Joyce Post: "Once Beverly left for good, he abandoned the Tiburon house, and moved in with me in my little home in San Rafael. He said he was never going back to that house again because it reminded him too much of her, so he asked, 'Would you mind taking your sister and videotape my whole house, so that I can decide what I want to bring from the place?' So, of course, we're amateurs, and we just walked through the house, filming the kitchen and all the rooms and everything.

"He didn't like my house, thought it was very, very small, but he lived here. It was a little three-bedroom, one-bath, stucco house on the flats of San Rafael. It's nothing spectacular at all. It's just a cute little house. And then once we remodeled the kitchen into a beautiful, working kitchen, it was like it became like his house. The kitchen is 500 square feet, so what I did was put a million dollar saddle on a jackass. But we did it the way he wanted it. Well, actually, we did it the way *I* wanted it. I just let him think we did it the way he wanted it.

"We did that because he liked to eat, and because he would like to watch me eat. At breakfast, we would be discussing dinner, and at dinner we would be discussing lunch for the next day. And it was nothing for him to all of a sudden go on a whim and go up and get me four live lobsters and everything else. In '86 he was unable to cook, his hands had started to get arthritic so he would direct me in preparing everything."

Carol Lynn Fletcher: "Joyce's house in San Rafael is 1300 square feet, maybe. Three bedrooms, one-and-a-half baths. The kitchen is the heart of the house and Joyce *loves* to cook. So Paul built her a new kitchen and lived there during the construction. We tried to stay as quiet as possible in the mornings so he could sleep, but that was difficult. Joyce and I worked on it along with others, and she and I hung the wallpaper. That is what we did for a living at the time.

"He loved his nightshirt and hung around the house in that a lot. Joyce and I also loved his nightshirts. We went to the men's department and got some for ourselves. I wore mine for years. Joyce still has hers.

"Joyce cooked dinner late. They would eat around 10 p.m. She went to bed before Paul, who went to bed around 2 to 4 a.m. and woke up at about 1-ish. On studio days Paul had to be up early and that was hard for him. All of his gigs earlier in his career meant getting home very late and his sleep patterns reflected that. But he was up and nervous on those days. His mood reflected that as well. He wouldn't eat. He was very serious about his work and although he looked very relaxed, at the studio beforehand was another story. He always looked very dapper with his watch fob hanging out of his vest pocket. He definitely had his own style and it suited him.

"Sometimes I would drive him to the studio along with Joyce. Those were fun days for me. I was amazed at the way he would do a 'warm-up' for the clients. They were always polite, but nervous, because the warm-

Paul Frees and Joyce Post.

up was on their time and Paul's fees were not cheap. Interestingly, the look on their faces changed when he actually got into the studio and did the work. He could have it done in fifteen minutes, sometimes less. They still paid him for the hour but he never went over that when I was there, even with the warm-up. It makes me think that he knew that it wouldn't take him long so he gave the clients their money's worth by doing a little stand-up for them.

"When we would go out for dinner, he would go into some routine that sounded so polished by its delivery that it was a challenge to figure out if he was ad-libbing or doing a time-tested routine. He did five minutes about a parking meter we were standing next to outside an Italian restaurant in Mill Valley that had three of us laughing so hard we almost soiled ourselves. My God, it was funny. I wish I could remember the story but no matter, I remember the laughing and it was glorious.

"He didn't like going to the movies. I did force him to see *Top Gun*. He politely told me that he liked it, but he didn't really. He really liked being at home. He was a homebody in the truest sense of the word. Probably because he was out and about so much in his career that home was the greatest place to be.

"But he didn't like to be alone for days on end. He needed to be with people. I think he was a very lonely person with an enormous talent that distanced him from companionship. He felt that companionship with Joyce, although their relationship wasn't a walk in the park. They loved each other so much it is hard to describe. Sometimes their love appeared painful. There was always something in the middle of their love that seemed to keep them from enjoying it completely. It wasn't about another person, it was just an energy that, to this day, I can't pinpoint. Maybe I'm hallucinating, I don't know.

"My compassion for his loneliness was apparent to him. The only person who could rectify those feelings was Paul. He was unable to. Those of us who loved him knew about it not because he mentioned it, but because it was apparent even though he thought he concealed it. I can't imagine what it must be like to be that talented and not feel like anyone really knew you. A handful of us did. I can't speak for or about anyone else. *I* do know this. He was a magnificent human being, who loved his work and had fun doing it. More importantly, he loved his kids, he loved his friends, and was generous with himself to others. All of that and none of that keeps the loneliness at bay.

"He was so open and so closed. He was so fun and so sad. He put on a good façade, but underneath was someone who wanted to be loved just like you and me. I think his talent got in the way of that ultimately. I think his talent made him lonely. I don't know. I just loved him for all that he was.

"One day, he and I were talking at Joyce's, as we had what seemed like a hundred times before, and we started talking religion. I mentioned that I thought that religion was overrated and that I was reading a book by Ernest Holmes. That is when he told me that he knew Holmes and was a minister, ordained and everything, as I recall. We both believed that the truth is the truth and you can't change the truth. As hard as you try to change it, the truth is the truth. This was wonderful for me because no one in my family was into anything remotely spiritual and I now had Paul, the person I admired the most, to talk with about it. I called him Honey. He called me Lynski.

"We'd bicker about his career because I remembered more of what he had done than he did. He'd say, 'I lived it, and you remember it. Between the two of us, I bet we know everything there is to know about show business.' We would talk about movies, TV and radio until the wee hours of the morning. Others around us would get bored and leave because we were talking about showbiz like two little old retired engineers. We had so much in our collective heads that when we talked about it, there was no room in our conversation for someone who couldn't keep up. We were so happy to have each other to talk to about it.

"I loved the fact that he loved attention. The more I got to know him, the more I found that he was not only interesting - he was interested. He loved attention, yes, but he loved interacting more. He was so brilliant that, when he had a captive audience of any size who wasn't intimidated by his shtick, that was when he felt comfortable enough to reveal a deeper side of himself. That is the person I got to know. His brilliance didn't frighten me off in the least."

"What supported his artistic ways," says Fred, "was no doubt a 'softness' on the inside. Dad cried a lot, depending on the circumstances. He definitely had an artistic temperament. He could get angry from time to time, but his mood was generally consistent when I visited him. His public face was a confident 'superman,' but at home, he was just a teddy bear."

"We now finally had our life together," recalls Joyce Post. "Paul was waiting for the divorce to be final in two weeks, and he asked me if I'd marry him. Of course, my daughter was grown up, and I consented."

Then she and Paul had what she called "a silly argument" that prompted Paul to move back into his Tiburon home. Peter Davis: "He stayed there, kind of trying to resume his way of life, but of course, he was alone then. There was no one staying with him. I think he might have been there maybe a month, a month and a half, at which time he had often asked, 'Hey, why don't you move in here with me and stay here so there's someone around and I don't feel so lonely.' I know for a fact that he was very lonely being there in his last days. Probably a week to two weeks before his death, we talked a great deal about dying and the whole life he had lived and things like that. Me, not thinking too much about that, I didn't pick up on some of the classic signs that he was going to take his life. Basically, he was trying to prepare me to be the only one that would find him because I was a fireman, and I could deal with it a lot better than anyone else.

"The night before or the night that he actually died, he tried calling me. I think I was one of the last phone calls he made, because it came up on his phone records when the police checked, but I was at the firehouse that night. I never did get a message the next day. I just had a blank message on the machine that someone had called and hung up.

"I didn't think much about it until the day he was discovered. Joyce had called me, and said she'd been trying to get a hold of him for a day and a half, that there was no answer, and that she was worried. I said I'd go down there and just check. The minute I walked in, I knew. I opened his door. The alarm wasn't on, and there was a radio playing classical music throughout the house, and I knew. I went down and found him in his bedroom. He'd overdosed on pain medication."

"It is interesting," says Fred Frees, "that some people attributed my father's ill health to his weight. This may be partially true. And it is understandable that people believed that his weight was the cause of his death, because that is what they were led to believe. But that is not the case. My father's death was by his own hand. The coroner determined that the death of Paul Frees was suicide. It was Charles Stern (who himself has since passed away) who decided to release to the press that the cause of his death was heart failure. At the time, it was felt by some that this would protect his dignity and reputation, and I agreed. But I have since come to believe that the truth is more important to my father's memory than an obfuscation of that truth.

"My father had a large quantity of prescription medicines because of his health. His death was due to an overdose of these medicines. Whether the overdose was intentional or not is still unclear, but the coroner obviously felt that it was intentional. However, this would not have been the first time he took too many pills. He had flirted with this danger before. He used to say to me, 'Someday they're gonna find your old man…' (meaning they would find him lying dead in his room; and that's exactly what happened). I would respond by saying, 'Oh, stop saying that,' but he was unfortunately too accurate about this one prediction (and it had nothing to do with psychic abilities).

"On one hand, if my father accidentally overdosed, it would have followed a pattern which he had previously set and his life could have been saved if he hadn't been alone when it happened. On the other hand, if my father intentionally took his own life, then it is understandable when all is considered from his point of view. There is nothing to fear by admitting that he may have committed suicide. Unlike today, the ancient Romans considered it a dignified and noble act. And I refuse to stand in judgement of a decision my father may have made, whatever his motivations."

Joyce Post: "The coroner's office, given the fact that he was a high profile case, withheld the death certificate for maybe three weeks, four weeks, six weeks, until the media frenzy had died down. I saw the coroner's note to the assistant: suicide. He said, 'Do you have any objections to putting suicide on the death certificate?' So, it's on the death certificate.

"Beverly had them investigate me, thinking that I had murdered him. So, I was a murder suspect for about fifteen minutes. He had been talking about taking himself out since the day I met him. He said, 'If I ever go, it's going to be because I'm taking myself out.' And he was always saying, through all the years, 'Oh, I've got angina. I'm going to die of a heart attack. I've got bad this, bad that, bad this, bad that.' The coroner's results said he probably would have lived easily another 25 years; his heart was in great shape, and so was his liver, though he drank very heavily. So, throughout his life, he was always sick or thought he was sick, and all the results showed there was absolutely nothing wrong with him.

"He was angry at me, because I guess I was his last hope, if you know what I mean. He had finally found me. He used to call me his magic lady. We were finally able to be together. His divorce was going to be final, and we were at last going to be able to live together in peace and privacy. He had cut down on his work, was not doing really very much of anything, and then we had that stupid fight. I think it was the ultimate 'fuck you' to me that he killed himself, which sounds egotistical on my part. He went in and changed his will three days before he took himself out. His suicide note just said, 'Goodbye.' That's all it said.

"It took me years to get over that. It really, really did. For me, it was like a dream come true that finally the really incredible love that we shared was going to be ours forever. Saying that just doesn't even put a dent in it. And he's dead. The whole thing was tragic. Horrible. I went into a fit of depression and locked myself in the house for almost a year. I didn't go anywhere. I really miss him. He was my sweetheart."

"I flew up with my uncle Dave for Dad's funeral service," recalls Fred Frees, "just two days after his death. The casket was open, and I saw him laying in there. I remember thinking that he actually looked pretty good; peaceful and wearing one of his fancy suits.

"But, when they closed the lid, that was hard.

"And when I went to the Tiburon house, I found an extensive collection of rather disturbing articles which Dad had clipped out of magazines; all about heart attacks and heart failure. So, obviously, these things worried him, even if they were unwarranted.

"As for changing his will three days before he died, I only found out about that years later from Charles Stern. Apparently, I had been excluded from his will since the time I testified in court when I was fifteen. Even though it was Charles' idea to put me back in (he told me), I still regard it as a way of Dad telling me that he had forgiven me.

"But, never ever did I ever doubt that he loved me."

Paul Hersh Frees died on November 2, 1986 of an overdose of pain medication. Five days later, one of two memorial services was given at 3 p.m. at Temple Emmanuel in Beverly Hills, with Daws Butler, Lucille Bliss, Bill Schallert, Casey Kasem, and many other co-workers and friends in attendance. Lorne Greene spoke of playing cards with Frees at his house; when Paul ran out of betting money, he just went out to the mailbox and got another check. He also talked about being troubled by a series of phone calls from a stunning, sexy voice, during his *Bonanza* years. The caller turned out to be Frees doing a woman's voice.

June Foray gave a touching speech at Paul's memorial service. She spoke eloquently and picturesquely on this colorful character, ending thus: "A short time ago, after watching a particularly uproarious Bullwinkle segment, I was stunned again by Paul's phenomenal and unique artistry and felt compelled to telephone him in Tiburon to tell him so. Here was a mid-western American, playing a Russian playing a Texan. A remarkable, exquisitely funny performance. Unmercifully, Ma Bell kept ticking off those message units for almost an hour. But words simply tumbled out uncontrollably while we reminisced, laughed and cried. He was profoundly appreciative of the fact that I was a fan as much as a friend.

"Well, Boris dollink, you are up there with Moose, and I am down here with Squirrel…An ironic Bullwinkle episode, isn't it, Paul? Our cast has been diminished. But we're with each other forever on celluloid—and in our hearts."

At the services Joy Terry Frees had Cole Porter and George Gershwin played. Contributions in Paul's name were asked to be sent to the American Heart Association.

Carol Lynn Fletcher: "Paul never wanted to be remembered as the Pillsbury Doughboy. I said that he would be and he'd just roll his eyes.

"I got to hear him talk about his kids which he did with great reverence and always with a sparkle in his eye. He loved them so very much. Whether they felt that from him or not, I always thought they were so fortunate to be loved like that.

"At his funeral, while paying condolences to his kids, I said to each of them, 'He loved you so much.' I heard Joyce say it too. They didn't know me. I don't think that they knew who Joyce was either. They both looked surprised. That was the first and the last time I saw them and that is all I said. He loved them so much."

Peter Davis: "In my office right now, I have a framed autographed picture of Paul Frees. It says 'To my second son Peter, look forward to the past. Live. Paul Frees – 1985.' He's sitting in a rather tall pink chair. He's wearing dark sunglasses and a white three-piece suit."

Eddie Brandt: "A lot of people didn't like him at all. They said he was too stuck up, but he was entirely the opposite if you knew him well, if you knew him right. It's like meeting a movie star at the wrong time, and you piss them off. If you meet them at the right time, they'll talk to you all day. He didn't have enough time to spend hours talking to every person on the street. But if he'd had the time, he would have. He was my closest friend."

Joyce Post: "He was a great man, and the side that he showed to the public was the side he wanted to be remembered for, I'm sure. But the side that I saw was Paul Frees, the man.

"He told me many, many stories. My God, the stories were amazing. I mean, this was someone that I took care of. It was like taking care of a 12-year-old, and I loved it. I loved him. He was incredible. That's a stupid, dumb word, but he was *incredible.*"

Fred Frees: "My father was everything one would expect from a human being. He was contradictory. He was gentle but he had a temper. He was generous and he was selfish. He was experienced and he was naive. He was simple and he was complex. He was powerful and he was vulnerable.

"But his dignity is intact. His reputation is secure. And the one thing that was the key to his enormous success was something that he once told me when I was about 12 years old. He told me, 'Never lose your zest for life.' Of all the things he ever said to me, this was the one thing that he insisted that I promise never to forget. And I did promise. And I have never forgotten.

"It was his zest for life that drove him. And whether he ended his life intentionally or not, it does not diminish, in the least, that unquenchable zest. That is what made him my father. That is what made him Paul Frees."

Afterword:
An unabashed fan recalls the Master
by Keith Scott

IT SOMETIMES SEEMED as though Paul Frees had come to Earth from another planet. The man was not merely extravagantly gifted; he had about him a mysteriously impenetrable aura. I noticed it even in my childhood— his uniquely sonorous voice for "Oliver Wendell Clutch" on the TV cartoon show *Calvin and the Colonel* was oddly, joltingly striking. And when I slowly discovered it was also Frees enacting those truly oddball vocal characterizations on Jay Ward's splendid series *Rocky and His Friends* (one moment an impression of the effete British character actor Henry Daniell in a *Peabody* episode, the next his klutzy Captain Peachfuzz, or a manic German villain, or the funny, plummy Inspector Fenwick) I was hooked: I had to find out more about this man, whose bag of vocal tricks was so different from the norm.

Indeed that was the mystery: he even seemed different to the majority of actors providing multiple voices—a class apart. That vocal timbre carried with it the hint of several cultures. Was he slightly, what…European? Continental? And how could he go from that rumblingly deep, sonic velvet, to the giggling high tones of the Pillsbury Doughboy, with no sign of the distorting strain that so often mars today's barely average cartoon voices?

Beyond animation, I soon discovered Paul Frees could do far more: his straight narration was also instantly striking (today, only a few others like William Conrad and Orson Welles can really stand alongside Frees as that period's top dramatic orators). When Frees hit a project for which he felt some empathy he was often the best thing in it: his Jay Ward recordings, his Rankin-Bass role of Burgermeister Meisterburger, even a virtually unseen B-movie, *The Night Walker*, that contains one of his finest narration jobs.

As time went on I also discovered Frees lurking in vintage recordings: his near-forgotten singing ability was almost thrown away, but on one old Spike Jones single, *Deep Purple* (for which he sends up jazz great Billy Eckstine), Paul Frees hits a climactic note that is as operatically rich and ringing as any basso profundo ever achieved.

And then there was radio. Paul Frees's work is well preserved in the vast legacy of radio shows unearthed over the last thirty years. Just twenty-four when he started in this greatest of all training grounds, by 1947 Frees was given a shot at the audio big time by William N. Robson, an important, flamboyant, dramatically gifted director. Robson went back to the medium's early days as director on *The Columbia Workshop*, and he kick-started the careers of many brilliant actors with distinctive voices (Frank Lovejoy, Elliott Lewis). Sensing something unique in this Frees kid, he cast Paul in *Escape*, a classy transcontinental show that, in its earliest days, adapted classic literary tales of adventure and horror.

Here, Frees was thrown in the deep end. Handed several lead roles - *The Fall of the House of Usher*, *Taboo*, *Wild Oranges*—often supported by performers twice his age, he came through strikingly. To listen fifty-five years later is to marvel at this young man's flair for the dramatic. In one show called *Ancient Sorceries* (Algernon Blackwood's eerie tale of lycanthropy), Frees evokes a world of unease in one tiny scene. His character has just been warned not to alight at the misty, lonely village of Moulton. Underscored by a lone woodwind invoking a mournful Welsh tune, Frees (in the oddly transatlantic voice he adopted for many of these European-based tales), softly remarks, "I made my way from the busy train platform, when suddenly, for no good reason—I shivered," as the music changes to a portentous counter-melodic sting. It's essentially a corny line, but Frees simply does wonders with this material. In just seven seconds, a palpably gothic feeling of unease is planted in the listener. While it was obvious in later decades that Frees could be infuriatingly lazy with his talent, here he proved he could really act; indeed it is tempting to think of what could have been, had radio survived.

But it is most likely his animated cartoons for which Paul Frees will be remembered. There were only three other male cartoon voice artists from Frees's era who stand the test of time for me as great animation actors; and the four of them will likely remain unsurpassed, for, sadly, today we have entered a media-saturated, hipper-than-thou, insufferably smug and often mean spirited era where prime-time amateurism reigns, and even basic performing skills are scorned as seeming "dated."

Frees's three outstanding comrades-in-voice were Mel Blanc, Daws Butler and Bill Scott. Each was a brilliant interpretive talent; yet it is apparent with hindsight that none of them matched the sheer range of vocal artistry that Paul Frees boasted. As his son Fred points out in this book, while Frees was their equal in the creation of vibrant, funny, and *believable* cartoon characters, he alone could also announce, narrate and sing (okay, to split hairs, Blanc and Scott could also sing, but only as required in cartoons—not the way Frees could; and though Daws Butler began as a young impressionist like Frees, he couldn't match Paul's awesome mimic's range). In fact, had he been temperamentally inclined, Frees could have made a solid living in each single category. Fortunately for us, he chose to be too versatile, and thus became virtually unclassifiable.

As a teenager I became so all-consumingly influenced by these four artists that I determined to enter the field of audio acting and cartoons, and, most importantly, to meet my heroes. Daws Butler, truly the nicest man I have ever known in showbiz, was my (eventually literal) teacher, but Frees was my mischievous, spiritual role model; if a true role model is someone to whom you aspire, while realizing deep down you can never match, then that is what happened the moment I heard Paul's Ghost Host in Disneyland's *The Haunted Mansion*: although intentionally campy and melodramatic, it remains in my opinion the single greatest job of narration I've ever heard.

I had the great good fortune to see Frees in action at two recording sessions. In 1973, he invited me to a session at Radio Recorders where he was doing Jolly Green Giant commercials. What a thrill for a nineteen year old to see the master at work, holding court, cracking jokes, and yes, being the obnoxiously funny audio court jester yet again. Six years later, my ultimate reward occurred when Bill Scott told me to be at TVR studio one afternoon to watch a Jay Ward session featuring himself, Daws Butler, and Paul Frees (doing tracks for Quaker cereals). When I entered the lobby, Frees was already kidding with Ward, showing off a new voice he was working on: that of an outrageous gay, black holdup-man. In that two hours, he was silly, infuriating, hilarious; to this day in my mind, he remains completely unforgettable.

It's high time the real story of Paul Frees was told, not just for his countless fans who wondered about this man from the first time they heard him, but for the many industry folk who often totally misunderstood him. Ben Ohmart has done a sterling job in presenting the sweeping saga of Frees's colorful life, especially considering the author's major stumbling block - the passing of so many who were major players in Frees's tale. Within these pages is a great showbiz story, daubed often with touching human strokes, revealing in word pictures just who this hilarious, child-like, insecure, arrogant, tiny but towering talent really was.

It's a timely tribute to one of the greatest and most neglected performers in the history of American entertainment. Sadly, Paul Frees represents the type of talent who has virtually disappeared in our instantly disposable new Millennium; but while he was a product of his time, his immense body of outstanding voice-work remains happily accessible, to hopefully inspire and teach (though even now one can almost hear him adopting his most Welles-ian tones, and declaiming, "Yes, but no one will ever topple the Emperor!").

The great June Foray, in this book's Foreword, mentions Frees being in Heaven: if so, God is no doubt yelling, "Shut up, Paul!!"

Sydney, Australia
December 2003

Photos

A radio show with Jimmy Stewart.

The Thing.

The Company She Keeps.

Dragnet.

His Majesty, Paul Frees

CONGRATULATIONS TO:
Award Winning Announcer
PAUL
FREES

and
PLAYHOUSE PICTURES
for placing
FIRST
in the
Television Commercial Series
at the
**INTERNATIONAL
BROADCAST
AWARDS**

CONGRATULATIONS
also to
PAUL
FREES
for being selected as
the Announcer of this
year's SARA LEE commercials
scheduled for the
**MOTION PICTURE
ACADEMY AWARDS**
telecast on April 8.

We salute
PAUL
FREES
one of the leading exponents
of today's
"NEW SOUND"
in Announcing.

P.S. The Walt Disney "Symposium of
Music" Short Subject nominated
for an Academy Award is another
of Paul's numerous voice credits.

CHARLES H. STERN AGENCY
1680 North Vine Street
Hollywood 28, California
HO. 6-4304

REPRESENTING LEADING TALENT
FOR
RADIO & TV COMMERCIALS

PRESENTING----

THE

OUTSTANDING TALENTS

OF

PAUL FREES

The 27th Day.

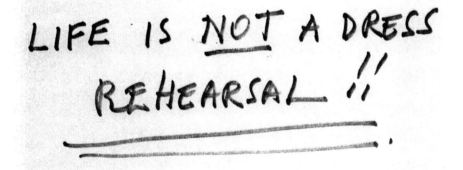

References

BOOKS

BeatleToons: The Real Story Behind the Cartoon Beatles by Mitch Axelrod

Careless Love: The Unmaking of Elvis Presley by Peter Guralnick

The Enchanted World of Rankin/Bass: A Portfolio by Rick Goldschmidt

The Encyclopedia of Animated Cartoons by Jeff Lenburg

The Moose That Roared by Keith Scott

On the Air: The Encyclopedia of Old-Time Radio by John Dunning

Spike Jones: Off the Record by Jordan R. Young

Unsold Television Pilots 1955-1989 by Lee Goldberg

MAGAZINES

The Commercial Actor, 1977-78

Frostbite Falls Far-Flung Flier

Los Angeles Herald-Examiner, March 3, 1963 "TV's Insurance Policy"

Los Angeles Times, November 28, 1970 "Paul Frees and His Poster People"

Pittsburgh Press, November, 1962 "Man of Many Voices"

Radio Life, October 31, 1948

Radio Life, December 1, 1950

The TV Collector, January-February 1987

WITS "Talking Trivia" 6/27/82

MISCELLANEOUS

Gary Owens Show interview with Frees – October, 1970

Gene Nelson interview with Frees – 1972

Jack Roth interview – October, 1975

John Dunning interview with Frees – April 25, 1982

Keith Scott phone interviews with Frees – 1972, 1973, 1981

Morgan White interview with Frees – June 27, 1982

Justin Humphreys interview with Robert Cornthwaite – 2003

Credits

(This list, while certainly comprehensive, cannot hope for completeness at enumerating a career as vast as that of Paul Frees. It is merely a guide to all known Frees credits. There are undoubtedly several hundred more undiscovered radio shows, and literally thousands of TV and radio commercials not included. Anyone with extra credits for Paul Frees is urged to contact the author.)

RADIO

1945	A Man Named Jordan
April 2, 1945	Lux Radio Theatre (Swanee River)
September 3, 1945	Sherlock Holmes (The Case of the Limping Ghost)
October 18, 1945	Maxwell House Coffee Time (with Burns and Allen)
1945-46	The Adventures of Sherlock Holmes
1945-48	The Dick Haymes Show
January 3, 1946	Rogue's Gallery (The Stark McVey Case)
January 21, 1946	Sherlock Holmes (The Telltale Pigeon Feathers)
May 6, 1946	Sherlock Holmes (The Man with the Twisted Lip)
July 1, 1946	The Whistler (Solid Citizen)
July 8, 1946	The Whistler (The Confession)
August 12, 1946	The Whistler (Stolen Murder)
September 12, 1946	Miss Sherlock (Wilmer and the Widow)
September 16, 1946	The Whistler (The Brass Ring)
September 23, 1946	The Whistler (Stranger in the House)
September 30, 1946	The Casebook of Gregory Hood (The Washington D.C. Murder)
October 11, 1946	The Alan Young Show (The Cucamonga Killer)
October 24, 1946	Suspense (Dame Fortune)
October 29, 1946	Half Hour to Kill (Blackout; audition)
November 7, 1946	Suspense (Easy Money)
December 5, 1946	Suspense (The House In Cypress Canyon)
December 23, 1946	The Whistler (Next Year Is Mine)
January 18, 1947	The Ghost Walks (Power of Attorney)
February 3, 1947	The Whistler (Seven Steps to Murder)

February 20, 1947	Suspense (Always Room At The Top)
April 10, 1947	Suspense (Community Property)
May 19, 1947	The Whistler (Hasty Conclusions)
June 2, 1947	The Whistler (Caesar's Wife)
July 9, 1947	The Whistler (The Two Lives of Colby Fletcher)
August 18, 1947	Escape (The Fourth Man)
August 21, 1947	The Voyage of the Scarlet Queen (The Story of the Eight Historic Periods)
September 6, 1947	Hawke Larabee (The Actor)
September 10, 1947	The Whistler (The Bridge on Black Mountain)
September 24, 1947	The Henry Morgan Show
October 1, 1947	Escape (The Most Dangerous Game)
October 10, 1947	Spotlight Revue
October 16, 1947	The Voyage of the Scarlet Queen (Ah Sing and the Balinese Beaux Arts Bal)
October 18, 1947	Hawke Larabee (The California Kid)
October 22, 1947	Escape (Fall of the House of Usher)
October 31, 1947	Spotlight Revue
November 5, 1947	Escape (Evening Primrose)
November 12, 1947	Escape (The Young Man with the Cream Tarts)
November 26, 1947	Escape (The Country of the Blind)
December 3, 1947	Escape (Taboo)
December 17, 1947	Escape (Wild Oranges)
December 18, 1947	The Adventures of Ellery Queen (The Melancholy Dane)
December 21, 1947	California Caravan (How Santa Came to Simpson's Bar)
December 24, 1947	Escape (Back for Christmas)
December 31, 1947	The Whistler (The First Year)
1947-48	The Private Practice of Dr. Dana
January 3, 1948	Suspense (The Black Curtain) [1st hour show]
January 4, 1948	The Adventures of Sam Spade (The One Hour Caper)
January 7, 1948	Escape (Second Class Passenger) [East Coast broadcast]
January 10, 1948	Escape (Second Class Passenger) [West Coast broadcast]
January 21, 1948	The Whistler (Twelve Portraits of Marcia)
January 29, 1948	First Nighter (A Writer in the Family)
February 5, 1948	The Adventures of Ellery Queen (Bubsy)
February 8, 1948	Escape (Snake Doctor) [East Coast broadcast]
February 12, 1948	Family Theater (Out of the Wilderness)
February 14, 1948	Escape (Snake Doctor) [West Coast broadcast]
February 15, 1948	Escape (Ancient Sorceries) [East Coast broadcast]
February 15, 1948	The Last Water Hole (documentary)
February 21, 1948	Escape (Ancient Sorceries) [West Coast broadcast]
February 22, 1948	Escape (How Love Came to Professor Guildea) [East Coast broadcast]

February 28, 1948	Escape (How Love Came to Professor Guildea) [West Coast broadcast]
February 28, 1948	Escape (The Grove of Ashtaroth) [East Coast broadcast]
(unknown)	Follow That Man (The Trail of the Terrified Temptress)
(unknown)	Crusade for Freedom (The Tank That Jan Built)
March 6, 1948	Escape (The Grove of Ashtaroth) [West Coast broadcast]
March 7, 1948	Escape (Jimmy Goggles, the God) [East Coast broadcast]
March 13, 1948	Escape (Jimmy Goggles, the God) [West Coast broadcast]
March 21, 1948	Escape (Misfortune's Isle) [East Coast broadcast]
March 27, 1948	Escape (Misfortune's Isle) [West Coast broadcast]
1948	The Player (Jack the Giant Killer)
1948	The Player (Murder at Tammerlane)
1948	The Player (The Missing Mr. Dillon)
1948	The Player (Johnny Dynamite)
1948	The Player (The Professor Goes to a House Cleaning)
1948	The Player (Mirage)
1948	The Player (First Citizen of the Bowery)
1948	The Player (Curse of the Jonker Diamond)
1948	The Player (Solo Flight)
1948	The Player (The Professor Goes to a Wrestling Match)
1948	The Player (It's All in the Deal)
1948	The Player (Reward for Sanchez)
1948	The Player (Fate Upsets a Plan)
1948	The Player (The Pinwheel Role)
1948	The Player (The Prophesy)
1948	The Player (They Do It In Books)
1948	The Player (Frozen Justice)
April 1, 1948	The Adventures of Ellery Queen (The Vanishing Crook)
April 4, 1948	The Eternal Light (The Physician of Birkenau)
April 5, 1948	Let George Do It (The Smugglers)
April 11, 1948	The Eternal Light (The Man Who Remembered Lincoln)
April 18, 1948	The Eternal Light (The Passover of Rembrandt Van Rijn)
April 22, 1948	The Adventures of Ellery Queen (Murder by Installments)
April 25, 1948	Escape (The Fourth Man)
May 18, 1948	Remember ("My Old Flame")
May 24, 1948	Murder and Mr. Malone (The Charles Morgan Case)
June 7, 1948	Let George Do it (Have Some Excitement)
June 20, 1948	Shorty Bell

June 27, 1948	Escape (The Country of the Blind)
July 4, 1948	Escape (A Tooth for Paul Revere)
July 5, 1948	Box 13 (The Haunted Artist) [West Coast broadcast]
July 8, 1948	Suspense (The Last Chance) [1st as announcer]
July 15, 1948	Suspense (Summer Night) [announcer]
July 22, 1948	Suspense (Deep Into Darkness) [announcer & actor]
July 29, 1948	Suspense (The Yellow Wall-Paper) [announcer]
August 5, 1948	Suspense (An Honest Man) [announcer]
August 9, 1948	Our Miss Brooks
August 12, 1948	Suspense Beware the Quiet Man [announcer]
August 15, 1948	The Adventures of Sam Spade (The Critical Author Caper)
August 19, 1948	Suspense (Crisis) [announcer]
August 26, 1948	Suspense (Song of the Heart) [announcer]
August 29, 1948	The Adventures of Sam Spade (The Lawless Caper)
August 30, 1948	Box 13 (Last Will and Nursery Rhyme) [West Coast broadcast]
September 2, 1948	Suspense (The Morrison Affair) [announcer]
September 9, 1948	Suspense (The Big Shot) [announcer]
September 11, 1948	Jeff Regan (Cain and Abel and the Santa Maria)
September 16, 1948	Suspense (Hitch-Hike Poker) [announcer]
September 23, 1948	Suspense (Celebration) [announcer]
September 26, 1948	The Adventures of Sam Spade (The Dick Foley Caper)
September 30, 1948	Suspense (The Man Who Wanted To Be Edward G. Robinson) [announcer]
October 2, 1948	Jeff Regan (The Man with the Key)
October 7, 1948	Suspense (Night Cry) [announcer]
October 9, 1948	Jeff Regan (Too Many Mrs. Rogers)
October 10, 1948	NBC University Theatre (An American Tragedy)
October 14, 1948	Suspense (A Little Piece of Rope) [announcer]
October 21, 1948	Suspense (Give Me Liberty) [announcer]
October 24, 1948	NBC University Theatre (They Stooped to Folly)
October 31, 1948	Rocky Jordan (The Bartered Bridegroom)
November 4, 1948	Suspense (Death Sentence) [announcer]
November 7, 1948	Rocky Jordan (Count Me Out)
November 11, 1948	Suspense (Muddy Track) [announcer]
November 18, 1948	Suspense (Sorry, Wrong Number) [announcer]
November 20, 1948	Jeff Regan (The Pilgrim's Progress)
November 25, 1948	Suspense (The Screaming Woman) [announcer]
November 28, 1948	The Adventures of Sam Spade (The Quarter Eagle Caper)
November 29, 1948	The Railroad Hour (New Moon)
December 2, 1948	Suspense (The Hands of Mr. Ottermole) [announcer]
December 6, 1948	Box 13 (Daytime Nightmare) [West Coast broadcast]
December 9, 1948	Suspense (The Sisters) [announcer]
December 10, 1948	Spotlight Revue (with Peter Lorre)

December 12, 1948	Box 13 (The Haunted Artist) [East Coast broadcast]
December 16, 1948	Suspense (No Escape) [announcer]
December 23, 1948	Suspense (Holiday Story) [announcer]
December 30, 1948	Suspense (Break-Up) [announcer]
1948-49	Doorway to Life
1948	The New Adventures of Michael Shayne (The Man Who Lived Forever)
1948	The New Adventures of Michael Shayne (The Case of the Bloodstained Pearls)
1948	The New Adventures of Michael Shayne (The Case of the Gray-Eyed Blonde)
1948	The New Adventures of Michael Shayne (The Pursuit of Death)
1948	The New Adventures of Michael Shayne (The Case of the Deadly Dough)
1948	The New Adventures of Michael Shayne (The Case of the Popular Corpse)
1948	The New Adventures of Michael Shayne (The Case of the High Priced Twins)
January 6, 1949	Suspense (To Find Help) [announcer]
January 13, 1949	Suspense (The Too-Perfect Alibi) [announcer & acted in]
January 15, 1949	The Adventures of Philip Marlowe (The Black Halo)
January 16, 1949	NBC University Theatre (All the King's Men)
January 17, 1949	The Railroad Hour (Naughty Marietta)
January 20, 1949	Suspense (If the Dead Could Talk) [announcer]
January 27, 1949	Suspense (The Thing in the Window) [announcer]
February 3, 1949	Prowl Car (The Wilshire Werewolf; audition)
February 3, 1949	Suspense (Backseat Driver) [announcer]
• February 6, 1949	Box 13 (Last Will and Nursery Rhyme) [East Coast broadcast]
February 10, 1949	Suspense (De Mortuis) [announcer]
February 12, 1949	Escape (The Lost Special)
February 13, 1949	Rocky Jordan (Red Stands for Blood)
February 17, 1949	Suspense (Catch Me If You Can) [announcer]
February 19, 1949	The Adventures of Philip Marlowe (The Flying Trapeze)
February 24, 1949	Suspense (Where There's a Will) [announcer]
February 27, 1949	Screen Director's Playhouse (The Night Has a Thousand Eyes)
February 28, 1949	Box 13 (The Clay Pigeon) [West Coast broadcast]
March 3, 1949	Suspense (The Lovebirds) [announcer]
March 6, 1949	The Prudential Family Hour of Stars (Impact)
March 10, 1949	Suspense (Three O'Clock) [announcer]
March 11, 1949	The Philip Morris Playhouse (The Lady from the Sea)
March 17, 1949	Suspense (Murder Through the Looking Glass) [announcer]
March 19, 1949	The Adventures of Philip Marlowe (The Dancing Hands)

March 24, 1949	Suspense (Dead Ernest) [announcer & acted in]
March 27, 1949	Rocky Jordan (Everything Shipshape)
March 31, 1949	Suspense (You Can't Die Twice) [announcer]
April 2, 1949	Pat Novak for Hire (Joe Feldman)
April 7, 1949	Suspense (Noose of Coincidence) [announcer]
April 9, 1949	The Adventures of Philip Marlowe (The Name to Remember)
April 10, 1949	The Adventures of Sam Spade (My Quiet Friend)
April 10, 1949	Rocky Jordan
April 13, 1949	Special Care Program (Aftermath)
April 14, 1949	Suspense (Murder in Black and White) [announcer]
April 21, 1949	Suspense (The Copper Tea Strainer) [announcer]
April 23, 1949	The Adventures of Philip Marlowe (The Cloak of Kamehameha)
April 24, 1949	Rocky Jordan (Consignment for Naples)
April 28, 1949	Suspense (The Lie) [announcer]
May 5, 1949	Suspense (Death Has a Shadow) [announcer]
May 8, 1949	Rocky Jordan (Lady in Disguise)
May 12, 1949	Suspense (The Light Switch) [announcer]
May 15, 1949	Box 13 (Daytime Nightmare) [East Coast broadcast]
May 17, 1949	The Green Lama (The Man Who Never Existed; audition)
May 19, 1949	Suspense (Consequence) [announcer]
May 22, 1949	The Whistler (The Fatal Fraud)
May 26, 1949	Suspense (The Night Reveals) [announcer]
May 29, 1949	Frank Race (The Enoch Arden Adventure)
May 29, 1949	Rocky Jordan (The Make-Up Man)
June 2, 1949	Suspense (The Ten Years) [announcer]
June 5, 1949	The Green Lama (The Man Who Never Existed)
June 5, 1949	Rocky Jordan (The Man They All Loved)
June 9, 1949	Suspense (Lunch Kit) [announcer]
June 10, 1949	Dragnet (Quick Trigger Gunman)
June 12, 1949	The Green Lama (The Man Who Stole a Pyramid)
June 12, 1949	Rocky Jordan (The Man from Damascus)
June 16, 1949	Suspense (The Trap) [announcer]
June 19, 1949	The Green Lama (The Girl with No Name)
June 19, 1949	Rocky Jordan (The Big Ditch)
June 23, 1949	Suspense (Ghost Hunt) [announcer]
June 26, 1949	The Green Lama (Million Dollar Chopsticks)
June 30, 1949	Suspense (The Day I Died) [announcer]
July 2, 1949	Richard Diamond (Bert Kalmus Frame-up)
July 3, 1949	The Green Lama (The Last Dinosaur)
July 9, 1949	Richard Diamond (Escaped Prisoners)
July 15, 1949	Screen Director's Playhouse (Yellow Sky)
July 16, 1949	The Green Lama (The Return of Madame Pompadour)

July 23, 1949	The Green Lama (Tapestry in Purple)
July 30, 1949	The Green Lama (The African Diamond Affair)
July 31, 1949	Rocky Jordan (Barlachi)
August 6, 1949	The Green Lama (The Gumbo Man)
August 7, 1949	Box 13 (The Clay Pigeon) [East Coast broadcast]
August 7, 1949	Rocky Jordan (Gold Fever)
August 12, 1949	Screen Director's Playhouse (Jezebel)
August 13, 1949	The Green Lama (The Case of the Dangerous Dog)
August 14, 1949	Rocky Jordan (Cairo Vendetta)
August 18, 1949	Dragnet (The Big Affair)
August 18, 1949	Escape (Snake Doctor)
August 20, 1949	The Green Lama (The Adventure of the Perfect Prisoner)
August 28, 1949	Rocky Jordan (The Lady from Istanbul)
September 1, 1949	Suspense (Nightmare) [announcer]
September 4, 1949	Rocky Jordan (A Stranger to the Desert)
September 8, 1949	Suspense (Chicken Feed) [announcer]
September 11, 1949	The Whistler (Brief Pause for Murder)
September 15, 1949	Suspense (Last Confession) [announcer]
September 17, 1949	Gene Autry's Melody Ranch
September 19, 1949	The Railroad Hour (Tribute to Nacio Herb Brown)
September 21, 1949	The Croupier (The Roman; audition)
September 22, 1949	Suspense (Experiment 6-R) [announcer]
September 29, 1949	California Caravan (The Saga of Charlie Parkhurst)
September 29, 1949	Suspense (Blind Date) [announcer]
October 2, 1949	The Prudential Family Hour of Stars (Love Affair)
October 2, 1949	Rocky Jordan (Pattern for Revenge)
October 3, 1949	Screen Director's Playhouse (The Senator Was Indiscreet)
October 6, 1949	Suspense (The Defense Rests) [announcer]
October 9, 1949	Rocky Jordan (The Man with No Name)
October 13, 1949	Suspense (Account Payable) [announcer]
October 16, 1949	Rocky Jordan (The Quest for Traneeneh)
October 20, 1949	Suspense (Goodnight Mrs. Russell) [announcer]
October 21, 1949	Crime Correspondent (The Chair for Dino; recorded audition)
October 23, 1949	Rocky Jordan (The Diorite Bowl)
October 27, 1949	Pursuit (The Vicarage)
October 27, 1949	Suspense (Momentum) [announcer]
October 29, 1949	The Adventures of Philip Marlowe (The Green Witch)
November 1, 1949	Escape (Flood on the Goodwins)
November 2, 1949	Rocky Jordan (The Big Heist)
November 3, 1949	Suspense (The Search for Isabell) [announcer]
November 4, 1949	Crime Correspondent (The Chair for Dino, actual broadcast)

November 6, 1949	NBC University Theatre (Dodsworth)
November 6, 1949	Rocky Jordan (Black Ball)
November 8, 1949	Escape (Plunder of the Sun)
November 10, 1949	Suspense (Murder of Aunt Delia) [announcer]
November 13, 1949	Rocky Jordan (The Strange Death of Van Dorn)
November 17, 1949	Suspense (The Red-Headed Woman) [announcer & actor]
November 20, 1949	Rocky Jordan (The Big Heist)
November 22, 1949	Escape (Maracas)
November 24, 1949	Suspense (The Long Wait) [announcer]
November 29, 1949	Escape (Letter from Jason)
December 1, 1949	Suspense (Mission Completed) [announcer]
December 6, 1949	Escape (Command)
December 8, 1949	Suspense (For Love or Murder) [announcer]
December 9, 1949	Screen Director's Playhouse (Call Northside 777)
December 10, 1949	Richard Diamond (Ghost Story)
December 11, 1949	Rocky Jordan (The Veiled People)
December 13, 1949	Escape (Bordertown)
December 15, 1949	Suspense (The Flame Blue Glove) [announcer]
December 18, 1949	The Whistler (Patroness of Murder)
December 20, 1949	Escape (Figure a Dame)
December 22, 1949	Suspense (Double Entry) [announcer]
December 23, 1949	Screen Director's Playhouse (Miracle on 34th Street)
December 25, 1949	The Whistler (Letter from Cynthia)
December 29, 1949	Suspense (The Bullet) [last as announcer]
1949	Favorite Story (Enoch Soames)
1949	Favorite Story (How Much Land Does a Man Need?)
1949	Tomorrow (Civil defense special, starring Orson Welles)
1949-50	The Damon Runyon Theatre
1949-50	Jeff Regan, Investigator
(unknown)	The Hallmark Playhouse
1950s	The Bob Hope Show
January 7, 1950	Richard Diamond (The Butcher Shop)
January 8, 1950	NBC University Theatre (Manhattan Transfer)
January 8, 1950	Rocky Jordan (Smokescreen)
January 10, 1950	Escape (The Vanishing Lady)
January 15, 1950	Rocky Jordan (Loomis Affair)
January 17, 1950	Escape (The Sure Thing)
January 22, 1950	NBC University Theatre (At Heaven's Gate)
January 24, 1950	Escape (Treasure, Inc.)
January 29, 1950	Rocky Jordan (An Air of Death)
January 31, 1950	Escape (Present Tense)
February 3, 1950	Screen Director's Playhouse (The Sea Wolf)

February 5, 1950	Rocky Jordan (Return of Toni)
February 6, 1950	Dangerous Assignment (Missing Japanese Weapons)
February 7, 1950	Escape (The Outer Limit)
February 12, 1950	Rocky Jordan (Madame Dulac's Daughter)
February 14, 1950	Escape (Two if by Sea)
February 21, 1950	Escape (The Red Mark)
February 23, 1950	Beyond This World (audition)
February 24, 1950	A Day in the Life of Dennis Day
February 28, 1950	Escape (The Man Who Won the War)
March 5, 1950	Rocky Jordan (The Secret of Wong Lee)
March 10, 1950	Escape (Port Royal)
March 24, 1950	Escape (Danger at Matecumbe)
March 27, 1950	Dangerous Assignment (Desert Sheik Controls Uranium)
March 28, 1950	The Adventures of Philip Marlowe (The Sword of Cebu)
March 31, 1950	Escape (Green Splotches)
April 5, 1950	Richard Diamond (The Kali Statue)
April 7, 1950	Screen Director's Playhouse (The Fighting O'Flynn)
April 9, 1950	NBC University Theatre (The Nazarene)
April 9, 1950	Rocky Jordan (Holiday Weekend)
April 16, 1950	Rocky Jordan (Adventure in Zakazik)
April 28, 1950	Escape (Something for Nothing)
May 1, 1950	The Railroad Hour (Sally)
May 5, 1950	Escape (The Man Who Stole the Bible)
May 12, 1950	Escape (The Rim of Terror)
May 17, 1950	Dangerous Assignment (Lecturing Professors)
May 19, 1950	Escape (Pass to Berlin)
May 24, 1950	Dangerous Assignment (Murdered Burmese Correspondent)
May 26, 1950	Escape (Command)
May 28, 1950	Rocky Jordan (A Song in the Nile)
May 31, 1950	Dangerous Assignment (Drugged Diplomat)
June 2, 1950	Escape (Mars Is Heaven)
June 4, 1950	Rocky Jordan (Word of a Bishop)
June 5, 1950	The Railroad Hour (Review of 1937)
June 7, 1950	Dangerous Assignment (International Smear Campaign)
June 16, 1950	Escape (Serenade for a Cobra)
June 18, 1950	Rocky Jordan (Shakedown)
June 19, 1950	The Railroad Hour (Review of 1934)
June 23, 1950	Escape (Sundown)
June 25, 1950	Operation Danger (audition)
June 25, 1950	Rocky Jordan (Dilemma)
June 30, 1950	Escape (Blood Bath)

July 1, 1950	T-Man (Show Business Is No Business)
July 2, 1950	Rocky Jordan (The Dead Kalim)
July 7, 1950	Escape (A Shipment of Mute Fate)
July 9, 1950	Jeff Regan (She's Lovely, She's Engaged, She Eats Soybeans)
July 9, 1950	Rocky Jordan (Interlude with Lorraina)
July 14, 1950	Escape (Shark Bait)
July 16, 1950	NBC University Theatre (Treasure of Franchard)
July 20, 1950	The Line-Up (Johnny Turanto Murder)
July 21, 1950	Escape (Yellow Wake)
July 26, 1950	Dangerous Assignment (Oriental Guerilla Leader)
July 30, 1950	Rocky Jordan (The Money Changers)
August 4, 1950	Escape (Two Came Back)
August 4, 1950	The Adventures of Philip Marlowe (The Parrot's Bed)
August 10, 1950	Dragnet (The Big Actor)
August 10, 1950	The Line-Up
August 11, 1950	Escape (The Red Forest)
August 19, 1950	Tales of the Texas Rangers (Fool's Gold)
August 20, 1950	Rocky Jordan (The Man from Damascus)
August 25, 1950	Escape (Crossing Paris)
August 27, 1950	NBC University Theatre (Hedda Gabbler)
August 27, 1950	Rocky Jordan (Dr. Markoff's Discovery)
September 3, 1950	The Whistler (Whirlwind)
September 6, 1950	Dangerous Assignment (Balkan Mine Disaster)
September 8, 1950	This Is Your FBI (The Swing Shift Racketeers)
September 13, 1950	Dangerous Assignment
September 25, 1950	Lux Radio Theatre (Good Sam)
September 27, 1950	Dangerous Assignment (Fugitive in Latin America)
September 29, 1950	Dangerous Assignment (Forged Papers)
September 30, 1950	Tales of the Texas Rangers (Clean-Up)
October 15, 1950	Tales of the Texas Rangers (Dead Giveaway)
October 20, 1950	The Man Called X (One Way to Macassar)
October 26, 1950	Presenting Charles Boyer (Cheese and Castle)
October 26, 1950	Suspense (Too Hot to Live)
October 27, 1950	Dr. Kildare (The Chinese Grandfather)
October 29, 1950	Tales of the Texas Rangers (Soft Touch)
November 10, 1950	Escape (Earth Abides, Part 1)
November 12, 1950	The Adventures of the Saint (The Dame on the Doorstep)
November 17, 1950	Escape (Earth Abides, Part 2)
1950	Jeff Regan (Some Enchanted Carhop)
1950-51	Bold Venture
1950-51	A Day in the Life of Dennis Day
January 26, 1951	Dr. Kildare (Acute Anemia)
February 3, 1951	Dangerous Assignment (Nazi Fugitive)

February 10, 1951	Dangerous Assignment (The Kroner Cutlass)
February 23, 1951	Enchanted Room (The Mona Lisa; audition)
March 22, 1951	Screen Director's Playhouse (The Great Lover)
March 24, 1951	The Man Called X (The Missing Witness)
April 4, 1951	NBC Presents Short Story (Honor)
April 5, 1951	Screen Director's Playhouse (The Damned Don't Cry)
April 5, 1951	Suspense (Murder in G-Flat)
April 6, 1951	The Adventures of Sam Spade (The Danny Shane Caper)
April 7, 1951	The Man Called X (Land Reclamation Project)
April 8, 1951	Tales of the Texas Rangers (Bad Blood)
April 13, 1951	The Adventures of Sam Spade (The Civic Pride Caper)
April 21, 1951	The Man Called X (National Easter Party)
April 22, 1951	Tales of the Texas Rangers (Canned Death)
April 27, 1951	The Adventures of Sam Spade (The Hail And Farewell Caper)
April 28, 1951	Dangerous Assignment (Outlaw Balkan Radio Station)
May 17, 1951	Suspense (Another Man's Poison)
May 18, 1951	Dangerous Assignment (Operation Hotfoot)
June 8, 1951	Night Beat (The Search for Fred)
June 22, 1951	The Man Called X (Free Newspaper Owner Murdered)
June 27, 1951	Rocky Jordan (The Beach of Stones)
June 28, 1951	Suspense (The Case for Dr. Singer)
July 3, 1951	Dangerous Assignment (Latin American Party Leader Murdered)
July 4, 1951	Rocky Jordan (The Lady from Tangier)
July 5, 1951	Rocky Jordan (Voice Tests)
July 7-September 8, 1951	Mr. Aladdin
July 8, 1951	The Whisperer (Teatime for Teenagers)
July 10, 1951	Dangerous Assignment (China Sea Contraband)
July 11, 1951	Rocky Jordan (The Genacos Affair)
July 15, 1951	The Whisperer (Attempted Murder of Newsman)
July 16, 1951	Romance (China Run)
July 22, 1951	The Whisperer (Hippety Hoppy)
July 29, 1951	The Whisperer (Policeman in Danger)
August 1, 1951	Escape (The Gladiator)
August 1, 1951	Rocky Jordan (The Marcouf Plan)
August 26, 1951	The Whisperer
August 1951	Pete Kelly's Blues (Little Jake the Altar Boy)
September 2, 1951	The Whisperer
September 9, 1951	The Whisperer
September 16, 1951	The Whisperer

September 23, 1951	Broadway Is My Beat (Tom Keeler Murder)
September 23, 1951	The Whisperer
September 30, 1951	The Whisperer
October 2, 1951	This Is the Story (Hometown USA)
October 6, 1951	Broadway Is My Beat (The Lily Nelson Murder Case)
October 21, 1951	Silent Men (Empire of Pip the Blind)
November 14, 1951	The Halls of Ivy (The Late Student)
November 21, 1951	Perfect Crime (audition)
December 2, 1951	Tales of the Texas Rangers (The Dead Giveaway)
December 30, 1951	Romance (Mail Order Bride)
1951-52	Operation Underground
January 9, 1952	Wild Bill Hickock (The Two-Faced Horny Toad)
January 10, 1952	Hollywood Star Playhouse (The Frontier)
January 16, 1952	The Halls of Ivy (Art Exhibit)
January 29, 1952	The Man Called X (Swindling Racket)
February 2, 1952	The Man in Black (The Price of the Head; 2nd audition)
February 3, 1952	Silent Men (The Big Kill)
February 4, 1952	The Railroad Hour (The East Wind)
February 10, 1952	Silent Men (Blood Money)
February 17, 1952	The Black Book (On Schedule)
February 24, 1952	The Black Book (My Favorite Corpse)
March 2, 1952	The Black Book (The Vagabond Murder)
March 3, 1952	Lux Radio Theatre (Young Man with a Horn)
March 25, 1952	Those Young Bryans (audition)
March 26, 1952	Wild Bill Hickock (Jokes and Gunsmoke)
April 16, 1952	Silent Men (The Torch)
April 23, 1952	Silent Men (Food and War)
April 27, 1952	Hollywood Star Playhouse (Nor Gloom of Night)
April 27, 1952	The Whistler (Saturday Night)
May 2, 1952	Wild Bill Hickock (Jingles, the Ladies Man)
May 10, 1952	I Cover Hollywood (audition)
May 15, 1952	Night Beat (The Death of Riley)
May 16, 1952	The Pendleton Story (The Privateer)
May 18, 1952	Hollywood Star Playhouse (The Safari)
May 19, 1952	Lux Radio Theatre (The Magnificent Yankee)
May 21, 1952	Silent Men (Sabotage)
May 28, 1952	I Was a Communist for the FBI (Traitor for Hire)
May 28, 1952	Silent Men (The Green Sedan)
June 10, 1952	Safari (The Bull Elephant; audition)
June 19, 1952	Night Beat (Railroaded)
June 21, 1952	Gunsmoke (Heat Spell)
June 26, 1952	Night Beat (The Reformer)
July 13, 1952	Tales of the Texas Rangers (Finger Man)
July 20, 1952	Tales of the Texas Rangers (Round Trip)

August 17, 1952	Tales of the Texas Rangers (Cover-Up)
August 25, 1952	Dangerous Assignment (Port Said)
September 4, 1952	Night Beat (Bomb on the Denver Plane)
September 7, 1952	Tales of the Texas Rangers (Alibi)
September 25, 1952	Romance (Bayou Song)
October 3, 1952	Wild Bill Hickock (The Wolf of Ghost Mountain)
October 11, 1952	Broadway Is My Beat (Louise Downing Murder)
October 17, 1952	I Confess (Teenage Runaway; audition for the series that became *Confession*)
October 20, 1952	The Railroad Hour (Naughty Marietta)
October 22, 1952	Dangerous Assignment (The Butterfly Chasers)
November 3, 1952	Lux Radio Theatre (Viva Zapata)
November 3, 1952	Suspense (Frankenstein)
November 9, 1952	Escape (The Return)
November 12, 1952	Dangerous Assignment (Impersonating a Dead Foreign Agent)
November 15, 1952	Broadway Is My Beat (The Kenny Purdue Murder Case)
November 17, 1952	Suspense (Death and Miss Turner)
November 19, 1952	Dangerous Assignment (Munich Sanatorium)
November 26, 1952	Wild Bill Hickock (The Red River Mutiny)
December 10, 1952	Dangerous Assignment (Hungarian Prison Camp)
December 12, 1952	Wild Bill Hickock (Joke Book Bandits)
December 22, 1952	Lux Radio Theatre (Les Miserables)
December 24, 1952	Dangerous Assignment (Lecturing Professors)
December 29, 1952	Lux Radio Theatre (Westward the Women)
December 31, 1952	Dangerous Assignment (Stolen Atomic Secrets in Trieste)
1952-53	I Was a Communist for the FBI
January 7, 1953	Dangerous Assignment (South Pacific Gun Runners)
January 17, 1953	Broadway Is My Beat (The Joseph Brady Murder Case)
January 21, 1953	Dangerous Assignment (Leak of Strategic Materials)
January 21, 1953	Wild Bill Hickock (The Voice in Hawkins Well)
February 4, 1953	Dangerous Assignment (Scientist Held Prisoner in Greece)
February 18, 1953	Dangerous Assignment (Political Kidnap in Tokyo)
March 2, 1953	Wild Bill Hickock (Big Welcome at Shady Rest)
March 4, 1953	Dangerous Assignment (Witness to Nazi Killings)
March 11, 1953	Dangerous Assignment (International Stolen Information Bureau)
March 16, 1953	Suspense (The Mountain)
March 18, 1953	Dangerous Assignment (Oslo)
March 21, 1953	Broadway Is My Beat (The Mary Varden Murder)
March 23, 1953	Lux Radio Theatre (Fourteen Hours)

March 29, 1953	Escape (The Invader)
April 1, 1953	Dangerous Assignment (Agent in Venezuela)
April 8, 1953	Dangerous Assignment (Tutor to Ten-Year-Old in Paris)
April 15, 1953	Wild Bill Hickock (The Big Cleanup)
April 23, 1953	On Stage (Skin Deep)
April 25, 1953	Gunsmoke (The Soldier)
April 29, 1953	Dangerous Assignment (South Pacific Sabotage)
May 20, 1953	Dangerous Assignment (Norway Pipeline)
May 27, 1953	Wild Bill Hickock (The Whining Arrow)
June 8, 1953	Suspense (The Mystery of the Marie Celeste)
June 10, 1953	Wild Bill Hickock (The Little Dude)
June 18, 1953	On Stage (An Ideal Couple)
June 24, 1953	Dangerous Assignment (Damascus Prisoner Exchange)
July 1, 1953	Dangerous Assignment (Dead Crime Boss in Canada)
July 5, 1953	Confession (Doris Kane)
July 5, 1953	Escape (A Source of Irritation)
July 6, 1953	Crime Classics (The Shrapnelled Body of Charles Drew, Senior)
July 12, 1953	Confession (Martin Everett)
July 19, 1953	Confession (Anna Carlson)
July 20, 1953	Crime Classics (The Death of a Picture Hanger)
July 26, 1953	Confession
August 2, 1953	Confession (Esther Phillips)
August 9, 1953	Confession (Peter W. Greer)
August 9, 1953	Escape (Three Skeleton Keys)
August 10, 1953	Crime Classics (The Axe and the Droot Family: How They Fared)
August 16, 1953	Confession
August 16, 1953	Escape (The Thirteenth Truck)
August 23, 1953	Confession
August 25, 1953	Mr. President (Timothy Webster, Counter Agent)
August 30, 1953	Confession
September 6, 1953	Confession (George S. Andress)
September 13, 1953	Confession (Roger S. Chapman)
September 28, 1953	Lux Radio Theatre (The President's Lady)
September 30, 1953	Crime Classics (The Bloody, Bloody Banks of Fall River)
October 14, 1953	Wild Bill Hickock (The House on Windy Hill)
October 26, 1953	Suspense (Dutch Schultz)
November 2, 1953	Lux Radio Theatre (Because of You)
November 4, 1953	Broadway Is My Beat (The Paul Holland Murder Case)
November 7, 1953	Gunsmoke (Stolen Horses)

November 9, 1953	Lux Radio Theatre (Thunder on the Hill)
November 11, 1953	The Family Theater (The Martians and the McCoys)
November 15, 1953	The Whistler (Fading Star)
December 7, 1953	Lux Radio Theatre (Man on a Tightrope)
December 9, 1953	Wild Bill Hickock (Silk Hat and Hogan's Donkey)
December 12, 1953	Gunsmoke (The Cast)
December 20, 1953	The Eternal Light (Face to Face with Gabriel)
December 23, 1953	Wild Bill Hickock (The Tangled Rope)
January 4, 1954	Lux Radio Theatre (The Day the Earth Stood Still)
January 28, 1954	The Roy Rogers Radio Show (The Land of Blue Shadows)
February 1, 1954	Suspense (Never Follow a Banjo Act)
February 24, 1954	Crime Classics (The Good Ship Jane: Why She Became Floatsam)
February 28, 1954	The Edgar Bergen and Charlie McCarthy Show
March 9, 1954	Rocky Fortune (Incident in a Bar)
March 9, 1954	Rocky Jordan (The Confession)
April 13, 1954	Fibber McGee and Molly
April 16, 1954	That's Rich (Astronomy)
May 3, 1954	Suspense (The Giant of Thermopylae)
May 15, 1954	Wild Bill Hickock (The Rimrock Rainmaker)
June 10, 1954	Escape (Benchillina and the Fisherman)
June 17, 1954	Escape (Bloodwaters)
June 24, 1954	Escape (Judgement Day at Crippled Deer)
June 29, 1954	Suspense (Too Hot to Love)
July 1, 1954	Escape (The Dark Wall)
July 10, 1954	Escape (The Birds)
July 17, 1954	Escape (Eye of Evil)
August 7, 1954	Romance (Flight to Athens)
August 12, 1954	That's Rich (Movie Usher)
September 19, 1954	Mr. and Mrs. North (Operation Murder)
September 25, 1954	Escape (The Heart of Kali)
November 6, 1954	Romance (Inheritance of Susan)
November 24, 1954	Wild Bill Hickock (The Old Hometown)
January 27, 1955	The Cisco Kid (The Cattle Train)
February 8, 1955	Lux Radio Theatre (The War of the Worlds)
October 8, 1955	Romance (Sir Henry, Part I)
October 15, 1955	Romance (Sir Henry, Part II)
December 1, 1954	Wild Bill Hickock (Six-Gun Serenade)
December 15, 1954	Wild Bill Hickock (The .35 Caliber Killer)
December 21, 1955	The Family Theater (The Juggler of Our Lady)
December 27, 1955	Suspense (The Mystery of the Marie Celeste)
January 8, 1956	NBC Radio Theatre (The Snake Pit)
January 21, 1956	Romance (Old Army Buddy)
March 23, 1956	Yours Truly, Johnny Dollar (The Jolly Roger Fraud Matter)

August 25, 1957	CBS Radio Workshop (Sweet Cherries in Charleston)
September 8, 1957	Suspense (Old Army Buddy)
October 13, 1957	Heartbeat Theater (Out of the Darkness)
December 22, 1957	Gunsmoke (Twelfth Night) [Frees is in the Armed Forces Radio commercial]
January 19, 1958	Heartbeat Theater (Columbia Street)
January 26, 1958	Heartbeat Theater (A Million Laughs)
March 2, 1958	Heartbeat Theater (The End of the Trail)
March 9, 1958	Heartbeat Theater (Safe at First)
June 29, 1958	Heartbeat Theater (The Kidnapping of Kirby Dent)
April 12, 1959	Heartbeat Theater (Memory of Tomorrow)
August 16, 1959	Suspense (Like Man, Somebody Dig Me)
December 27, 1959	Heartbeat Theater (Yuan Tan)
February 28, 1960	Heartbeat Theater (The City That Was)
November 20, 1960	Yours Truly, Johnny Dollar (The Double Deal Matter)
December 2, 1960	Broadway Is My Beat
July 8, 1973	Same Time, Same Station
April 19, 1974	Recollections: An Evening with William N. Robeson
April 25, 1982	Old Time Radio (Paul Frees)
April 4, 1984	Bradbury 13 (The Ravine) [narrator]
April 9, 1984	Bradbury 13 (Night Call, Collect) [narrator]
April 16, 1984	Bradbury 13 (The Veldt) [narrator]
April 23, 1984	Bradbury 13 (There Was an Old Woman) [narrator]
April 30, 1984	Bradbury 13 (Kaleidoscope) [narrator]
May 7, 1984	Bradbury 13 [narrator]
May 14, 1984	Bradbury 13 (The Screaming Woman) [narrator]
May 21, 1984	Bradbury 13 (A Sound of Thunder) [narrator]
May 28, 1984	Bradbury 13 (The Man) [narrator]
June 4, 1984	Bradbury 13 (The Wind) [narrator]
June 11, 1984	Bradbury 13 [narrator]
June 18, 1984	Bradbury 13 (Here, There Be Tigers) [narrator]
June 25, 1984	Bradbury 13 (The Happiness Machine) [narrator]

SHORT THEATRICAL CARTOONS

(Name of film series is listed first, followed by cartoon title, Frees' character(s) when known, and releasing company)

1950	(Pluto) Primitive Pluto (Primo) (Walt Disney/RKO)
1951	(Tom & Jerry) Jerry's Cousin (Cousin Muscles) (MGM)
	(Tom & Jerry) Sleepy-Time Tom (Cat) (MGM)

1952	(Barney Bear) Busybody Bear (Barney, Buck Beaver) (MGM)
	(Tom & Jerry) Cruise Cat (Ship's Captain) (MGM)
	(Tom & Jerry) Little Runaway (MGM)
	(Barney Bear) The Little Wise Quacker (Barney) (MGM)
1953	(Barney Bear) Barney's Hungry Cousin (Barney) (MGM)
	(Barney Bear) Bird Brain Bird Dog (Barney) (MGM)
	(Barney Bear) Cobs and Robbers (Barney, Joe Scarecrow, others) (MGM)
	(Barney Bear) Half-Pint Palomino (Barney) (MGM)
	(Barney Bear) Heir Bear (Barney, Gopher, Tax Collector) (MGM)
	(Tom & Jerry) The Missing Mouse (Radio Announcer) (MGM)
	TV of Tomorrow (Narrator) (MGM)
	(Barney Bear) Wee-Willie Wildcat (Barney, William Wildcat) (MGM)
1954	(Tom & Jerry) Baby Butch (MGM)
	The Farm of Tomorrow (Narrator) (MGM)
	(Droopy) Homesteader Droopy (Narrator) (MGM)
	(Barney Bear) The Impossible Possum (Barney) (MGM)
	(Barney Bear) Sleepy-Time Squirrel (Barney Bear, Jimmy Squirrel) (MGM)
1955	Cellbound (Prisoner, Warden, The Little Wife) (MGM)
1956	(Tom & Jerry) Blue Cat Blues (Narrator) (MGM)
	(Tom & Jerry) Downbeat Bear (Radio Announcer) (MGM)
	In the Bag (Walt Disney/BV)
1958	(Ham & Hattie) Picnics Are Fun (UPA/Columbia)
	(Ham & Hattie) Sailing & Village Band (UPA/Columbia)
	(Ham & Hattie) Spring (UPA/Columbia)
	(Ham & Hattie) Trees & Jamaica Daddy (UPA/Columbia)
1959	(Donald Duck) Donald in Mathmagic Land (Narrator, other voices) (Walt Disney/BV)
	Eyes into Outer Space (Walt Disney/BV)
	Goliath II (Mouse) (Walt Disney/BV)
	(Hickory, Dickory & Doc) Mouse Trapped (Doc) (Lantz/Universal)
	Noah's Ark (Noah, God) (Walt Disney/BV)
	(Cartune) Space Mouse (Lantz/Universal)
	Spring & Saganaki (UPA)

1960	(Woody Woodpecker) Bally Hooey (Lantz/Universal)
	(Woody Woodpecker) Bats in the Belfry (Lantz/Universal)
	(Woody Woodpecker) Fowled-Up Falcon (Lantz/Universal)
	(Cartune) Freeloading Feline (Doc) (Lantz/Universal)
	(Loopy de Loop) Tale of a Wolf (Hanna-Barbera/Columbia)
	Witty Kitty (Doc, cat) (Lantz/Universal)
1961	(Chilly Willy) Clash and Carry (Wally Walrus) (Lantz/Universal)
	(Cartune) Doc's Last Stand (Doc) (Lantz/Universal)
	(Donald Duck) Donald and the Wheel (Walt Disney/RKO)
	(Cartune) Tin Can Concert (Lantz/Universal)
	(Chilly Willy) Tricky Trout (Lantz/Universal)
1962	Corny Concerto (Doc) (Lantz/Universal)
	(Cartune) Fowled-Up Birthday (Charlie Beary) (Lantz/Universal)
	(Comic King) The Hat (Famous Studios)
	(Comic King) Keeping Up with Krazy (Ignatz Mouse, Officer Pupp) (Famous Studios)
	(Comic King) The Method and Maw (Famous Studios)
	(Beary Family) Mother's Little Helper (Charlie Beary) (Lantz/Universal)
	(Comic King) Mouse Blanche (Ignatz Mouse, Officer Pupp) (Famous Studios)
	(Cartune) Pest of the Show (Doc) (Lantz/Universal)
	(Cartune) Punch Pooch (Doc) (Lantz/Universal)
	(Comic King) Snuffy's Song (Barney Google, Snuffy Smith) (Famous Studios)
	A Symposium on Popular Songs (Walt Disney/BV)
	(Comic King) Take Me to Your Gen'rul (Barney Google, Snuffy Smith) (Famous Studios)
1963	(Beary Family) Charlie's Mother-in-Law (Charlie Beary) (Lantz/Universal)
	(Beary Family) Goose Is Wild (Charlie Beary) (Lantz/Universal)
	(Woody Woodpecker) Stowaway Woody (Lantz/Universal)
1964	(Beary Family) Rah, Rah, Ruckus (Charlie Beary) (Lantz/Universal)
	(Beary Family) Roof-Top Razzle Dazzle (Charlie Beary) (Lantz/Universal)

1965	(Beary Family) Bugged in a Rug (Charlie Beary) (Lantz/Universal)
	(Beary Family) Davey Cricket (Charlie Beary) (Lantz/Universal)
	(Goofy) Freewayphobia (Narrator) (Walt Disney/ BV)
	(Goofy) Goofy's Freeway Troubles (Walt Disney/ BV)
	(Inspector) The Great De Gaulle Stone Robbery (Three-Headed Villain) (Mirisch/Geoffrey/DFE/ UA)
	(Beary Family) Guest Who? (Charlie Beary) (Lantz/ Universal)
	(Pink Panther) Pinkfinger (Mirisch/Geoffrey/DFE/ UA)
	(Pink Panther) Pink Panza (Mirisch/Geoffrey/DFE/ UA)
	(Pink Panther) Sink Pink (Mirisch/Geoffrey/DFE/ UA)
1966	(Inspector) Ape Suzette (Mirisch/Geoffrey/DFE/UA)
	(Inspector) Cirrhosis of the Louvre (Commissioner) (Mirisch/Geoffrey/DFE/UA)
	(Inspector) Cock-a-Doodle Deux-Deux (Commissioner) (Mirisch/Geoffrey/DFE/UA)
	(Beary Family) Foot Brawl (Charlie Beary) (Lantz/ Universal)
	(Inspector) The Pique Poquette of Paris (Spide Pierre) (Mirisch/Geoffrey/DFE/UA)
	(Inspector) Plastered in Paris (Commissioner) (Mirisch/Geoffrey/DFE/UA)
	(Inspector) Reaux, Reaux, Reaux Your Boat (Mirisch/Geoffrey/DFE/UA)
	(Inspector) That's No Lady, That's Notre Dame (Commissioner) (Mirisch/Geoffrey/DFE/UA)
	(Inspector) Unsafe and Seine (Commissioner, waiter, customers) (Mirisch/Geoffrey/DFE/UA)
1967	The Bear That Wasn't (Narrator) (MGM)
	(Inspector) Bomb Voyage (Commissioner) (Mirisch/ Geoffrey/DFE/UA)
	(Inspector) Le Escape Goat (Commissioner) (Mirisch/Geoffrey/DFE/UA)
	(The Amorous Adventures of Juan Novarro) The Magic Peartree (Juan Novarro) (Murakami/ Wolf/Bing Crosby Productions)
	(Beary Family) Mouse in the House (Charlie Beary) (Lantz/Universal)

(Inspector) Le Quiet Squad (Commissioner) (Mirisch/Geoffrey/DFE/UA)

(Inspector) Sacre Bleu Cross (Hassan the Assassin) (Mirisch/Geoffrey/DFE/UA)

(Beary Family) Window Pains (Charlie Beary) (Lantz/Universal)

1968   (Beary Family) Jerky Turkey (Charlie Beary) (Lantz/Universal)

(Beary Family) Paste Makes Waste (Charlie Beary) (Lantz/Universal)

1969   (Beary Family) Charlie's Campout (Charlie Beary) (Lantz/Universal)

(Beary Family) Cool It, Charlie (Charlie Beary) (Lantz/Universal)

The Good Friend (Murakami/Wolf/AFI)

(Beary Family) Gopher Broke (Charlie Beary) (Lantz/Universal)

1970   (Beary Family) The Bunglin' Builder (Charlie Beary) (Lantz/Universal)

(Beary Family) Charlie in Hot Water (Charlie Beary) (Lantz/Universal)

(Beary Family) Charlie's Golf Classic (Charlie Beary) (Lantz/Universal)

(Beary Family) The Unhandy Man (Charlie Beary) (Lantz/Universal)

1971   (Beary Family) Charlie the Rainmaker (Charlie Beary) (Lantz/Universal)

(Beary Family) Moochin' Pooch (Charlie Beary) (Lantz/Universal)

1972   (Beary Family) A Fish Story (Charlie Beary, Junior) (Lantz/Universal)

(Beary Family) Let Charlie Do It (Charlie Beary) (Lantz/Universal)

(Beary Family) Rain, Rain Go Away (Charlie Beary) (Lantz/Universal)

(Beary Family) Unlucky Potluck (Charlie Beary) (Lantz/Universal)

Films

1948   The Lady from Shanghai (Dubs for Orson Welles in one scene) (Columbia)

Force of Evil (Elevator Operator) (MGM/Enterprise)

1949   Red Light (Bellhop) (United Artists/Pioneer)

1950	Atoll K/Utopia (Narrator) (Fortezza Films)
	The Company She Keeps (Court Clerk) (RKO)
	Hunt the Man Down (Packy Collins) (RKO)
	The Toast of New Orleans (Narrator, Dubbed a Voice) (MGM)
1951	His Kind of Woman (Corley) (RKO/Howard Hughes)
	The People Against O'Hara (Voice of Frank Corvac) (MGM)
	A Place in the Sun (Reverend Morrison) (Paramount)
	The Thing from Another World (Dr. Vorhees) (RKO/Winchester Pictures)
	When Worlds Collide (Narrator, President's voice, Misc. Bit Voices) (Paramount)
1952	Assignment: Paris (Narrator, Hungarian Radio Announcer) (Columbia)
	The Big Sky (Louis McMasters) (RKO/Winchester Pictures)
	Cripple Creek (Narrator) (Columbia/Resolute Productions)
	The Las Vegas Story (District Attorney) (RKO/Howard Hughes)
	Million Dollar Mermaid (Bandleader) (MGM)
	The Star (Richard Stanley) (20th Century-Fox)
1953	Let's Do It Again (Dubs for Ray Milland) (Columbia)
	The War of the Worlds (Opening Narrator, Radio Reporter) (Paramount)
1954	Dragnet (Warner Bros.)
	Riot in Cell Block 11 (Monroe) (Monogram/Allied Artists)
	Suddenly (Benny Conklin, voice of TV announcer) (UA/Libra Productions)
1955	The Man with the Golden Arm (Voice of TV Commentator) (UA/Carlyle Productions)
	Prince of Players (Romeo) (20th Century-Fox)
	The Rains of Ranchipur (Sundar) (20th Century-Fox)
	The Scarlet Coat (Narrator) (MGM)
	Son of Sinbad (Mahmud) (RKO)
1956	Away All Boats (Misc. Voices) (Universal)
	Earth vs. the Flying Saucers (Narrator, Alien Voice) (Columbia)
	Francis in the Haunted House (Francis, the Talking Mule) (Universal)
	The Harder They Fall (Priest, Dubbing) (Columbia)
	Rodan/Sora no daikaijû Radon (Police Chief, Others) (Toho)

1957	The 27th Day (Newscaster Ward Mason) (Columbia/Romson Productions)
	Beginning of the End (Announcer Voice, Voice of Helicopter Pilot) (Republic/AB-PT Pictures)
	The Cyclops (Vocal Effects) (Allied Artists/B&H Productions)
	The Deadly Mantis (Narrator) (Universal-International)
	Jet Pilot (Lt. Tiompkin) (Universal-International/RKO-Howard Hughes, 1950)
	The Monolith Monsters (Narrator) (Universal-International)
1958	Gigi (Dubbed men with Louis Jordan) (MGM)
	Last of the Fast Guns (Mexican Voices) (Universal-International)
	Raw Wind in Eden (Dubs Carlos Thompson & Old Man) (Universal-International)
	Space Master X-7 (Dr. Charles T. Pommer) (20th Century-Fox/Regal Films)
	A Time to Love and a Time to Die (Voice of soldiers and Misc. Voices) (Universal-International)
1959	Attack of the Jungle Women (Narrator, Paul Limon) (Barjul International Pictures/Sampson)
	The H-Man/Bijo to Ekitaimingen (Misc. Voices) (Columbia)
	Li'l Abner (Radio Announcer) (Paramount/Panama-Frank Productions)
	Operation Petticoat (Dubbed Voices) (Universal-International/Granarte Co.)
	The Shaggy Dog (Narrator, Psychiatrist) (Walt Disney/BV)
	The Snow Queen/Snezhnaya koroleva (Voice of Ol' Dreamy, The Raven) (Universal-International)
	Some Like it Hot (Josephine's Speaking Voice, Voice of Funeral Director, Misc. Voices) (UA/Mirisch-Ashton)
1960	The Beatniks (Writer/Director/Composer, Misc. Voices) (Glenville)
	Bells Are Ringing (Misc. Voices in song "Drop That Name") (MGM)
	Jack the Ripper (U.K., 1959) (Narrator) (Paramount)
	Pollyanna (Voice of Barker) (Walt Disney/BV)
	Spartacus (Voices of Soldiers) (Universal)
	The Sword and the Dragon/Ilja Muromets (Voice of Kalin)
	The Time Machine (Voice of The Talking Rings) (MGM)
	Where the Boys Are (Narrator) (MGM)

1961	The Absent-Minded Professor (Pilot, Radio Announcer, Misc. Voices) (Walt Disney/BV)
	Atlantis, The Lost Continent (Narrator, Misc. Voices) (MGM)
	I Bombed Pearl Harbor/Taiheiyo no Arashi (Toho/Parade)
	The Last War/Senkai Dai Senso (Toho)
	Not Tonight Henry (Foremost Films)
	One Hundred and One Dalmations (Dirty Dawson) (Walt Disney/BV)
1962	The Four Horsemen of the Apocalypse (Voice of Resistance Driver) (MGM)
	Gay Purr-ee (Meowrice, Railway Cat, Misc. Voices) (Warner Brothers)
	The Magic Sword (Voice of a German Knight) (United Artists)
	The Manchurian Candidate (Narrator) (United Artists)
	A Public Affair (Narrator) (Parade)
	Taras Bulba (Narrator) (United Artists)
	Tower of London (Opening Narration) (United Artists)
	The World's Greatest Sinner (Voice of Snake) (Frenzy Productions)
1963	The List of Adrian Messenger (Misc. Voices) (Universal)
	PT-109 (Warner Brothers)
	The Thrill of It All (Voice of TV Announcer) (Universal)
1964	Blood and Black Lace/Sei Donne per I'Assassino (Dubs Male Leads) (Woolner/Allied Artists)
	The Carpetbaggers (Narrator) (Paramount)
	The Disorderly Orderly (Opening Narration)
	Flight from Ashiya/Ashiya Kara No Hiko (U.S. Version Narrator) (Daiei/United Artists)
	The Incredible Mr. Limpet (Crusty the Crab) (Warner Brothers)
	Mary Poppins (Singing Horse) (Walt Disney/BV)
	The Night Walker (Opening Narration) (Universal)
	Robin and the Seven Hoods (Public Address Voice) (Warner Brothers)
	The Sword of Ali Baba (Narrator, Misc. Voices) (Universal)
1965	Once a Thief (Voice of Drug Dealer) (MGM)
	The Outlaws Is Coming (Narrator, Mirror's Voice) (Columbia)

Requiem for a Gunfighter (Narrator) (Embassy Pictures)

The War Lord (Narrator, Dwarf's Voice, Misc. Voices) (Universal)

1966   Grand Prix (Speaking Voice of Toshiro Mifune, Misc. Voices) (MGM)

The Man Called Flintstone (Rock Slag, Bo-Bo, Triple X, Mario, Shady Character) (Hanna-Barbera/ Columbia)

Maya (Misc. Voices) (MGM)

The Ugly Dachshund (Speaking Voice of Dick Wessel) (Walt Disney/BV)

1967   In Cold Blood (Radio Announcer, Misc. Voices, Interviewer, Interviewee) (Columbia)

Good Times (Misc. Voices) (Columbia)

King Kong Escapes/Kingu Kongu no Gyakushu (Dubbing Director, Misc. Voices) (Toho/Universal)

The St. Valentine's Day Massacre (Narrator, Ben Bernie on Radio) (20th Century Fox)

Tarzan and the Valley of Gold (Misc. Voices) (AIP)

1968   Guns for San Sebastian/La Bataille de San Sebastian (Voice of Mr. Cayetano, Misc. Voices) (Cipra Films)

Wild in the Streets (Narrator) (American International Pictures)

1969   The Comic ("Newsreel" Voice in Restaurant) (Columbia)

On Her Majesty's Secret Service (Dubs for Gabriele Ferzetti) (United Artists)

1970   Beneath the Planet of the Apes (Closing Narrator) (20th Century-Fox/APJAC)

Colossus: The Forbin Project (Voice of Colossus) (Universal)

Horror of the Blood Monsters (Dubs Filipino Cavemen)

Patton (Misc. Voices) (20th Century-Fox)

Tora! Tora! Tora! (Voice of Japanese Ambassador in Washington scenes) (20th Century-Fox)

1971   The Abominable Dr. Phibes (Off-Screen Singer of "The Darktown Strutters' Ball" in Party Scene) (AIP)

1973   The Day of the Jackal (Dubs Voices) (MCA)

Dillinger (Voice on Radio, Post-Credit Voice) (AIP)

Shaft in Africa (Speaking Voice of Aldo Sambrell) (MGM/Shaft Prods.)

1975   Doc Savage: The Man of Bronze (Narrator) (Warner Brothers)

The Milpitas Monster (Narrator) (VCI)

1976	Midway (Speaking Voice of Toshiro Mifune) (Universal/Mirisch)
1979	The Bushido Blade (Speaking Voice of Toshiro Mifune) (Rankin/Bass)
	Rudolph and Frosty's Christmas in July (Winterbolt) (Rankin/Bass)
1982	The Last Unicorn (Talking Cat) (Rankin/Bass)
	The Challenge (Speaking Voice of Toshiro Mifune) (CBS/Embassy Pictures)
1983	Twice Upon a Time (Narrator, Voices of Chief of State, Judges, Bailiff)
1984	Nothing Lasts Forever (Misc. Voices) (MGM/Broadway)
1986	The Fantasy Film Worlds of George Pal (Narrator) (Arnold Leibovit Entertainment)
1987	The Puppetoon Movie (Arnie the Dinosaur, Pillsbury Doughboy) (Arnold Leibovit Entertainment)

Short Films/Documentaries

1966	Birth of a Legend (Narrator) (Mary Pickford Corporation)
1977	Hardware Wars (Narrator)
1980	The Day after Trinity: J. Robert Oppenheimer and the Atomic Bomb (Narrator) (KTEH San Jose) (Documentary)
1982	The Case of Dashiell Hammett (Narrator) (Documentary)
	Routes of Exile: A Moroccan Jewish Odyssey (Narrator) (Documentary)

Movie Trailers (Narrator)

1949	The Cowboy and the Indians (Columbia)
1953	Donovan's Brain (United Artists)
1957	Back from the Dead (20th Century-Fox)
	Forty Guns (20th Century-Fox)
	Love in the Afternoon (AA)
	The Monster from Green Hell (Distributors Corporation of America)
	Sweet Smell of Success (United Artists)
	The Unknown Terror (20th Century-Fox)
1958	The Haunted Strangler

	Monster on the Campus (Universal-International)
	The Return of Dracula (United Artists)
	A Time to Love and a Time to Die (Universal-International)
1959	The Hideous Sun Demon (Pacific International)
	Return of the Fly (20th Century-Fox)
1960	Thirteen Ghosts (Two Different) (Columbia)
	The Time Machine (MGM)
1961	Atlantis, The Lost Continent (MGM)
	Black Sunday (Radio Spots)
	The Pit and the Pendulum (AIP)
1962	Varan the Unbelievable
1963	Twice-Told Tales
1967	The Best of Laurel and Hardy
	Spree
1971	The Abominable Dr. Phibes (AIP)
1972	The Doberman Gang (Fox-Rank/Rosamond)
	Sweet Sugar
1973	Beyond Atlantis
	The Manhandlers
	Il Plenilunio delle vergini (The Devil's Wedding Night)
	Terminal Island
1977	Fantasia (Reissue)
1979	Midnight Madness
1984	Nothing Lasts Forever (MGM/Broadway)

TELEVISION

As Regular

1953	Carson's Cellar (Regular Skit Player) (NBC)
1955-60	The Millionaire (Voice & Hand of John Beresford Tipton) (CBS)
1956-57	The Gerald McBoingBoing Show (CBS)
1957	Disneyland (ABC):
	"Cosmic Capers"
	"Mars and Beyond" (Narrator)
	"Your Host, Donald Duck"
1958-63	Naked City (Narrator) (ABC)
1958-59	Rescue Eight (Narrator, Creator) (Syndicated)
1958-59, 1962	Bozo the Clown (Syndicated)
1958-61	Walt Disney Presents (ABC):
1959	"Duck Flies Coop" (Radio Announcer)
1960	"Moochie of Pop Warner Football" (Stanley Wickershaft)

1959-61	Matt's Funday Funnies (Voices, Writer) (ABC)
1959-61	Rocky and His Friends/The Bullwinkle Show (Boris Badenov, Capt. Peachfuzz, Cloyd, Inspector Fenwick, Misc. Voices) (ABC/NBC)
1960	Mister Magoo (Tycoon Magoo, Misc. Voices)
1961-62	The Alvin Show (Various Voices) (CBS)
1961-62	Calvin and the Colonel (Oliver Wendell Clutch) (ABC)
1961-62	The Dick Tracy Show (Flat Top, Go Go Gomez, Officer Heap O'Calorie, Misc. Voices) (Syndicated)
1961-62	Top Cat (Various Voices) (ABC)
1961-69	Walt Disney's Wonderful World of Color (Ludwig Von Drake) (NBC):
1961	"An Adventure in Color/Donald in Mathmagic Land" (Ludwig Von Drake)
1961	"The Hunting Instinct" (Ludwig Von Drake)
1961	"Inside Donald Duck" (Ludwig Von Drake)
1961	"Kids Is Kids" (Ludwig Von Drake)
1961	"The Nine Lives of Elfego Baca" (Dubs Voices in Four Episodes)
1961	"Title Makers"
1961	"Nature's Half Acre" (Alien Voice)
1962	"Carnival Time" (Ludwig Von Drake)
1962	"Man Is His Own Worst Enemy" (Ludwig Von Drake)
1962	"Von Drake in Spain" (Ludwig Von Drake)
1963	"Fly with Von Drake" (Ludwig Von Drake)
1963	"Inside Outer Space" (Ludwig Von Drake)
1963	"A Square Peg in a Round Hole" (Ludwig Von Drake)
1963	"Three Tall Tales" (Ludwig Von Drake)
1963	"The Truth About Mother Goose" (Ludwig von Drake)
1964	"The Ballad of Hector, the Stowaway Dog" (Off-Camera Voices)
1964	"In Shape with Von Drake" (Ludwig Von Drake)
1964	"Mediterranean Cruise" (Ludwig Von Drake)
1964	"A Rag, a Bone, a Box of Junk" (Ludwig Von Drake)
1966	"Music For Everybody" (Ludwig Von Drake)
1963	Beetle Bailey and His Friends/ King Features Trilogy (Barney Google, Snuffy Smith, Ignatz Mouse, Officer Pupp, Mr. Kolin Kelly)
1963-64	Fractured Flickers (Various Voices) (Syndicated)
1963	Krazy Kat (Ignatz Mouse, Officer Pupp)
1963	Tintin (Various Voices)
1964-65	The Famous Adventures of Mr. Magoo (Various Voices)

1964-67	The Adventures of Hoppity Hopper (Narrator, Fillmore the Bear) (Syndicated/ABC)
1965-68	The Beatles (John Lennon, George Harrison, Misc. Voices) (ABC)
1965	The Secret Squirrel Show (Squiddly Diddly, Morocco Mole) (NBC)
1966-68	Frankenstein Jr. and the Impossibles (Narrator, Fluid Man, Misc. Voices)
1966	Laurel and Hardy
1966	Uncle Waldo's Cartoon Show (Fillmore the Bear) (ABC)
1966-69	Super Six (Brother Matzo-Riley, Misc. Voices) (NBC)
1967-68	The Atom Ant/Secret Squirrel Show, The (Morocco Mole, Squiddly Diddly) (NBC)
1967-70	The Fantastic Four (Ben Grimm, The Thing, Dr. Doom, Misc. Voices) (ABC)
1967-70	George of the Jungle (Ape, Narrator, Commissioner, Weevil, Fred, Plumtree, Baron Otto Matic, Misc. Voices) (ABC)
1967	Justice League of America (Kyro, Guardian of the Universe) (ABC)
1967	The Superman/Aquaman Hour of Adventure (ABC)
1967-68	Super President (James Norcross/Super President, Narrator) (NBC)
1968	The Arabian Knights (Bakaar)
1968-69	The New Adventures of Huckleberry Finn (Various Voices) (NBC)
1968-70	The Banana Splits Adventure Hour (Evil Vangore, Sazoom) (NBC)
1969-70	Dudley Do-Right and His Friends (Inspector Fenwick, Others) (ABC)
1969-81	The Wonderful World of Disney (NBC):
1970	"Nature's Strangest Oddballs" (Ludwig Von Drake)
1969-78	The Pink Panther Show (Commissioner, Misc. Voices) (NBC)
1971-73	The Jackson 5 (Many Voices) (ABC)
1972-74	The Osmonds (Fugi) (ABC)
1974-76	Run, Joe, Run (Narrator) (NBC)

Guest

1950's	My Friend Irma (Irma's Boyfriend)
1953	The Jack Benny Program (Episode with Marilyn Monroe)
1954	G.E. Theatre ("Foggy Night") (CBS)

1954	Lux Video Theatre (January 28th; "A Place in the Sun")
1954	Studio 57 ("Step Lightly, Please") (Dumont)
1955	Big Town ("Hostage of the Law") (NBC)
1955	The Mickey Rooney Show (February 12, 1955) (NBC)
1955	TV Reader's Digest ("France's Greatest Detective") (ABC)
1955-59	Love That Bob (Actor in "Bob Becomes a Stage Uncle" episode)
1956	The Mickey Mouse Club (Voices of Carl and Sheriff in "Boys of the Western Sea") (ABC)
1956-57	Dragnet ("The Big Fall Guy" and "The Big Dip" episodes)
1956	Jane Wyman Presents the Fireside Theatre (Emcee in episode "Ten Percent")
1957	The Adventures of Jim Bowie ("German George") (ABC)
1958-61	The Tales of Texas John Slaughter (Dubs Voices in Two Episodes)
1958	Steve Canyon (Durkel in "Operation Towline" Episode)
(unknown)	John Wilson's Magic Tinderbox
1965	The Joe Pyne Show (Interviewed Guest)
1967	A Salute to Alaska (Narrator)
1968	Get Smart (*Casablanca* episode; Voices of Sydney Greenstreet and Peter Lorre)
1968	Pacifically Speaking (Moby Duck)
1970	Johnny Carson Presents Sun City Scandals (the "vocal counterpart of Howard Hughes")
1970	Mr. Magoo's Holiday Festival
1970	Nanny and the Professor ("Voice of the 30s" in "The Great Broadcast of 1936" episode)
1972	Hawaii Five-O (Voice of Goro Shobata in "Odd Man In" Episode, and Voice of McGarrett Imposter in "The Ninety-Second War: Part 1" Episode)
1978-79	Battlestar Gallactica (Various Voices) (ABC)
1978-79	Buck Rogers (Various Voices) (NBC)
1980	Rah! Rah! Woozy! (Narrator)
1984	Knight Rider (Voice of Evil Car) (NBC)

Specials

1962	Mr. Magoo's Christmas Carol (Old Fezzlwig, Undertaker, Charity Man, Man with Eyepatch, Tall Man with Top Hat) (NBC)

1967	The Cricket on the Hearth, The (Uriah, Sea Captain) (NBC)
1968	The Mouse on the Mayflower (Captain Jones, William Bradford, Quizzler, Scurv) (NBC)
1968	The Little Drummer Boy (Ali, Others) (NBC)
1969	Frosty the Snowman (Santa Claus, Traffic Cop, Others) (CBS)
1970	Santa Claus Is Comin' To Town (Burgermeister Meisterburger, Grimsby, Assorted Townspeople & Soldiers) (ABC)
1971	Here Comes Peter Cottontail (Santa Claus) (ABC)
1972	Willie Mays and the Say-Hey Kid (Iguana) (ABC)
1976	The First Easter Rabbit (Zero, Spats) (ABC)
1976	Frosty's Winter Wonderland (Jack Frost) (ABC)
1976	Rudolph's Shiny New Year (Santa Claus, General Ticker, Aeon, Humpty Dumpty, Benjamin Franklin) (ABC)
1977	Nestor, the Long-Eared Christmas Donkey (Nestor's Master, Olaf) (ABC)
1978	The Stingiest Man in Town (Ghosts of Christmas Past & Present, charity collector)
1979	Jack Frost (Kubla Kraus, Father Winter) (NBC)
1984	Donald Duck's 50th Birthday (Ludwig Von Drake)
1986	Disney's DTV Valentine (Narrator, Ludwig Von Drake)

TV Movies

1970	The Mad, Mad, Mad Comedians (Harpo & Chico Marx, W.C. Fields, Others) (ABC)
1971	The Point (The King, Leafman, Oblio's Father, Assorted Villagers, Pointed Man's Right Head)
1977	The Hobbit (Bombur, Troll #1) (NBC)
1980	The Return of the King (Goblin, Elrond) (ABC)
1987	The Wind in the Willows (Wayfarer) (ABC)

DISCOGRAPHY

Albums

1956	Exploring the Unknown *RCA*
1959	The Shaggy Dog *Disneyland Records*
1959	Spike Jones in Hi-Fi
1960	Bells are Ringing *Capitol*
1960	Rocky and His Friends *Golden*

1960	The Snow Queen (Soundtrack)
1961	Professor Ludwig Von Drake *Disneyland Records*
1961	Serious Music (Frank Zappa)
1961	Stan Freberg Presents the United States of America *Capitol*
1962	Big Red *DisneylandRecords*
1962	Gay Purr-ee *Warner Brothers*
1964	Les Poupées de Paris *RCA*
1964	Twin of the Jolly Green Giant *Singlette Records*
1965	Huckleberry Hound Tells Stories of Uncle Remus *Hanna-Barbera*
1965	Monster Shindig *Hanna-Barbera*
1965	Pecos Bill *Disneyland Records*
1965	Tinpanorama *Buena Vista*
(unknown)	Laffter Sweet and Profane *Epic*
(unknown)	Pixie & Dixie with Mr. Jinks Tells the Story of Cinderella (45rpm) *Hanna-Barbera*
1967	Cricket on the Hearth *RCA*
1967	Goofy Grape Sings! *Mark 56*
1968	Great Moments with Mr. Lincoln *Disneyland Records*
1970	Paul Frees and The Poster People *MGM*
1970	Santa Claus Is Comin' to Town *MGM*
1971	The Abominable Dr. Phibes soundtrack *AIR*
1971	Here Comes Peter Cottontail (Promo)
1976	The First Easter Rabbit (Promo)
1976	Frosty's Winter Wonderland *Disneyland*
1977	The Hobbit *Vista Records*
1995	Classic Disney, Volume 1 *Walt Disney Records*

Songs

137th Infantry March (written by Saul H. Frees and Raymond Schmidt. Published March 1, 1941)

Across Our Great Big Nation (written by Harold Alfred Fimberg, Paul Frees, Sidney Miller, Larry Orenstein, Bert J. Pellish, Ruby Raksin)

Another Good Day Is Done (written by Paul Frees, Sidney Miller, Ruby Raksin)

Bermuda Bells (words and music by Paul Harcourt Frees. Copyright November 30, 1953)

The Clown (written by Paul Frees, Ruby Raksin)

The Comedian (words and music by Paul Frees. January 19, 1954. Kavelin Music Corp.)

Dancers of the Past (written by Paul Frees, Ruby Raksin)

Dancing Fool (written by Paul Frees, Ruby Raksin)

Deep Purple (1952)

Don't Be Afraid of the [unknown] (written by Harold A. Fimberg, Paul Frees, Sidney Miller, Larry Orenstein, Bert J. Pellish, Ruby Raksin)

Everybody Wants To Be [unknown] (written by Paul Frees, Ruby Raksin)

First, Last and Always (written by Saul H. Frees and Raymond Wendell Schmidt. Unpublished, but copyrighted April 5, 1943)

Fly the Flying Carpet Line (written by Harold A. Fimberg, Paul Frees, Sidney Miller, Larry Orenstein, Bert J. Pellish, Ruby Raksin)

Folks at Home (written by Paul Frees, Ruby Raksin)

For Fifty Boxtops (written by Paul Frees, Sidney Miller, Ruby Raksin)

From Time to Time (written by Saul H. Frees and Raymond Wendell Schmidt. Unpublished, but copyrighted April 5, 1943)

A Girl (written by Paul Frees, Tony Romano. Performed by A. Hassiler, F. Lane)

Give Yourself a Break (written by Paul Frees, Ruby Raksin)

Hand in Hand (words by Paul Frees, music by Stanley Black. Copyright June 2, 1966)

Hollywood Soliloquy (written by Paul Frees, Ruby Raksin.

How Come We're Up in the [unknown] (written by written by Paul Frees, Sidney Miller, Donald O'Connor, Larry Orenstein, Bert J. Pellish, Ruby Raksin, Walter Scharf)

I'm Drowning My Sorrows (written by Eddie Brandt, Paul Frees. Published

I'm Gonna Get Away (written by Paul Frees, Ruby Raksin)

I'm Having a Breaking [unknown] (written by Eddie Brandt, Paul Frees.

I'm Ready (written by Paul Frees, Eddie Brandt)

I've Got Nothing To Do [unknown] (written by Paul Frees, Ruby Raksin)

If You're Bumping into [unknown] (written by Harold A. Fimberg, Paul Frees, Sidney Miller, Larry Orenstein, Bert J. Pellish, Ruby Raksin)

It Is Madness (written by Saul H. Frees and Raymond Wendell Schmidt. Unpublished, but copyrighted May 3, 1943)

It's a Good Good Morning (written by Paul Frees, Ruby Raksin)

Jet-Zoom (words and music by Stepin Fetchit & Paul Frees; words, music and arrangement by Ruby Raksin. Copyright July 21, 1955)

Keep Him in Mind (words by Paul Frees, music by Bob Thompson. Westmont Music. Copyright January 19, 1976 and September 7, 1976)

Kids Collects Those Boxtops (written by Paul Frees, Sidney Miller, Ruby Raksin)

The Late, Late Movies (Part I and II) (from 1959 album *Omnibust*)

Let's Look into Our [unknown] (written by Harold A. Fimberg, Paul Frees, Sidney Miller, Larry Orenstein, Bert J. Pellish, Ruby Raksin)

Life Is Like a Game of [unknown] (written by Paul Frees, Ruby Raksin)

Little Child (from 1956 album *Dinner Music, For People Who Aren't Very Hungry*)

Ma-na-ma-Nootsy (words by Paul Harcourt Frees, music by Ruby Raksin. Copyright January 26, 1955)

Mother Love (words and music by Paul Frees & Ruby Raksin. Copyright July 21, 1955)

Move Over Brother (words and music by Paul Frees & Ruby Raksin. Copyright July 21, 1955)

My Gal Tuesday (written by Saul H. Frees and Raymond Wendell Schmidt. Unpublished, but copyrighted April 22, 1943)

My Old Flame (1947)

Pleasure (words and music by Paul Frees. April 28, 1953. Goday Music Corp.)

Popcorn Sack (1947)

Portrait of a Fool

Road to Reno (written by Saul H. Frees and Harry E. Short. Unpublished, copyrighted October 6, 1941)

Sixty Million Miles (written by Harold A. Fimberg, Paul Frees, Sidney Miller, Larry Orenstein, Bert J. Pellish, Ruby Raksin)

The Skin Diver (written by Paul Frees, Eddie Brandt)

So I Fell in Love with [unknown] (written by Harold A. Fimberg, Paul Frees, Sidney Miller, Larry Orenstein, Bert J. Pellish, Ruby Raksin)

Space Girl (written by Jack Marshall)

Sweet Sweet Love (written by Eddie Brandt, Paul Frees)

Taxes (words and music by Paul Frees and Ruby Raksin. Copyright May 27, 1954)

Tell Me Why (1956)

Then in a While (written by Harold A. Fimberg, Paul Frees, Sidney Miller, Larry Orenstein, Bert J. Pellish, Ruby Raksin)

There'll Be a Boo Boo [unknown] (written by Harold A. Fimberg, Paul Frees, Sidney Miller, Larry Orenstein, Bert J. Pellish, Ruby Raksin)

Time Goes By (written by Harold A. Fimberg, Paul Frees, Sidney Miller, Larry Orenstein, Bert J. Pellish, Ruby Raksin)

Too Young (1951)

The Voice in the Wind (words and music by Paul Harcourt Frees. Arranged by Walter K. Gross. Copyright December 28, 1953)

Wanted a Softer Saddle (written by Paul Frees, Ruby Raksin)

Wear a Pair of Miller's [unknown] (written by Harold A. Fimberg, Paul Frees, Sidney Miller, Larry Orenstein, Bert J. Pellish, Ruby Raksin)

What's the Thing That [unknown] (written by Harold A. Fimberg, Paul Frees, Sidney Miller, Larry Orenstein, Bert J. Pellish, Ruby Raksin)

What Would You Do? (written by Saul H. Frees (words) and Raymond Wendell Schmidt. Unpublished, but copyrighted April 5, 1943)

When a Soldier Says Goodbye (written by Saul H. Frees and Raymond Wendell Schmidt. Unpublished, but copyrighted May 3, 1943)

While Building Our Home [unknown] (written by Harold A. Fimberg, Paul Frees, Ruby Raksin)

Why Did You Have to [unknown] (written by Harold A. Fimberg, Paul Frees, Ruby Raksin)

Why Must It Be Like This? (written by Saul H. Frees and Raymond Wendell Schmidt. Unpublished, but copyrighted April 5, 1943)

Year Right Now Is Not [unknown] (written by Harold A. Fimberg, Paul Frees, Sidney Miller, Larry Orenstein, Bert J. Pellish, Ruby Raksin)

You Can Be a Spaceman (written by Paul Frees, Sidney Miller, Ruby Raksin)

You Can Be Anything You [unknown] (written by Paul Frees, Ruby Raksin)

You're a Society Clubman (written by Harold A. Fimberg, Paul Frees, Sidney Miller, Larry Orenstein, Bert J. Pellish, Ruby Raksin)

DISNEYLAND/WORLD ATTRACTIONS

1966	Adventure Thru Inner Space (Narrator)
1966	Great Moments with Mr. Lincoln (Narrator, Voices in Film)
1967	Pirates of the Caribbean (Most of the Male Voices)
1969	Haunted Mansion (Ghost Host)
(unknown)	Main Street USA

COMMERCIALS

3M

Alcoa Aluminum

American Republic Insurance Company

American Trauma Society (for using seatbelts)

Armour

Atlas Batteries

Busch Gardens

Cap'n Crunch (barefoot pirate)

Chicken of the Sea

CKLW

Going to the Movies for Chun King

Cocoa Krispies (Ogg the Caveman)

Cornflakes (Cantata for Cornflakes)

Dianne Feinstein mayoral campaign

Fantastic Animation Festival (TV)

Foremost Big and Krispie

Foremost Dairies

Freeze It

Fuller O'Brien Paints

Gibraltar Savings and Loan

S.I. Hayakawa senatorial campaign

Hungry Tiger Restaurant

Jolly Green Giant (Sprout)

Johnson's Wax

Jovan

Kellogg's Fruit Loops (Tucan Sam)

KFRC "Close Encounters" promo

Kitchens of Sara Lee

KHJ (Los Angeles)

KTVU
Lang Laboratories
LeSeur (as Little People)
Lysol
Man, Myth and Magic (magazine)
Mark Wilson's Magic Circus
Mattel Toys
Mazda
Midland CB
Mobil Oil Corporation (documentary narrator)
Mr. Goodwrench (General Motors)
Nutesome's Ice Cream
Nestle's
Pepsi
Perrier
Pillsbury Doughboy
Pittsburgh Paints (PPG Industries) (Peacock)
Raid
RKO General Radio Stations
Schlitz Lite (for Cunningham & Walsh, NY)
Shell No-Pest Strips
Steak and Ale Inn
Super Pops (Big Yella)
Tuff N' Ready Towels
Waffle Whiffer
Wang
WXLO

AWARDS

1960	Clio (for Housewife, a 20-second TV commercial for Minneapolis Gas Company, with Barbara Ford)
1960	Clio (for Newlyweds, a 60-second TV commercial for Minneapolis Gas Company, with Barbara Ford and Julyie Bennett)
1960	Clio (for Old Movie Kitchen, a 60-second TV commercial for Seven-Up)
1960	Clio (for Tiger, a 60-second TV commercial for Calo Pet Food, with Shep Menken and Art Ballinger. Directed by Tex Avery)
1961	Clio (for What to Buy, a 60-second TV commercial for Kellogg's Snack-Pak, with Jim Conway, Daws Butler, Bryan Bruns, Thurl Ravenscroft, Betty Bryan, and Betty Leach)

1970	Clio (for Mr. Cow, a 60-second TV commercial for Tootsie Pops, with Paul Winchell, Frank Nelson, Buddy Foster, Ralph James, and Herschel Bernardi)
1974	Clio (for Take a Ride, a 60-second radio commercial for Datsun, with Mark Lindsay)
1978	Northern California Broadcasters Association Award
1980	Clio (for I Survived Skylab, a 60-second radio commercial for CKLW Skylab)

IBA Awards (several)

PAINTINGS

3M

PAINTINGS *(Titles aren't official, merely the author's descriptions)*

A Cello Player (on paper, framed drawing in color)
Elderly Gentleman at Sea (on canvas, framed oil)
An Elderly Lady
An Elderly Lady in Chair (on panel, framed acrylic)
An Elderly Person (on canvas, framed oil, 1986)
A Fisherman with Ship in Bottle (on canvas, framed oil, 1969)
A Gentleman (framed acrylic on panel)
A Gentleman (on panel, gilt framed acrylic, signed in lower right corner)
A Gentleman Playing Piano (on paper, gilt framed drawing)
Horse Race (on panel, framed acrylic)
Interior Scene with Various Figures Gambling (on panel, gilt framed acrylic)
A Lady (on canvas, framed oil)
A Lady at the Piano (on canvas, framed oil)
A Lady in Profile (on panel, framed drawing, 1952)
A Lady with Flowers (on panel, framed acrylic)
A Man with Child (on canvas, framed acrylic)
A Native Woman (on canvas, framed oil)
A Nude (on panel, framed oil)
Nudes (two framed drawings)
An Older Gentleman (on paper, framed drawing)
An Older Gentleman with Apple (on canvas, framed oil)
Painter holding pallet & paintbrush
A Pirate (framed oil painting)
A Polar Bear (on canvas, framed oil)
Portrait (on panel, framed acrylic)
Portrait of an Elderly Person (on canvas, framed oil, 1970)
Portrait of an Elderly Person (on panel, framed acrylic)

A Reclining Nude (on panel, framed oil)
A Samurai Wrestler (on canvas, framed oil)
A Soldier (on canvas, framed oil)
A Soldier with Rifle (on panel, framed acrylic)
A Soldier with Young Boy (on panel, framed acrylic)
Three Gentlemen about to Duel (on panel, framed acrylic)
Two Children with Flowers (on canvas, framed oil)
Two Wrestlers (on panel, framed acrylic)
A Young Child (on panel, framed acrylic)
A Young Child (on panel, framed acrylic, signed in upper right corner)
A Young Couple (on canvas, framed pastel)
A Young Girl (on canvas, framed oil)

Appendix:
The Beatniks 45s
and Press Kit

Peter Breck, star of TV's "Black Saddle" series, plays the title roll of a Beatnik in Barjul International Pictures' "THE BEATNIKS" opening at the _____ Theatre.

1 COL. SCENE MAT NO. S-1-1

SYNOPSIS
(not for publication)

For "kicks" and spending money, a gang of young men and women spend their time robbing and terrorizing a suburban community. Mr. Bayless, (Charles Delaney), a TV agent and talent scout overhears Eddie, (Tony Travis), sing to the accompaniment of a juke box. Impressed with the quality of Eddie's voice, Bayless offers Eddie a guest spot on a TV station in the city. In true beatnik style, Bayless is ridiculed and sent on his way. However, a seed of unconscious desire is sown within Eddie . . . he would like to accomplish something with his life. The seed grows, knawing within him.

Deciding to take the "opportunity" under the guise of "kicks", Eddie and his gang appear at the TV station. Singing a number, Eddie becomes an immediate success. The possibility of a decent way of life gives Eddie the motive and courage to break away from the gang. They will have none of it, particularly Moon, (Peter Breck), a real cool, bestnik, psycho-killer, he threatens violence. Vacillating, Eddie becomes involved in a murder that Moon commits which strips the gang to their naked, fearful emotions and brings Eddie face to face with himself. Aided by Helen, (Joyce Terry), Bayless' secretary who is in love with him, Eddie is able to completely see right from wrong, and break away from the gang. However, he becomes a prime target for Moon, who intends to kill him. In a final tense and dramatic stale, Eddie jeopardizes his life and sacrifices his own freedom to bring Moon to justice, thus ending the terror reign of the gang.

CREDITS . . . "THE BEATNIKS"

TONY TRAVIS............as EDDIE	A GLENVILLE PRODUCTION
PETER BRECK............as MOON	Written and Directed........by PAUL FREES
KAREN KADLER....... as IRIS	Original Story........KENNETH HERTS and
JOYCE TERRY........ as HELEN	JOYCE TERRY
	Produced........by KENNETH HERTS

Karen Kadler, former Universal Picture Starlet, faces her psychotic assailant in a tense moment from the motion picture "THE BEATNIKS" now playing at the _____ Theatre.

1 COL. SCENE MAT NO. S-1-2

BEATNIK "KICK" CURRENT RAVE WITH TEENERS AND EGGHEADS

"Resentment and rejection of parental authority." Dr. R. A. Richmond says. Speaking before a University body, the noted Los Angeles psychologist stated that the current craze tagged "Beatnik" could be more harmful than the Rock and roll or gold-fish swallowing crazes.

After viewing the "THE BEATNIKS," now screening at the _____ theatre, Dr. Richmond described the beatniks portrayed in the picture as "psychopaths, with strong exhibitionistic tendencies", who would have been labeled "Crazy Hoodlums" in the early thirties. Dr. Richmond also "tagged" the picture as very informative and entertaining.

FROM ALLEYWAYS AND IVORY TOWERS MARCHES THE BEATNIK

[...] law of America comes as the "craze" for the youth of this nation. Described by some as a means of expression, by others as the flouting of authority, the term, beatnik, nevertheless has become a national byword. "THE BEATNIKS," now playing at the _____ theatre, is shocking in its revelation of one phase of Beatnikism.

BEATNIK COUNTERPARTS LODGED IN BASTILLE?

Peter Breck, young actor portraying the Psycho-Killer in the Picture "THE BEATNIKS," soon to run at the _____ theatre, discovered many a "Chill" in his visits to the wards for the criminally insane. These "chills" were the result of studying, in preparation of his role, the two incarcerated. In Peter's own words, "It's frightening to realize that many of these youths have committed crimes far beyond anything that could be shown on the motion picture screen.

TONY TRAVIS TILTS TEENERS IDOLS!

Heralded as having an outstanding voice, Tony Travis is, today a young man on his way up. Having scored a couple of hit albums, Tony is moving amongst the top teenage favorites. Playing the role of a "beatnik" leader in the film "THE BEATNIKS" his starring role proves a fine singing ability and talent. The story, "THE BEATNIKS," now screening at the _____ theatre, is the shockingly dramatic record of beatniks who terrorize a community.

SOCIOLOGIST SAYS BEATNIKISM MATURITY

A noted sociologist, Professor Joseph Roberts, after viewing the picture, "THE BEATNIKS," at a special screening, stated that the beatnik "kick," as long as it stays within the "Socio-Legal" boundries, was the healthy sign of youth ripening into sociological maturity and their desire for strong economic identification.

Professor Roberts also made it clear that while the picture depicted a lower economic group of Psuedo-Beatniks, and tended toward violence, it nevertheless was forcefully dramatic in its shocking [...]

AUTHORITIES ENTER FRAY ON BEATNIK STUDENTS CRY

Stating emphatically, that many of the young men and women of today are just plain delinquents going under the guise of Beatnikism or as University students across the nation describe it "Intellectual Expressionists of expression." Juvenile authorities of the County of Los Angeles join the Professors in the controversy in stating, "The beatnik is definitely an immature individual." However, some police feel that any student beatnik crawls are well behaved and co-operative. Ed. [...]

BEATNIKS COPY CAMPUS CRAZE?

Los Angeles, California

Not to be outdone by the egghead variety of students who have been seeing records filling phone booths and cars to "world beating" capacity, "Beatniks" completely crammed a small Supreme Cafe on Sunset Blvd. late last night.

Alarmed, Jerome Pernell, owner of the small cafe called police after several station wagon loads of "beatniks" piled into the coffee shop. By the time police arrived, there wasn't even standing room. "Beatniks" were swaying in chant like one mass of jello. Cops consumed "cool cats" to "cut out." "Coffee for cops, cafe cost." "Crazy, Man."

PRODUCERS ANSWER STUDENTS BEATNIKISM "INSULT" CRY

Producers of the picture "THE BEATNIKS" at first declined to answer University of Southern California students on their cry of "Insult to beatnikism." However, after a storm of protests in which the students maintained, the producers had no right to portray beatniks from a criminal aspect, claiming "True Beatniks" exist only in the "intellectual" world of today. Producers took a dim view of this stoutly maintaining "beatnikism, beatnik, have their roots in the intellectual life of the campuses, and the picture "THE BEATNIKS" now playing over the country, does not represent the true form of "beatnikism" but is representative only of the self-styled "Beatniks."

This picture is currently playing at the _____ theatre.

RUSSIANS DISCLAIM BEATNIK DISCOVERY!

Claiming the word "beatnik" has no meaning in the Russian language, Russian newspapers today stated their "beatnikism" was just another name for "Capitolistic Hoodlumism." Students from Universities over the country rallied to defend the true beatnik meaning. Campus leader William Goldberg stated: "The terms beat, beatnikism, beatnik, have their roots in the intellectual life of the campuses and the picture "THE BEATNIKS" [...]

PLAYS FEMALE BEATNIK AS SEXY PSYCHOPATH

Karen Kadler, former Universal Pictures starlet and a Stanislavsky "Method" student, literally "beat" her way to the female lead in the picture "THE BEATNIKS" now playing at the _____ theatre.

Hearing of the role and not having played anything but unsophisticated and engenue roles before, Karen joined a "beat" crowd. Everything went well with the "cool" crowd until one of the leaders on a "kick" decided that the crowd should raid a nearby drug store for narcotics. The "Method" had never "axed" anyone on this sort of realism. Karen disappeared; later, anonymously reporting the incident to the L. A. Police.

At a preview of the picture Karen came face to face with the same leader. Giving her a stare and the beat gesture of "square" she disappeared into the crowd. Karen's outstanding performance has brought her many other fine roles.

ACTOR PAUL NEWMAN SAYS: "I'M NO BEATNIK"

Interviewed by the reporter of a national magazine, Paul Newman, star of such motion pictures as "THE LONG HOT SUMMER," "CAT ON A HOT TIN ROOF," and "PICNIC," disclaimed the "label" of "Beatnik".

"How I got the reputation of being a rebel, a beatnik, is something I don't understand. In this country, there's a tendency to believe you play the kind of a guy on the screen that you are in real life. And some actors, I suppose, live their screen roles in real life. Brother, I don't. I simply don't."

Exactly what the true definition or meaning of "beatnik" has not yet been determined. In Paul's case, he has been tagged as a rebel, for which the term "beatnik" has become the favorite synonym. The motion picture "THE BEATNIKS," first of its kind, is now screening at the _____ theatre.

Action and Suspense are the Keynotes as Karen Kadler and Peter Breck are ringleaders for a group of today's mutinous young Beatniks in the Barjul International Picture "THE BEATNIKS". This Pictures deals with the nation's newest craze, the "Beat" movement. "THE BEATNIKS" opens at the _____ Theatre on _____

2 COL. SCENE MAT NO. S-2-3

POWERFUL ROLE IN "BEATNIK" TRIGGERS MANY PARTS FOR PETER BRECK

A real psycho portrayal . . . that's the description everyone gives for Peter Breck in his portrayal of the Beatnik Character, Moon, in the picture, "THE BEATNIKS," now screening at the _____ theatre.

As Moon, Peter's beat-psycho performance is outstandingly dramatic in a vividness that leaves the audience in a cold sweat. After reading the script, Peter felt that the role would take intense work and complete industrialization with this type of psychoneurotic. Taking a number of days, Breck went to the P. N. ward of the Los Angeles County jail. There, talking with Psychologists, Psychiatrists and policemen, he learned of the many strange feelings and quirks of a psycho. Not satisfied, he also studied the dress, mannerisms and speech of the true and psucdo Beatnik. To quote Peter, "The knowledge just helped me to give an accurate portrayal, but it left a chill that should last the rest of my life."

A group of young Beatniks wait for a fight to start in this scene from the Barjul International Release, "THE BEATNIKS". Starring Tony Travis, Karen Kadler and Peter Breck, the story explodes on the screen as a group of today's rebellious generation wages a battle for their right to be heard. "THE BEATNIKS" opens at the _____ Theatre.

2 COL. SCENE MAT NO. S-2-4

★ $ENSATIONAL BEATNIK HERALD ★

3 DIFFERENT BEATNIK CARTOONS ON FRONT • SHIPPED ASSORTED

ENTIRE BACK BLANK FOR THE
IMPRINT AND SECOND FEATURE

★ ★

USE PLENTY OF
THESE HERALDS
plus
THIS GREAT
ATTENTION GETTING

40 x 60

IN YOUR
LOBBY
and
CASH IN ON
BIG PROFITS

ORDER FROM YOUR
NEAREST

BARJUL EXCHANGE

NEWSPAPER ADS!

2 COL. AD MAT NO. 2-7

TONY TRAVIS KAREN KADLER
PETER BRECK and JOYCE TERRY

3 COL. AD MAT NO. 3-5

FOR RESULTS, USE NEWSPAPER ADS!
It Will Pay You!

TONY TRAVIS KAREN KADLER
PETER BRECK and JOYCE TERRY

2 COL. AD MAT NO. 2-8

3 COL. AD MAT NO. 3-6

DESIGNED FOR REAL SHOWMEN!

EXPLOITATION!

THE MUTINOUS YOUNG...
MOCKING SOCIETY...!

3 COL. AD MAT NO. 3-9

2 COL. AD MAT NO. 2-10

1 COL. AD MAT NO. 1-12

TONY TRAVIS · KAREN KADLER

2 COL. AD MAT NO. 2-11

1 COL. AD MAT NO. 1-13

1 COL. AD MAT NO. 1-14

CATCHLINES

A PULSATING STORY OF
TODAY'S YOUTH!

THE DEFIANT YOUNG WHOSE
PASSWORD WAS MUTINY!

A NEW GENERATION . . . MOCKING THE
COURSE OF SOCIETY!

DESPERATE YOUTH . . . FIGHTING FOR
THEIR RIGHT TO BE HEARD!

YOUNG REBELS . . . LIVING VICARIOUSLY
IN THEIR NEW FOUND FREEDOM OF
SPEECH . . . SEDITION . SEX!

TODAY'S YOUTH . . . CAUGHT HALFWAY
BETWEEN DESIRE AND REALITY!

BORN OF WAR AND TURMOIL . . .
DEDICATED TO SETTLING A SCORE
WITH SOCIETY!

YOUNG ADULTS . . . LIVING A LIFE
OF NO TOMORROWS!

THE MUTINOUS YOUNG . . . APART AND
ALONE . . . WAGING WAR ON MODERN
CONVENTIONS!

THEY CAME FROM EVERY WALK OF
LIFE . . . THIS GENERATION CALLED
"THE BEATNIKS"

A MOTION PICTURE WITH INSIGHT
AND UNDERSTANDING!

EXPLOSIVE! DEFIANT! DEMANDING!

STUBBORN YOUTH . . . STRIKING BACK!

A CRAZE THAT IS SWEEPING THE
NATION!

REVEALING . . . REWARDING . . . A STORY
OF SUPPRESSED EMOTIONS!

LIVING BY THEIR CODE OF REBELLION
AND MUTINY!

TRAILERS AND ACCESSORIES
ARE AVAILABLE
THROUGH YOUR LOCAL
NATIONAL SCREEN SERVICE OFFICE

BEATNIK HERALDS

Take advantage of the dollar pulling Heralds. These heralds are like a page from Theater in their unique drawings coupled with the latest Beatnik Glossary and a back page for imprinting of the bottom half of the bill. These are sure-fire take home gimmicks that the "week before" audience will treasure, chuckle, and return to make their "box-office deposit" with you.

"BEAT THE BEATNIKS" CONTEST

A gone gimmick that has been tested and stamped with the "banking" seal of approval. Tie in with a local radio station that you've contracted for spot announcements. Have the Disc Jockey hustle enthusiasm for the Beatniks by telling the local theatre goers to rush on down to the lobby of your theatre and peek at the Beatnik Glossary on display in the lobby . . . THEN, as he mentions words from his copy of the glossary throughout the day, listeners are to call in and give the translation of the Beatnik word into the Kings English. In return, the listener receives a Beatnik record, passes, and a copy of the Glossary as a prize. It's fun and fruitful!

BEATNIK GLOSSARY

A 40x60 with a two column display of Beatnik words used throughout the country. Tie in this Glossary with the suggested radio Contest, and if there is no radio used, order your Glossary anyway as it is a terrific gathering spot for the audience as they munch on their popcorn and comment on the Glossary during your intermission!

BEATNIK RECORDS

Actual recording taken from the sound track of the picture featuring Tony Travis, the star of the picture. These records are available for premier space and are a wise investment in luring the younger generation into your theatre. Use them in the radio contest or any other type of 'give-away' gimmick that has proven successful in your area. Use them on your 'in theatre' sound system as a plug, in addition to your trailer, during intermission. These are 45rpm records that will win you lasting friends in the younger set as nothing makes them happier than to add another record to their collection . . . especially if it's a gift!

THE BEATNIKS ARE COMING!

Have local radio station make a short tape recorded announcement through an echo chamber with the announcer saying in a hush hush tone, "The Beatniks Are Coming." Play this as a teaser spot throughout the day. Another tried and true gimmick! It drives people nuts, but arouses their curiosity enough for them to come down to the theatre and BUY TICKETS!

A PIECE OF ICE!

. . . as large as the mold will hold. Get this from your local ice house or an exchange advertising gimmick. Have the largest block of ice possible delivered to your theatre and planted in front of the lobby on the street. Make sure you have it roped-off and properly displayed with signs advertising "THE BEATNIKS." If the ice is made especially for you, give the ice house some toy stuffed cats, large as you can get, and place them in the center of the block so that people can see them inside, then plaster signs all over reading something like "ALL COOL CATS DIG THE BEATNIKS" or any similar saying taken from a combination of words from the BEATNIK GLOSSARY. Don't pass up this gimmick!

A PHONE BOOTH AND FOREIGN CAR CONTEST

Get groups of young high school or college men and women to choose up teams and pile into a phone booth, located in front of the theatre, for a real 'on street traffic' stopper. The team piling the most into the booth, or a foreign car, which can be borrowed from a local agency for the exchange advertising, receives passes, the Beatnik Record, and copies of the Glossary. This has worked and is a barrel of fun for all. A great attention getter . . . especially on a shopping night when your streets are packed with shoppers!

TOP THE BEATNIKS CONTEST

An entry blank placed near the 40x60 BEATNIK GLOSSARY on display in the lobby. Have the patrons pick up their entry blanks (can also have radio station give them out if they get in on the contest) study the words on the BEATNIK GLOSSARY and then try to coin their own BEATNIK expression in one or two words and submit it for judging. 25 new words would be selected a day making 25 winners a day during the run of the show. The prizes again would be records, passes, and a copy of the glossary. Winners could be announced on the air each day and names and winning words posted in the lobby of your house. Prizes are to be picked up at the theatre.

FOR
**BEATNIK HERALDS, RECORDS,
AND GLOSSARY, ETC.**
ORDER DIRECT FROM
YOUR LOCAL
**BARJUL INTERNATIONAL PICTURES
EXCHANGE**

Index

Numbers in **bold** indicate photographs

#

27th Day, The 102, **292**, 316
2001: A Space Odyssey 202, 213-214

A

Abominable Dr. Phibes, The 217-218, **218**, 318, 320, 325
Adventure Thru Inner Space 92, 165-166, 328
Alias Smith and Jones 220-221
Allen, Steve 63-64, 260
Astaire, Fred 214, 216-217
Atom Ant/Secret Squirrel Show, The 160, 322

B

Banana Splits Adventure Hour, The 204, 322
"Barney Bear" 73, 86, 311
Barrymore, John 155
Barrymore, Lionel 62
Bartell, Harry 3, 42-43, 61
Beany and Cecil 204
"Beary Family, The" 143, 312-314
Beatles, The 169-171, 201, 212, 322
Beatniks, The 41, 123-126, **124**, **125**, **127**, 316, 333-340
Beginning of the End 102-103, 316
Benny, Jack 38-39, 74, 87, 211, 322
Big Sky, The **81**, 83, 315
Black Sunday 131, 320
Blanc, Mel 64, 102, 131, 145, 160, 258, 285
Blood and Black Lace **154**, 156, 317
Bogart, Humphrey 41, 52, 76, 77, 91-92, 159, 207, 217, 218-219, 250, 253, 258
Boltz, Ron 202-203
Border Incident 129
"Boris Badenov" ix, **105**, **107**, 108-109, 112, 113, 120, 165, 197, 219, 251, 265, 281, 321
Bozo the Clown 108, 320

Brandt, Eddie 3, 13, 48, 50, 76, 92-93, 119, 120-121, 123, 124-126, 273, 281, 326, 327
"Buddy Green" 5-13, **11**, **12**, **13**, 36, 50
Buffum, Ray 37, 83
Burton, Corey 3, 142
Butler, Daws ix, 41, 113, 114, 131, 134, 162, 175, 204, 205, 226, 247, 263, 280, 285, 329
Buttons, Red **144**, 145

C

Calvin and the Colonel 143, 283, 321
Cap'n Crunch ix, 109, 111, 155, **226**, 226, 328
"Captain Peter Peachfuzz" 104, **107**, 109, 283, 321
Carpetbaggers, The 156, 317
Case of Dashiell Hammett, The 261, 319
Carson's Cellar 87, 320
Church of Religious Science 130, 217
Colossus: The Forbin Project 202, 213-214, 318
Comic, The 205-206, 318
Commercial Actor, The 232-233, **239**, 241, 293
Confession 85-86, 307, 308
Colman, Ronald 76, 172, 217, 218, 219
Conrad, Bill (William) ix, x, 39-40, 42, 45, 56, 61, 110, 113, **153**, 155, 172, 232, 261, 283
Conried, Hans ix, 40, 41, 42, 91, 102, 110, 133, 154, 155, 172, 174, **246**, 250
Cornthwaite, Robert 37, 70, 294
Cricket on the Hearth 174, 324, 325
Crime Correspondent 58-59, **61**, **62**, 301
Curio Shop, The 80

D

Dangerous Assignment 61, 79, 303, 304, 305, 307, 308
Davis, Peter 3, 261-263, **262**, 277-278, 281
Day, Dennis 41, **248**, 251, 303, 304

Day After Trinity, The 259, , 319
Demon from Dimension X, The 83
Dick Tracy 143, 321
Disney, Walt 13, 74, 87, 92, 103, 111, 114, 115, 117, 118, 135, 139, 141, 159, 163, 164, 165, 166, 168, 169, 250, 268, 310, 311, 312, 313, 316, 317, 318, 320, 321, 322, 324, 325
Disneyland/world 78, 92, **93**, 96, 145, **162**, 163, 164, 165, 166, 167, 168, 181, 202, 209, 285, 328
Disneyland Records 117, 136, 167, 240, 324, 325
Disorderly Orderly, The 156, 317
Dobkin, Larry 45, 61
Doc Savage: The Man of Bronze 231, 318
Down to Earth 80
Dr. Kildare 62, 304
Dudley Do-Right 103, 109, 110, 161, 172, 322
Dunning, John 3, 17-18, 63-64, 261

E

Earth vs. the Flying Saucers 92, 315
Edgar Bergen Show, The 134
Edmiston, Walker 3, 133, 240
Escape 18, 38, 39-40, 42, 43, 128, 158, 284, 296, 297, 298, 299, 300, 301, 302, 303, 304, 305, 307, 308, 309
Exploring the Unknown 92, 324

F

Fang, the Wonder (?) Dog 217
Fantastic Four, The 200, 322
Fantasy Film World of George Pal, The 268, 270, 319
FBI (Dept. of Justice) 1, 85, **193**, 199-200, 203, 212
Fields, W.C. 207, 211, 212, 218, 224, 253, 324
First Easter Rabbit, The 238, 324, 325
Fishbein, Janice 3, 6-7, 146, 273
Fletcher, Carol Lynn 3, 226-228, 274-277, 281
Flight from Ashiya 156, 317
Flight of Dragons, The 265
Fong, Benson 97, 201
Foray, June ix-x, 3, 61, 86, 103, 108, 110, 112, 113, 117, 131, 134, 141, 143, 154, 162, 177, 204, 205, 206, **216**, 219, 234, 247, 260, 263, 280, 286
Fosselius, Ernie 2, 247-249
Fox and the Crow, The 64
Fractured Fairy Tales 109
Fractured Flickers 154-155, 321
Frankenstein Jr. and the Impossibles 171, 322

Frankie Vendetta 129
Freberg, Stan 3, 61, 117, **140**, 141-142, 204, 238, 247, 259, 325
Freddy 128
Frees, Dave 3, 5-6, 8, 9, 12, 16-17, 19, 99, 177, 179, 199, 202, 265, 279
Frees, Fred 1, 3, 8, 9, 17, 47-48, **48**, 78, **86**, 88, **93**, **94**, **95**, 95-99, **100**, 104-105, 126, 129-130, 132-133, 135, 141, 151, 159-160, 164, 168-169, 171, 176, 191-194, 199, 200-202, 212, 217, 220, 221, 250, 253, 257, 264, 273, 277, 278-280, 282, 285
Frees, Helen 3, 6, 19, 94, 99, 179, 220
Frees, Joy Terry 3, 18, 45, 46-47, **66**, 70, 74, **75**, 78, **86**, 87, 88-89, 93-94, **95**, 95, 99, 103, 104, 123, 124, 126, 129, 132, 146, 156, 190-191, 192, 194, 281
Frees on 2 **87**, 87
Frees, Sabrina 2, **48**, **146**, **147**, 147-151, 176, 178-181, 220, 255-257, 273
Frees, Sarah and Abraham (Paul's parents) 5-8, **5**, **6**, 130
Front Page 61
Frosty the Snowman 206, 217, 240, 324
Frosty's Winter Wonderland 240, 324, 325

G

Gay Purr-ee **143**, **144**, 145-146, 317, 325
George of the Jungle ix, 110, 172, 322
Gerald McBoingBoing Show, The 91, 320
Get Smart 159-160, 323
Glason, Billy 173
Godfrey, Arthur 63
Grand Prix 239, 240, 318
Great Moments with Mr. Lincoln 165, 166-167, 325, 328,
Green Lama, The 43, 55-57, **58**, **60**, 300, 301
Greene, Lorne 94, 105, 106, 188, 280

H

Hall of Presidents, The 145
Harder They Fall, The 91-92, 315
Hardware Wars 2, **243**, 247-249, 250, 319
Haunted Mansion, The 4, 142, 145, 158, **161**, 164-166, 202, 285, 328
Hawkear: Frontier Scout 205
Hayward, Chris 3, 109-110, 154-155
Here Comes Peter Cottontail 219, 324, 325
Hobbit, The 250, 259, 324, 325
Hollywood Babysitter, The 75-76
Hoppity Hooper 109, 155

Horror of the Blood Monsters 213, 318
Hunt the Man Down 67, **68, 69**, 315

I

I Dream of Jeanie 161
"I'm Drowning in My Sorrows" 93
Immortal, The 205
Incredible Mr. Limpet, The 158, 317

J

Jackson Five Show, The 212-213
Jeff Regan, Investigator 54, 298, 302, 304
Joan of Arkansas 91
Johnny Carson's Sun City Scandals '72 226
Jones, Spike x, 3, 13, 48-51, **54**, 56, 74, 75-77, **91**, 92, 118-121, 284, 324
Justice League of America 171-172, 322

K

Karloff, Boris 114, 120, 152, 154, 207, 209, 210, 253
KECA **128**, 128
King Features Trilogy 154, 169, 321

L

Las Vegas Story, The 84, 315
Last of the Fast Guns 106, 316
Last Unicorn, The 260, 319
Late Late Late Movies, The 118-119
Laurel and Hardy 173-174, 322
Legend of Barnacle Bill, The 81
Leibovit, Arnold 3, 268, 269-271, 319
Lindner, Bob 2, 17, 168, 222-223, 224-225, 236-237, 238, 258-259
"Little Child (Daddy Dear)" 92, 326
Little Drummer Boy, The 204, 324
Lord of the Rings, The 250, 259
Lorre, Peter x, 37, 44, 49-50, 52, **53, 54**, 76, 77, 114, 154, 160, 162, 163, 164, 190, 207-208, 219, 298, 323
"Ludwig Von Drake" 55, 74, 120, 135-142, **136, 137, 138**, 190, 211, 268, 321, 322, 324, 325
Lux Radio Theatre ix, 295, 304, 306, 307, 308, 309

M

Macdonnell, Norman 18, 57, 79
Mad, Mad, Mad Comedians, The 211-212, 324
Man in Black, The (The Black Book) 78-79, 306
Man Named Jordan, A (Rocky Jordan) 37-38, 295, 298, 299, 300, 301, 302, 303, 304, 305, 309

Manchurian Candidate, The 144-145, 317
Marin County Sheriff's Department 179-186, **180**, 194, 195, 197, 198, 199, 225, 271, 272
Matty's Funnies with Beany and Cecil, see *Beany and Cecil*
McKennon, Dallas 131-132, 144, 269
Mellomen, The 145, 165
Midway 239-240, 319
Mifune, Toshiro 239-240, 255, 318, 319
Miller, Marvin 89-90
Miller, Sidney 325, 326, 327, 328
Million Dollar Mermaid 85, 315
Millionaire, The 2, **89**, 89-90, 104, 320
Miss Matrimony 80
Mister Magoo 131, 151-153, 217, 321, 323
Monster Shindig 162-163, 325
Moose That Roared, The 2, 112
Mouse on the Mayflower, The 204, 324
Mr. Aladdin 73-74, 83, 305
Mr. Magoo's Christmas Carol 151-152, 217, 323
Mr. Terrific 176
My Friend Irma 87, 322
Mystery Science Theatre 3000 103, 126
"My Old Flame" 49-50, 120, 297, 327

N

New Adventures of Huck Finn, The 205
Night Walker, The 158-159, 284, 317
Noah's Ark 117, 311
Not Tonight, Henry 131, 317

O

Osmonds, The 213, 322
Outlaws Is Coming, The 161, 317
Owens, Gary 3, 210-211, 294

Pal, George 81, 130, 231, 268-271, 319
Partners in Crime (Jeremiah Shade, Esq.) 80, 128
Paul Frees and the Poster People 207-210, **208**, 215, 218, 219, 325
Peabody's Improbable History 109, 111, 205
Perfect Crime, The 78, 306
Phineas T. Phox, Adventurer 102
Pirates of the Caribbean 159, 163-164, 165, 328
Place in the Sun, A 68, 109-110, 315, 323
Player, The **51**, 52-54, 78, 297
"Pillsbury Doughboy" 5, 158, 197, 209, 211, **211**, 220, 235, 266, 267, 269, 271, 281, 283, 319, 329
Point, The 219-220, 324
"Popcorn Sack" 48-49, 327

Post, Joyce 2, 3, 78, 194-199, 212, 226, 266, 271-272, 273-274, **275**, 276, 277, 278, 279, 281-282
Presley, Elvis 184, 212, 268
Price, Vincent 84, 99, 154, **157**, 217, **218**, 219, 272
Puppetoon Movie, The 269-270, **270**, 271, 319

Q

Quizreel **66**

R

Rah! Rah! Woozy! 263, 323
Raksin, Ruby 78, 325, 326, 327, 328
Rankin/Bass 3, 111, 174, 204, 206, 211-217, 219, 229, 238, 244, **246**, 250-252, 255, 259, 260, 264, 265, 283, 319
Rescue 8 106, 108, 126
Return of the King, The 259, 324
Riot in Cell Block 11 **84**, **85**, 85, 315
Robson, William N. 80, 128, 284
Rocky and His Friends ix, x, 2, 4, 108-113, 247, 283, 321, 324
Romance 61, 305, 306, 307, 309
Romano, Tony 87, 155-156, 326
Rooney, Mickey 133, 173, 214, **215**, 252, 323
Routes of Exile: A Moroccan Jewish Odyssey 260-261, 319
Rudolph's Shiny New Year **235**, 238-239, 324

S

Santa Claus Is Comin' to Town 4, 174, 214-217, **215**, 324, 325
Scoma, Al 3, **180**, 184, 224, 225, 239
Scott, Bill ix, 91, **105**, 108, 109, 111, 113, 114, 154, 155, 172, 205, 226, 258, 260, 263, 285
Scott, Keith 2, 8, 45, 80, 112, 234, 258, 283-286, 294
Shaggy Dog, The 114-116, 316, 324
Sinatra, Frank **82**, 85, 144
Skelton, Red **235**, 238
"Skin Diver, The" 48, **50**, 74, 327
Snow Queen 103-104, 316, 325
Some Like It Hot 118, 316
"Space Girl" 74, 327
Spacemaster X-7 **103**, 106
Spike Jones in Hi-Fi 119-120, 324
Sportsmen, The 48
St. Valentine's Day Massacre, The 175-176, 318
Stan Freberg Presents The United States of America Vol. 1 141-142, 325
Star, The 85, 315
Stephenson, John 43-44, 94-95, 134, **246**, 250

Stern, Charles 167, 209, 210, 232, 234, 237, 245, 246, 252, 253, 255, 258, 259, 264, 278, 280
Suddenly **82**, 85, 315
Super Chicken ix, 172
Super President and Spy Shadow 175
Suspense 38, 40-41, **43**, 43, 230, 295, 296, 298, 299, 300, 301, 302, 304, 305, 307, 308, 309, 310
Sword, The 102

T

Tamiroff, Akim **107**, 109
"Telltale Heart, The" 229-230
Tetley, Walter 41, 91, 111, 141
Thing from Another World, The 69-70, **71**, 315
Time Machine, The 130, 268, 316, 320
Time to Love and a Time to Die, A 105-106, 316, 320
Tinpanorama 159, 325
Tintin 131-132, 321
Toast of New Orleans, The 67, 315
Tom Slick ix, 172
"Too Young" 51, 74-75, 76, 327
Top Cat 134, 321
Truth or Consequences 219

W

War Lord, The 159, 318
War of the Worlds 85, 268, 309, 315
Ward, Jay ix, 102, 108, 109, 110, 111, 112, 113, **152**, 154, 155, 172, 205, 210, **216**, 217, 226, 263, 283, 285
Watts Gnu Show, The 113-114
Webb, Jack 42, 54, 70, 182
Welles, Orson x, 52, 80, 120, 133, 168, 190, 198, 200, 232, 255, 283, 286, 302, 314
Where the Boys Are 130, 316
Whisperer, The 79, 305, 306
Who Knows? 80-81
Wild in the Streets 203, 318
Willie Mays and the Say-Hey Kid 229, 324
Wind in the Willows, The 265, 324
Winters, Shelley 69, 203, **237**, 240, 252
Wonderful World of Disney, The 92, 322
Woody Woodpecker 143, 144, 312
World's Greatest Sinner, The 151, 317
Wright, Ben 55, 57, **58**, **60**
Wynn, Ed **107**, 109, 128, 172, 207, 209, 210

Y

Young, Doug 173
You're the Boss 80

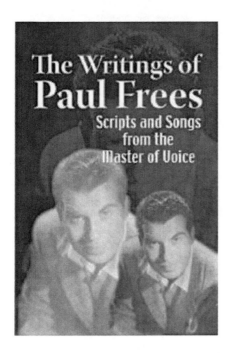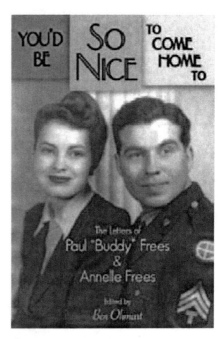

CPSIA information can be obtained at www.ICGtesting.com
Printed in the USA
LVOW05s0806231213

366418LV00001B/18/P